Changing Child Care

The Children Act 1989 and the Management of Change

The National Children's Bureau was established as a registered charity in 1963. Our purpose is to identify and promote the interests of all children and young people and to improve their status in a diverse society.

We work closely with professionals and policy makers to improve the lives of all children but especially children under five, those affected by family instability and children with special needs or disabilities.

We collect and disseminate information about children and promote good practice in children's services through research, policy and practice development, publications, seminars, training and an extensive library and information service.

© National Children's Bureau, 1993

All rights reserved. No part of this publication may be reproduced, stored in a retrieval system or transmitted in any form by any person without the written permission of the publisher.

ISBN 1 874579 07 5

Published by the National Children's Bureau, 8 Wakley Street, London EC1V 7QE. Telephone 071 278 9441

Typeset, printed and bound by Saxon Graphics Ltd, Derby.

Contents

Foreword	v
Acknowledgements	viii
1. Child care and the management of change	1
2. Crisis and change in social services	7
3. BACC's philosophy and method: a framework for managing change	34
4. The history of BACC	56
5. A strategy for child care	80
6. Services for children in need	113
7. Looking after Birmingham's children	143
8. Changing child care: the management of change	162
References	185
Appendix 1: Birmingham Action on Child Care: A Chronology	195
Appendix 2: Extract from the BACC *Outline*	210
Appendix 3: The interpretation of 'children in need'	216
Appendix 4: BACC publications	219
Appendix 5: Birmingham Action on Child Care Team	223
Appendix 6: Membership of the Advisory Group	225
Index	226

Foreword

Providing a child care service adequate and sensitive enough to meet the multiplicity of needs for which it is required will never be easy. It could be said to be the most difficult of all the tasks which local authorities have to carry out through their social services functions. In addition universal family and childhood problems are intensified by the circumstances of very large, densely urban and multicultural societies like Birmingham. Mistakes are made, standards are difficult to maintain, and scandals can occur.

There have been too many scandals in child care services in recent years. Inquiries, national and local, have analysed how they arose and recommended what should be done to prevent their recurrence. Remedial action has not always followed.

This book records an unusual and important attempt by Birmingham City Council and its Social Services Department to face up to problems, learn their lessons and implement far-reaching changes for the better. The Department had been through reorganisations. It had drastically reduced its residential child care facilities without concurrently providing adequate alternatives and, like many other local authorities, had given staff support, training and management a low priority. In the late 1980s, the Department was faced with a bad press, locally and nationally, and growing concern about standards.

The Director of Social Services, Adrianne Jones, supported by her Committee, took a courageous and imaginative approach to their dilemma. They decided to undertake a positive experiment which would incorporate not just investigation of the problems facing them, but a parallel and integral initiative to develop ways of remedying them and building up standards and provision to a high standard. The emphasis was on action – BIRMINGHAM ACTION ON CHILD CARE (BACC) was the title given to the project.

Cynics inside and outside the Department were sceptical that the Project could succeed where previous changes had failed. It was clear from the start that the task would be very difficult. Crisis and constant change were dimensions of the scene in which BACC would operate. The economic environment was already tough and major national developments, particularly the Children Act 1989, would have to be navigated. In addition a department already bruised by reorganisation should not face further restructuring. Such constraints were daunting.

The planning of the Project from the outset brought together a number of important factors which helped it to establish itself and to achieve its goals. It had clearly defined aims and objectives; its personnel from the Project Director to the administrative support staff were protected from day to day operational demands; and it had direct access to the Director and a seat at the table with the Departmental Management Team.

In addition, it had an Advisory Group which brought together not only representatives of all relevant services and interests in Birmingham but also a group of nationally known individuals who lent their support and experience to the BACC Team. Within the city, heads of other departments gave friendly support and understanding. Within the Social Services Department, participation and communication were key notes of all the Project's activities and achievements. As a matter of principle, the style of the Project was to try to model within itself the methods and practice which it was to promote within the child care service. Careful thought was given in planning and design to integrate theory and practice and effective ways of achieving change were demonstrated through the Project's own behaviour and work.

I was delighted to be asked to act as Chairman of the Advisory Group and Consultant to the Project Team. Members of the Advisory Group gave support and encouragement and acted as a sounding board and reference point for the Project's work; some travelled many miles to participate, not only in the Group's meetings but also in the work of task groups set up by the BACC Team; and they assisted in making the Project's work known on the national as well as the local scene.

Working with the BACC Team, led by Paul Sutton, was an experience I shall always recall with pleasure and satisfaction. There was a spirit of determination to face and resolve problems combined with realistic appraisal of constraints and imagination to find ways to overcome them. The methods used by the Team led to communication with and involvement of very large numbers of people in the Social Services Department and elsewhere. By doing so the Project's messages were clearly heard and produced results.

It has been depressingly fashionable in recent years to argue that a child care service required to give attention to individual need and provide sensitive delivery, cannot be done well by local authorities. Birmingham Action on Child Care gives the lie to this and demonstrates how much can be achieved even by a few people in a local government context if the leadership, thoughtfulness and imagination are available.

I commend this book, written on behalf of the Project by Gill Coffin, who was involved in the creative thinking throughout, to managers, practitioners, policy makers, and many others who are concerned to improve and develop public services. It has messages for a wider audience than social services.

Barbara Kahan OBE
Chairman of the Advisory Group of Birmingham Action
on Child Care and Consultant to the Project.
Chair, National Children's Bureau.

February 1993

N.B.
Throughout this book, 'the Department' and 'the Social Services Department' refer to Birmingham Social Services Department. When these terms do not have initial capitals, they refer to departments and social services departments in general. The term 'child care' (two words), unless otherwise qualified, refers to the care of children and young people under 18.

Acknowledgements

I am indebted to the BACC Editorial Group, Ben Brown, John Clarke, Neil Grant, Barbara Kahan, Sheila McGrath, and Paul Sutton, for their help and support throughout the year, and to the Group and David Berridge, Janette Bird, Roger Bullock, Adrianne Jones, Michael Little, and Jean Packman for reading the manuscript at various stages. I want to thank everyone who provided me with information and comments, especially Louise Bessant, Billy Foreman, Neil Grant, Stephanie Hart, Adrianne Jones, Gill Jones, Jane Middleton, Paul Sutton and Ruth Walsh. I am very grateful to Adrianne Jones, Director of Birmingham Social Services, for giving me the time and personal encouragement to undertake this task, and to both Paul Sutton and Barbara Kahan for their constant support. Finally, I must thank my colleagues in the Social Services Department – Barbara Elsom and Pat Barr – and my family – Betty, Harish, Joseph, Rajesh, Sam, Veena and William – for their patience and understanding while I have been absorbed in writing.

Gill Coffin
Sparkhill, Birmingham
February 1993

1: Child care and the management of change

The management of radical change in any organisation is difficult. The public provision of child care services is problematic – few local authorities have escaped censure for their handling of social work services in recent years. Birmingham Action on Child Care faced both tasks.

The Project was set up in 1989 by Birmingham Social Services Department to:

establish new objectives, priorities and resources which will enable the child care service to make a clear and positive response to future demands. [Birmingham Social Services Department, 1988d]

Whilst it was initially a response to internal concerns about quality of services, BACC's work was also structured by the requirements of the Children Act 1989 and the National Health Service and Community Care Act 1990. In three years, the small Project Team made an major impact on the department, and this book sets out to consider not only what was achieved, but how. Central to BACC's approach was the involvement of people in an open process of exploration which brought about a commitment to change. The Project demonstrated that even in a climate of restricted resources, change can be achieved in local government, but that the process is crucial to successful outcomes.

Birmingham is the largest urban local authority in Great Britain, with a population of just under one million. It is a multi-ethnic city – about one fifth of the total population are Black or minority ethnic people. In recent years, the city's industrial base has been severely affected by economic restructuring and recession, and unemployment has been consistently high. As a result, in 1992 the City Council's Anti-Poverty Unit estimated that half the population lived in or on the margins of poverty. (This was based on a broad definition of poverty which included lack of access to employment, education, recreation and social activities as well as low income.)

In 1993, Birmingham Social Services Department employed nearly 9,000 people, and had a net budget of £142 million of which approximately one third is spent on services for children and families. Management of such a large organisation would be difficult at the best of times, and for local government the period 1989-1992 was certainly not 'the best of times'. This context is important for understanding some of the problems faced by BACC.

The origins of Birmingham Action on Child Care

Social work with children received a consistently 'bad press' during the 1980s. Social workers were accused of doing too little too late to protect children from abuse, and, conversely, of intervening too much and too often in the lives of families. They received conflicting advice – not just from the media – but from the numerous official inquiries held during the years since the death of Maria Colwell in 1973. Working within a legislative framework which became ever more prescriptive, they were increasingly expected to use judgement and discretion in their dealings with families.

During the same decade, there were mounting concerns about standards of care and control in residential children's homes. There were those who argued that children's homes should be consigned to history – that institutional care was damaging, and all children and young people needing care from the state should be placed in foster or adoptive homes. Some of these concerns seemed only too well-founded when, in 1987 and 1988, Birmingham Social Services Department faced a series of allegations of abuse and ill-treatment of children by staff in several of its children's homes. Similar problems were surfacing in children's homes, boarding schools and community homes with education throughout the United Kingdom.

Birmingham's Director of Social Services, Adrianne Jones, believed that children's homes still had an essential part to play in a modern child care service, although she was determined that poor practice, ill-treatment and abuse would not be tolerated. At the same time, she acknowledged that the problems of the child care service were not confined to the residential care sector. A shortage of qualified social workers could be leaving children at risk in the community, and the foster care service was not able to find homes for all the children who needed them. She decided to establish a major project to review and reassess all the Department's services for children and families. The project was to have maximum freedom to undertake its task as well as a direct relationship with the Director herself. An advisory group, of people drawn from different fields and organisations, would guide the project and protect and enhance its independence.

This decision was strongly supported by the Social Services Committee, and Birmingham Action on Child Care (BACC) was conceived. By setting up the Project, the Director and Councillors sought to ensure that the City Council and the social services department took responsibility for finding out what had gone wrong and also for putting it right again.

Changing child care: means and ends

By 1988, two reorganisations of the Department in five years had left many staff wary of change. Some saw the new Project as just another inquiry making recommendations which would soon be forgotten. Others were ready to grasp the potential opportunity to look at the whole child care service and find ways to raise both standards and morale. Many were asking how this new Project would be different from previous initiatives. How could it make an impact when no new resources were promised?

The answer to these questions was to lie in the philosophy, method of work, and comprehensiveness of Birmingham Action on Child Care. From the start, bringing about change in an organisation the size of Birmingham Social Services Department was a formidable undertaking. The BACC Team began to realise that *how* they approached their task would influence the outcome; the process of change would, in part, determine the nature of the outcome.

This book describes and analyses an approach to the management of change in local government. It is not specific to the personal social services, but could be adapted and utilised in other contexts. It examines the development of policy and practice in child care from 1988 to 1992, through a major local authority's response to its own internal difficulties and to the implementation of the Children Act 1989. The impact of the Project on the Department's culture, its management structure, and the range of services it provided, are examined and combined with descriptions of the work which BACC undertook, its analysis of the child care services' problems and solutions, and critical accounts of its philosophy and methodology.

The context of the Project

Before looking at BACC's work, it is essential to understand the context in which the Project was operating. Chapter 2 provides a brief account of the history and dilemmas faced by the statutory child care services in the years since 1945. It describes in more detail problems faced by the residential care service in the 1980s, and gives a brief history of Birmingham Social Services Department's children's services in the 1980s. The Director's actions in response to difficulties in 1987-8 are set out, including the decision to set up Birmingham Action on Child Care. This decision is then set in the local government context, where change was taking place and financial and other stresses were being experienced. Some of the issues specific to the management of change in local government are described.

Birmingham Action on Child Care was charged by the Director with looking at the whole child care service. In response to this the Project Team conceptualised the child care service as a system, in which each part related to a greater or lesser extent to every other part. Understanding the system was one key to managing change. Using the 'systems model' also reinforced the view that change could not be imposed from the top, but must come from within the organisation, and be owned by the people throughout the system who would have to implement the Project's recommendations. Drawing on the experience of other departmental projects, the Team's approach to developing solutions, promoting best practice and managing change, was one which permitted involvement of staff and service users at all levels.

Chapter 3 sets out the key features of BACC's philosophy and methodology, and makes an assessment of the effectiveness of this approach.

Chapter 4 provides a mainly chronological and descriptive account of Birmingham Action on Child Care. It shows how the Project followed the typical lifecycle of a short term project, and introduces the range of work which the Project tackled. The historical account is located in the context of national developments in child care. Local and national media interest in the subject is recorded as a backdrop to events. The chapter provides a basis for more detailed description and analysis of BACC's work and methods which follow in chapters 5 to 7.

A strategy for child care

Although Birmingham Action on Child Care was conceived before the Children Bill – later the Children Act 1989 – was even announced in Parliament, by the time the Project Team began work the Bill had been published and it was clear that BACC would be in the forefront of the Department's effort to implement the Children Act.

Chapter 5 sets out the work BACC undertook in developing an implementation strategy for the Children Act, securing a corporate commitment, including resources, for the Act, and taking a lead role in developing training. It goes on to describe the strategic direction and policy framework for children's services developed by BACC, and shows how these led to proposals for residential and foster care services. With the demands made on the Department by both the Children Act 1989 and the National Health Service and Community Care Act 1990, the necessity for organisational change in the Social Services Department became clear. This chapter also sets out the thinking behind these changes and notes that the process followed by the Departmental Management Team in introducing changes was based on the methodology for managing change developed by BACC.

BACC produced a broad interpretation of 'children in need' – a key concept in the Children Act – which was adopted by the City Council. Effectively, this committed the city to developing a range of community services for children and families.

Chapter 6 begins by setting out some of the indicators of 'need' in Birmingham, and goes on to describe a range of work undertaken to ensure that children's needs were met. This included contributions to policy and practice designed to help ensure that services were appropriate for Black and minority ethnic children; various initiatives to enable children and young people to express their views and make complaints; work on improving day care services for pre-school children and young school children; measures to support children in their families; and provision of information about both rights and services.

Chapter 7 concentrates on the work which BACC undertook to improve children's homes and foster care. Recruitment and training of foster carers, procedures for dealing with allegations of abuse by foster carers, foster care for teenagers, provision of support to foster carers, and the funding of the service were all tackled. Given the Project's genesis in concerns about child care practice in children's homes, the residential care service was extensively examined by one of BACC's four topic groups. This major piece of work resulted in detailed recommendations for improving standards in children's homes and training for residential workers, whilst other work was undertaken on setting up a service for young people leaving the Department's care.

Finally, chapter 8 reviews the work undertaken by BACC, and assesses whether the Project was able to fulfil the expectations of the Director and Social Services Committee. It draws together BACC's achievements and examines indicators of their impact on the Department's policy and practice. It also sets out key features of BACC's approach to reviewing Birmingham Social Services Department's child care services and attempts to assess whether BACC's specific methodology and philosophy were crucial to the outcomes achieved. Finally, BACC's approach to the management of change is discussed as a strategy for local government.

2. Crisis and change in social services

> While the law changed slowly to meet new situations and to respond to new ways of looking at Society, Society itself remained remarkably and depressingly constant in the way in which children were treated and mistreated.
> [Poyser, 1990]

Child care in context

In December 1989, at the first meeting of the BACC Advisory Group, a presentation on the history of child care since 1948 was given by a member of the Social Services Inspectorate, Arran Poyser. Concentrating mainly on residential and foster care, he showed how many of the issues in child care in 1989 were remarkably similar to those of the immediate post-War years – problems of providing good substitute care for children, the importance of maintaining children in their own families, dilemmas to face in response to young offenders, and tensions between the impulse to rescue children from neglect and abuse and the will to provide preventive services. Change in how children in care were treated had been slow, and he suggested it had been achieved as much through gradual changes in how society itself approached childhood as through legislation. For example, in 1950, caning was routine in Approved Schools [Poyser, 1990]; by 1991, the authors of the Pindown Inquiry could condemn, with public support, staff who had sanctioned solitary confinement and deprivation for troublesome young people in Staffordshire children's homes [Levy and Kahan, 1991].

Poyser quoted the hopes expressed by one former Children's Officer in response to the Children Act 1948:

> I was convinced that the 1948 Act provided a charter for children, sweeping away the horrors of large children's orphanages, Dennis O'Neill situations, and the stigma attached to state care. The 1948 Act actually said that young children in care were entitled to everything available to young citizens not in care. It was our job to see that they got it. [Renier, 1990]

In December 1989, another Children Act had just received the Royal Assent and was to be implemented in October 1991. As social services departments prepared themselves to implement the new legislation, what lessons were there to be learnt from the history of child care since the War, and how could the principles embodied in the Children Act be put into practice in ways that would make a real difference to children and their families?

The message of that first Advisory Group meeting was that change was possible, but difficult and slow; and that in working with Birmingham Action on Child Care the participants were accepting a major challenge. Children's services were experiencing demoralisation resulting from lack of popular support in tackling very difficult tasks. A series of child abuse scandals had made headlines, and the media interpretation of the subsequent inquiry reports, from Maria Colwell in 1974 to Cleveland in 1988, blamed social workers. In Birmingham, allegations of abuse and malpractice in children's homes in 1987-8 and the growing concern about the severe pressure on children's services came together to prompt the Social Services Committee to establish Birmingham Action on Child Care.

This chapter sets out briefly the history of the state's intervention in child care since the end of the Second World War, and goes on to describe the specific problems experienced by residential child care services in Birmingham.

Themes in child care since 1945

> The public wants children protected from a variety of depredations; it wants parents' rights and family life to be safeguarded against unwarranted interference by the State; it wants to be protected from the unwelcome behaviour of older children; and it expects all this to be done quietly, smoothly, efficiently and effectively.
>
> [Parker et al., 1991]

There are a number of themes which stand out from a review of the history of statutory child care since 1945. These include:

- the balance between providing support and advice to parents with a view to keeping or returning a child home, and the need to protect the child and/or to find him or her substitute care, short or longer term;
- the problem of instability and uncertainty for children looked after by public bodies;
- establishing guidelines for the appropriate use of emergency action to protect children;
- the tension between the 'rights' of parents and the 'rights' of children;
- the merits and uses of fostering compared with residential care;
- attempts to divert children and young people from criminal activity, whilst keeping them out of care and custody, and at the same time reassuring the public that the 'problem of juvenile delinquency' was being addressed;
- revelations about the incidence of non-accidental injury of children; the extent of child sexual abuse; and abuse of children and young people in institutions.

The state has been involved in the care and protection of children since the Elizabethan Poor Law imposed certain duties on parents to provide for their children, and also empowered civil parish authorities to look after those whose parents could not do so. Modern child care law, however, has its origins in the Children Act 1948. As was often to be the case in the years that followed, this Act was passed after a national scandal – the death of a thirteen-year-old boy, Dennis O'Neill, at the hands of his foster parents while in the care of a local authority. Two inquiries followed – into the care of children by the state [Curtis, 1946] and into the specific circumstances leading to Dennis O'Neill's death [Monkton, 1945]. There were, however, other factors which also contributed to the passing of the Children Act 1948.

During the Second World War, the evacuation of families from major cities revealed standards of health and child care amongst a minority of families which gave rise to considerable concern [Philp, 1963]. After the war, many women who had been involved in war work were reluctant to relinquish their jobs to the returning servicemen and return to domesticity. Day nurseries which had been set up to enable women to contribute to the war effort were closed down. The importance of the family and the value of the mother-child relationship was re-emphasised during this period [Wilson, 1977]. Apart from stressing the value of family life, local authorities believed that keeping children with their families was cheaper than institutional or foster care. The Children Act 1948 required local authorities to set up children's departments to look after the best interests of children in their care as well as encouraging the return of children to their parents or wider family.

After the Second World War years, state day care for children was increasingly seen as a welfare service, for children or families considered to have special problems. Little provision was made for the children of working parents, and when employment increased again amongst mothers of young children during the 1980s, the demand was met by relatives (especially grandparents), childminders and private and voluntary day nurseries [Hennessy et al., 1992]. Although arguments for the provision of state day care for the children of working parents were increasingly put forward, local authority day nurseries were still largely seen as a social work resource. The appropriate role of state day care was – and continues to be – the subject of intense debate.

The Children Act 1948 reflected another aspect of the debate on the appropriate role of the state in child care. There was a tension between a policy of assisting natural families to care for their children at home and a policy of providing good, long term substitute care, a tension which was to continue during subsequent years. Greater powers to assist parents (Children and Young Persons Act 1963; Child Care Act 1980) went in tandem with increased powers to remove children from their parents (Children and Young Persons Act 1969) and to sever their ties with home (Children Act 1975).

The local authority shall, in all cases where it appears to them consistent with the welfare of the child to do so, endeavour to secure that the care of the child is taken over either (a) by a parent or guardian of his, or (b) by a relative or friend of his, being, where possible, a person of the same religious persuasion.

[Children Act 1948, Section 1(3)]

Interest and concern about child abuse was re-awakened by the death of Maria Colwell in 1973. After spending five years fostered by her aunt, six-year-old Maria was returned to her mother and step-father, only to be murdered by her step-father shortly afterwards. The Children Act 1975 included provisions reflecting the findings of the Inquiry into her death [Department of Health and Social Security, 1974]. Various administrative measures were taken by the Department of Health and Social Security to improve procedures for the protection of children, including the establishment of Child Protection Registers and the use of multidisciplinary case conferences.

Social services departments were established from 1970 to create a unified social work service following the recommendations of the Seebohm Committee [Seebohm, 1968]. The new generic departments were cautious about returning children home, and increasingly ready to take emergency action (place of safety orders) in cases of suspected child abuse or neglect. The numbers of children in care increased during the 1970s, with children once in care tending to stay for long periods. Children and young people of mixed parentage were particularly likely to be admitted to care [Bebbington and Miles, 1989], but social services departments often lacked policies or strategies to enable them to respond to the needs of multiracial communities. Social workers generally had little understanding of Black families or the needs of Black children at this time [Macdonald, 1991].

During the 1980s, however, the numbers of children in care fell substantially. This was in part a consequence of a decline in the overall population of children. There were, however, other reasons for the fall in the numbers of children cared for by local authorities. Much of the focus of policy makers and the media during the 1960s had been on 'juvenile delinquency'. It was felt that the existing system could not deal effectively with the most serious young offenders. Approved Schools were renamed Community Homes with Education and transferred to local authority control in the 1970s.

Research [Cornish and Clarke, 1976] suggested that residential care, especially where it removed the child or young person from his or her community, was not effective in the treatment of offending behaviour. Faced with the need to make economies, local authorities looked for community based alternatives for young offenders. At the same time, initiatives were underway to provide training and education to divert other children and young people from offending behaviour. The debate:

centred on the question of whether the offending child should be seen as an unsocialised individual in need of help and assistance or as a calculating transgressor in need of a formal sanction. [Giller, 1989]

Consequently, while the Children and Young Persons Act 1969 included provision for 'intermediate treatment' to be a condition of supervision orders, and as well as other measures to take children and young people out of the criminal courts, a change of government ensured that some parts of the Act were never implemented [Morris and Giller, 1987]. Nevertheless, alternatives to care and custody for young offenders were developed during the 1970s and 1980s by social services departments, the Probation Service and voluntary organisations, with the result that the number of children committed to care because they had been convicted of an offence declined substantially during the 1980s [NACRO, 1991]. In 1980, 15.4 per cent of children in care were committed to care on a criminal care order; by 1990, the percentage had fallen to 2.6 [Utting, 1991].

During the 1980s, public and professional concern focused increasingly on two issues: the over-use of compulsory powers to remove children, especially the use of place of safety orders, and the circumstances of children who remained for long periods in the care system. The publication in 1973 of *Children who Wait* [Rowe and Lambert, 1973] had drawn attention to the numbers of children under nine-years-old denied permanent home placements because of the hope that they would eventually return to their natural families. The emphasis on the child's natural family was held to be at the expense of the child's future; it was claimed that little effort went into planning, prevention, or rehabilitation at this time.

Rowe and Lambert's research had a significant impact on practice over the next fifteen years, leading to an emphasis on permanency planning, with strict timetables for rehabilitation home. Their findings were amongst the factors which led to the growing use of adoption for children in long term care as a means to secure 'permanency' for them [Thoburn, 1990]. In addition, adoption was used to secure the position of children in step-families and of children of single mothers who subsequently married. Thus, an adoption law primarily designed for the adoption of babies was increasingly used for the adoption of older children. Changing attitudes to the use of adoption led the Department of Health to institute a review of adoption law in 1990 [Department of Health, 1990].

In 1985 David Berridge's research on children's homes – the first major research study (other than studies of Approved Schools) to look at residential care for children – showed that residential provision was a positive experience for some children, especially teenagers. In some circumstances, it was the placement of choice, for example, where siblings needed to be kept together, where there were family links to be maintained, to provide reception and assessment facilities for children coming into care, and when foster placements broke down. The research also revealed, however, that some children experienced very little stability in substitute care as a whole, and had many moves and changes of carer [Berridge, 1985]. During the 1980s, the National Association of Young People in Care (NAYPIC) and the Family Rights Group both stressed the importance of listening to the views and experiences of children and their families. Young people from NAYPIC emphasised that residential care was the preferred option for some young people, especially those who for various reasons did not want another family to substitute for their own.

In the same year, the publication of the Department of Health funded *Social Work Decisions in Child Care* (known as The Pink Book) [Department of Health and Social Security, 1985] drew together the findings of nine research studies which demonstrated:

- that **admission to care** was often unplanned and haphazard, that compulsory powers were increasingly used but were often counterproductive, and that parents were rarely involved by social workers as equal partners;
- that little social work attention and planning took place immediately **after admission**, that family links were not encouraged, and that parents felt marginalised;
- that **practice** was deficient in a number of ways, assessments and records were often inadequate, social workers spent insufficient time in direct work with children, and reviews and case conferences were not as central as they should be to the decision-making process.

Another influential research study, *Lost in Care* [Millham et al., 1986], emphasised the importance of a child's first weeks in care – once children have been in care for over five weeks, their chances of returning home within two years decreased significantly. Maintenance of close contact with his or her family was the best indicator that a child would leave care rapidly. The research showed that many children in care lost contact with their natural families, yet children's psychological, social and educational well-being was enhanced by regular contact with their families, even if they were unlikely to return home.

The social worker's dilemma

During the 1980s a number of inquiries into the deaths of children concluded that social workers were not active enough in their efforts to protect children, paying too much attention to keeping the child at home or to the parents' needs [London Borough of Brent, 1985; London Borough of Greenwich, 1987; London Borough of Lambeth, 1987]. Concern about the over-use of social workers' powers to intervene was also expressed intermittently. In 1987, however, events in Cleveland produced a shift in the focus of attention, with many commentators concluding that social workers were intervening unnecessarily and arbitrarily.

> It has seemed that the primary concern addressed in the Beckford, Carlile, and Henry reports was that social workers did too little too late, while the primary concern addressed in the Cleveland report was that social workers did too much too soon.
>
> [Parton, 1989]

The Cleveland Inquiry [Butler-Sloss, 1988], which was set up in 1987 and reported in July 1988, arose as a result of an unprecedented rise in the diagnosis of child sexual abuse in Cleveland, mainly at Middlesbrough General Hospital. During five months of 1987, 121 children were diagnosed as having been sexually abused. Public and media concern focused on the manner of the diagnosis, the immediate action taken, and the subsequent handling of the cases. The Report criticised the use of emergency powers (place of safety orders) to remove children from their families without warning for further investigation; the denial of contact between parents and children; the failure of cooperation between agencies; and overreliance on a single diagnostic sign. Social workers and doctors were considered to have acted too hastily and on the basis of too little evidence, although the necessity at times to act immediately was also acknowledged.

> It is difficult for professionals to balance the conflicting interests and needs in the enormously important and delicate field of child sexual abuse.
>
> [Butler-Sloss, 1988 (The Cleveland Report)]

The Children Bill 1988, which was published in the same year as the Cleveland Report, attempted to resolve a number of the issues summarised here, by providing a coherent legal framework for statutory child care, with primacy for the welfare of the child, and the development of the concept of parental responsibility, rather than 'rights'. While it included provisions which were a direct result of the conclusions drawn by the Cleveland Inquiry, the main provisions of the Bill were the result of a long process of consultation and discussion, culminating in a White Paper issued in January 1987 [Department of Health and Social Security, 1987]. The Bill brought together for the first time public and private law relating to child welfare in a uniform and coherent framework. The Children Bill is considered in more detail in chapter 5.

While the main focus of public and professional concern during 1988 was growing evidence of child sexual abuse, a secondary issue was the state of residential care. An independent review of residential care was commissioned by the Department of Health and Social Security in 1985, in response to the widespread view that residential services were in a demoralised condition. The Review team was headed by Gillian Wagner and reported in 1988 [Wagner, 1988]. The report focused mainly on residential care for adults. Nevertheless, in its consideration of children's homes, it reiterated David Berridge's conclusion [Berridge, 1985] that residential care could be 'a positive choice' for some children, for example, to keep families together, or to deal with the breakdown of a foster placement. Some older children and young people, in evidence to the Review team, expressed a preference for residential care rather than fostering. Unfortunately, the Review Team's findings were somewhat overshadowed by the publication of the Cleveland Report at about the same time.

Professional awareness of poor conditions and abuse in residential care grew during the late 1980s, to reach a peak in 1991/92 with the publication of two reports into residential care for children [Levy and Kahan, 1991; Utting, 1991], and the establishment of the Howe Inquiry into the pay and conditions of residential workers [Howe, 1992], and the Warner Inquiry into their recruitment, selection and training [Warner, 1992]. Events in children's homes in Staffordshire, Leicestershire, Gwent, Sunderland, and North Wales, widely reported in 1989-1992, revealed that abuse of children in residential care could go undetected by management for long periods.

In Birmingham, however, allegations of abuse in residential child care were made as early as 1987, and were a major factor in the decision to set up Birmingham Action on Child Care. This chapter next examines the state of residential child care services in the late 1980s before considering the situation in Birmingham which preceded the establishment of BACC in 1989.

Residential child care in the late 1980s: a service in terminal decline?

The problems reported in Birmingham Social Services Department's residential child care service in 1987 were not unique. Changes in the child care service as a whole, the balance between age groups, the demands made on social services departments and on local authorities, new attitudes and perceptions all impacted on residential child care services. It was alleged that morale was low and conditions poor in many social services departments throughout England and Wales.

Nationally, provision of children's homes reduced dramatically during the 1980s. In England, the number of children in children's homes fell by over 60 per cent, from 29,300 residents in 1979 to 11,000 in 1989 [Howe, 1992]. There were a number of factors contributing to this decline – fewer children in the relevant age group, fewer children being looked after by local authorities, and greater use of foster care.

There was a substantial decrease of nearly 40 per cent in the numbers of children looked after by local authorities – in foster homes, children's homes, and other accommodation – during that period. This was partly accounted for by a decrease in the child population, but it was also due to changes in working methods by social services departments. This included strong pressures to keep children out of care (although not necessarily with corresponding preventive provision), diversionary work with young offenders, and reluctance to use the 'criminal care order'. In the 1980s the importance of maintaining children in their own families was stressed; moreover, the concept of 'family' was changing, with a wider range of family forms considered acceptable. This recognition may have supported acceptance of a wide range of family situations and placements as preferable to public care of all kinds, but specifically as preferable to residential care [Utting, 1991]. The Children Act 1989 reflected this view that the family is not a static, easily defined unit, and that families may take many forms and still provide environments in which children can thrive. Its provisions emphasised the need to support families in caring for their own children.

These national trends were replicated in Birmingham, where the number of children in care decreased from 3,758 at 31 March 1980 to 1,774 in 1991 – a fall of over 50 per cent. Again, this was partly due to a decline in the child population, especially in the age groups most likely to be looked after by the local authority. During the period, the number of children and young people aged 10 to 19 years in Birmingham fell by approximately 25 per cent (although it should be noted that the numbers of teenage children and young people in the city were predicted to rise again during the 1990s). There was, however, a real reduction in the use of all kinds of accommodation for children.

> The number of children in local authority care ... fell by nearly 40 per cent during the last ten years. [...] The overall population of children declined during that period but there was nevertheless a substantial decrease of 29 per cent in the number of children in care. Part of the reduction arose from changes in practice such as the virtual ending of care orders in criminal proceedings. An important part of the reduction, however, is due to improved preventive work by social services departments.
>
> [Utting, 1991].

There was also a significant change in how such children were looked after. Between 1979 and 1990, the number of children's homes provided by Birmingham Social Services Department decreased from 106 providing 1,619 places to 31 with 440 places. This represented a 73 per cent reduction in places. Whereas in 1979, 33 per cent of children looked after by Birmingham Social Services Department were accommodated in children's homes, in 1991, this had fallen to 25 per cent. The use of other kinds of non-family placements – boarding schools, hospitals, and community homes with education – also fell, from 20 per cent to 7 per cent. The difference was accounted for by fostering, which accommodated 28 per cent of children looked after by the authority in 1980 but over 50 per cent in 1991 [Birmingham Social Services Department, 1991a]. However, because of the decline in the numbers of children looked after, the number of children fostered remained roughly constant.

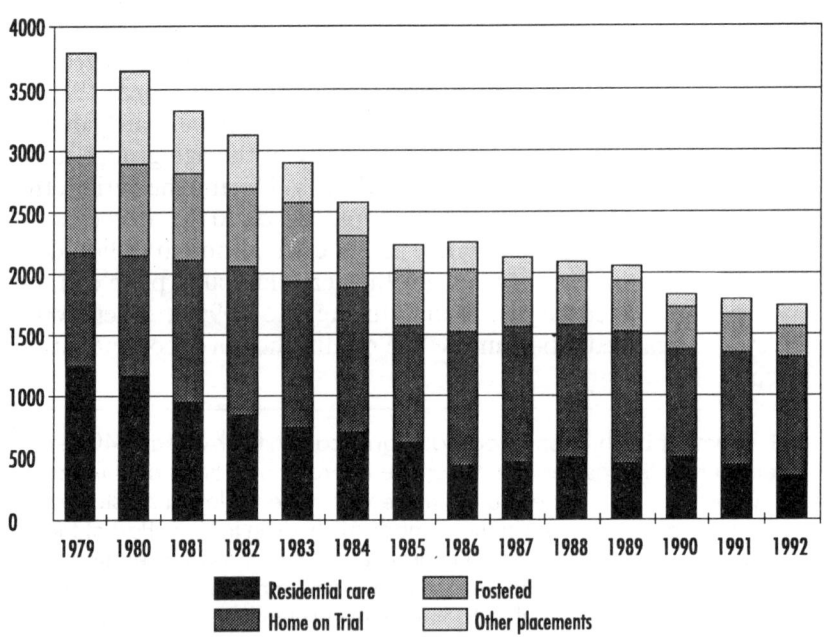

Total children in care by placement

Reduction in the use of residential care in Birmingham was facilitated by demographic changes, which reduced the numbers of children entering care. Adjustment to the changes was through closing children's homes, whilst maintaining approximately the same number of foster home places. Nevertheless, the proportion of children in foster care in Birmingham was, and remained, low in comparison with other authorities, an issue later to be addressed by Birmingham Action on Child Care.

Both the functions of residential child care and people's perceptions of it changed during the 1980s. Residential care came to be used as 'a last resort', when all other efforts to deal with a child's situation had been exhausted. In Birmingham, the 'challenge to care', described later in this chapter, was instituted to ensure that children were maintained in their families wherever possible. The result, however, was that residential care was *viewed* as a 'last resort' as well as used as one. This perception:

makes it very difficult for some establishments to have a positive set of common values because the implications of this are that residents are only present due to the failure of other alternatives or that nothing else can be done.
[Kelly, 1989]

The admissions process is very important in setting the tone of a placement, and may well determine its success or failure. Where residential care is seen as the last resort, admissions may often be the result of an emergency, unplanned, and with no preparation for either child or staff [ibid.].

Other factors help to stigmatise residential care. Traditionally, caring is women's work, and such work is invariably poorly paid and lacking in status. While women themselves recognise the range of complex skills and the high level of responsibility involved in running a home and caring for children and other dependent relatives, some of those who control resources – predominantly men – view home-making and caring as unskilled and undemanding work. Such perceptions lead to this type of work being poorly paid, and those working in it being given little recognition or training [Phillipson, 1989].

> Women's work has been caricatured as containing the ten deadly Cs ... catering, cleaning, coiffeuring, caretaking, care-giving, counterminding, clothes-making, clothes washing, clerking, and care of the sick. All of these are to be found extensively in residential work. But rarely are any of these activities seen as prestigious or worthy of substantial remuneration unless undertaken by men.
>
> [Phillipson, 1989]

Conversely, there was a trend to stress the value of care in the home, whilst still failing to acknowledge, other than with words, the work undertaken there by women. Since the Second World War there was growing emphasis on the importance of 'a normal natural family life' as the best place for children, including those children with severe disabilities who would in the past have been cared for in institutions. The implicit assumption that home is where people really like to live was also enshrined in the community care legislation. Such values made it difficult to justify the continued existence of residential care [Brown, 1989], and there were those who believed that children's homes had failed and should be phased out. In Warwickshire, the provision of children's homes was phased out completely, and the Social Services Director commented that:

Most directors are not very comfortable with the standards they provide [in residential homes]. All we have done in Warwickshire is to pose the question as to whether residential care is necessary for all but a very small number of youngsters. [Peter Smallridge, quoted in *Community Care*, 25 October 1990]

Although there were good reasons for challenging this view, the residual or redundant status of residential care was reinforced by such statements, as was, unfortunately, the low morale of the children and staff.

It is common knowledge in 1993 that staff in residential child care lack status, are poorly paid, and have received little or no training to undertake the work [Howe, 1992]. There is no recognised career structure for residential workers, and therefore those who acquire qualifications frequently leave the residential sector for fieldwork or other social work. Research undertaken for the Warner Inquiry into the selection, development and management of staff showed that 41 per cent of heads of homes employed by English local authorities, and only 6 per cent of care staff had a social work qualification [Warner, 1992]. On average, local authority staff had been in post for four years [Ibid.], but Utting postulated a polarisation between staff who had been in post for a short time and others who had been in residential work for a substantial period [Utting, 1991]. Despite 'the general perception ... of relatively young staff without life experience', the average age of heads of homes was 39 years, and of other care staff, 35 years [Warner, 1992]. The evidence suggests that residential care is used by some staff as a springboard to other social work careers.

Staff within homes are also often isolated, operating in a policy vacuum. Even where policies setting out the role and function of the residential sector within the child care service exist (and research suggests that in the 1980s such policies were rare), staff are often not aware of them [Utting, 1991; Department of Health, 1991b]. Both the Utting and Warner Inquiries concluded that many social services departments lacked management structures which helped and supported heads of homes in carrying out the complex task of managing a home. The Howe and Warner Inquiries found that residential establishments were often managed by middle managers with limited or no experience of residential work [Howe, 1992; Warner, 1992].

> ...children with long histories of disturbance or neglect, or with behavioural problems, are over-represented in homes.
> [Utting, 1991]

The reduction in residential care provision inevitably causes a concentration in the remaining homes of those children and young people who present the greatest problems. These include those considered too disruptive or damaged for fostering as well as those whose foster homes have broken down. In addition, because residential care is often used predominantly for teenagers, children's homes also cope with all the difficulties usually associated with young people at this stage in their lives [Utting, 1991]. The concentration of teenagers with long histories of disturbance or neglect, or with behaviour problems, compounds the difficulty of the residential task. Many children report stress caused by fellow residents – physical or verbal abuse, anxiety at others' behaviour, and bullying [Department of Health, 1991b]. A recent report shows that sexual abuse of children by other children is more common than was suspected, and that there can be special dangers for children in residential care [National Children's Home, 1992].

Research has also indicated that children from deprived backgrounds are much more likely to be looked after by a local authority at some time in their lives than children from more affluent backgrounds [Department of Health, 1991b]. As the Short Committee concluded as long ago as 1984, 'children in care are the children of the poor' [House of Commons: Social Services

Committee, 1984]. There are implications here for the provision of support to children in their own homes, as well as a question about how much support these children can realistically expect from their families while in care and when they are ready to leave.

> **The probability of admission to care**
>
> | **Child A** | **Child B** |
> |---|---|
> | Aged 5-9 | Aged 5-9 |
> | No dependence on social security benefits | Household head receives income support |
> | Two parent family | Single adult household |
> | Three or fewer children | Four or more children |
> | White | Mixed ethnic origin |
> | Owner occupied home | Privately rented home |
> | More rooms than people | One or more persons per room |
> | *Odds are 1 in 7,000* | *Odds are 1 in 10* |
>
> [Bebbington and Miles, 1989]

During the 1980s, there were also demographic pressures on social services departments throughout England and Wales, caused by increasing longevity. The growing population of frail elderly people, together with increasing expectations of support from other people with disabilities and from their carers, led local authorities to concentrate new resources on services for adults, rather than children's services. In part, this also reflected the reduction in the number of children in the population, but it led to a gradual shift in the balance of resources between the two major service areas. For example, in Birmingham, the health and special needs teams created in 1982 were resourced from generic teams which previously had worked mainly with children. Specifically, the money saved through the closure of children's homes was not retained to improve the quality of life in the remaining homes. (Since 1991 this trend has been reversed, and sums have been earmarked to upgrade these homes.) In the 1980s, the budget for community care services grew in real terms, whilst children's services simply kept pace with inflation.

Residential care is an expensive resource. Staff costs are the biggest element, but, in addition, the concentration of adolescents and of children with behavioural difficulties, together with a high turnover of population, lead to heavy expenses for provisions, clothing, redecoration, maintenance and repairs. Thus, although the number of homes run by Birmingham fell, residential care still accounted for over one-third of the Department's spending on children and families [Birmingham Social Services Department, 1991a].

This combination – of an expensive but declining service, with residual or (in some people's eyes) redundant functions, operating in a policy vacuum, undertaking work which was stigmatised and poorly paid, employing untrained, inexperienced and isolated workers, and dealing with a concentration of disturbed and disruptive teenagers from deprived backgrounds – was potentially explosive. It is, therefore, unsurprising that during the late 1980s, Birmingham Social Services Department was only one amongst a number of departments in Great Britain to uncover evidence of abuse and malpractice in its children's homes. What was significant about Birmingham was the firm and early action taken to deal with the emerging problems, and that the response tackled the problems of the residential sector in the context of reviewing the whole service to children and families.

The Director of Social Services, Adrianne Jones, in proposing to set up Birmingham Action on Child Care, recognised that the problems manifested in the city's children's homes could not be isolated from the way the whole children and families service was operated and managed. Change in one part of the service would have repercussions for other parts. For example, the emphasis on keeping children out of care combined with a preference for foster placement for most children under ten helped to create the loss of morale in residential child care. This was an unintended and therefore unmanaged consequence of change. In proposing to review and develop services for children and families to meet the needs of the 1990s, the Director was determined to manage the change effectively. The next section describes the events which led to recognition of a need to change and redevelop the service.

The genesis of Birmingham Action on Child Care

The decision to set up Birmingham Action on Child Care needs to be understood in the context of the history of Birmingham Social Services Department during the 1980s. During these ten years, as has been described, the number of places in residential care was reduced, and efforts were being made to manage and utilise the resources more effectively. Nevertheless, allegations made in 1987 suggested that staff in two homes had been able to operate abusive regimes over a long period without being detected.

In 1978, management of children's homes was transferred from Area Managers to four District Managers who were members of a newly established Care Services section. Referrals for placement in residential care were handled centrally by a placements officer. Concern at the number of children spending their childhood in residential care led the then Director of Social Services, Ronald Liddiard, to set up the Child Care Review Group (CCRG). Its task was to consider the role and functions of residential care, its ability to meet the needs of children, and the number of places required and their distribution. The Group expressed concern at the numbers of young children in children's homes and recommended that children aged under 11 should only be admitted to residential care 'in exceptional circumstances'. Four District Centres were established to undertake assessments, at the centres or at the child's own home.

The CCRG also introduced a procedure – known as the 'challenge to care' – which was designed to ensure that alternatives had been explored before a child was admitted to care. It gave District Managers power to refuse placements for children, and therefore complete control over these valuable resources. Whilst the 'challenge to care' ensured that expensive substitute care was not used unnecessarily, it had the function of giving residential care a 'last resort' role. Residential care was not seen as a positive experience, as a resource for children and families, but as a place to be avoided. Other ways of supporting families were not developed in its place, however. Parents under stress and asking for their child to be taken into care for a period were first given advice or counselling. Children would only be admitted to care when this had failed. Thus, some admissions took place at a moment of crisis and without planning, even though the family had been known to the Department for some time. CCRG also concentrated its work on the residential sector, making no parallel recommendations for foster care.

Recommendations made by CCRG to improve the use of and standards in children's homes were not implemented, however, because other concerns became more pressing. In 1982, the Social Services Committee asked the management consultants, Price Waterhouse, to undertake a review of the structure and management of the Department. At this time, the involvement of management consultants in the public sector was very unusual. Many staff were strongly opposed to the use of consultants whose main experience was in the private sector, and they expressed anger at not being consulted themselves. When the Director then set out plans for reorganisation which included dispersal of established teams and changes of social worker for many clients, many staff, with the support of their union, decided not to cooperate. Eventually, this led to a strike in 1982 which lasted several weeks and which involved all sectors of the service, including residential workers. The effects of the strike and lack of confidence in management led to demoralisation and cynicism in some staff.

When Adrianne Jones took up her post as Director in May 1985, she found the Department's reputation was poor. The death in 1985 of a child in the care of the department, Gemma Hartwell, and the murder of a social worker, Frances Bettridge, by a client in 1986 contributed to the atmosphere.

> When I arrived in Birmingham in 1985, my immediate impression was that the Department needed bringing up to date in its social work practice and that a more open management style was required.
>
> [Adrianne Jones, personal communication, 1993]

There had been a change in political control of the City Council and the new administration planned to decentralise services to parliamentary constituency level. One of the Director's first tasks, therefore, was to institute another reorganisation of the Department, which took place from 1987. Whilst attempts were made to ensure that staff were involved and informed, and that disruption was kept to a minimum, reorganisation was not popular. The process, however, enabled the Director to create a new management structure for the Department, and to appoint a Senior Assistant Director to oversee the day-to-day operations of the Department.

In April 1987, allegations of ill-treatment and abuse were made against the whole team of care staff at one children's home. First the Officer in Charge and Deputy were suspended and subsequently six other staff, while investigations took place. During the course of the subsequent police investigations, all but one of the staff resigned and left the Department; the other was given a final written warning.

Because of the police inquiry and the arguments of opposing solicitors, the whole process, however, was not concluded until June 1988. Late in 1987, in October, allegations of ill-treatment and abuse of children, and of sexual harassment of female staff, were made against senior staff at another children's home. These allegations resulted in suspensions, with subsequent resignations and dismissals of staff. The suspension of staff and the nature of their misconduct was widely reported in the press, both locally and nationally. Other, less sensational incidents in children's homes also now attracted media attention. Claims for compensation by some of the children involved ensured that the events remained 'live' over a long period.

> The ill-treatment of children by staff will not be tolerated. It is rare but it does happen. [These] are exceptional cases. They should not reflect badly on the work of the vast majority of staff which is of high quality.
>
> [Birmingham City Council, 1988]

The Director was determined to ensure that abuse and ill-treatment of children in the department's children's homes was not tolerated or allowed to persist undetected. A well-publicised complaints procedure for children was set up, with a telephone number straight through to the Director's office for children to use. In September 1988 the Director reported to the Social Services Committee on the actions she had taken in respect of conditions in children's homes, and informed Members that she had asked the Social Services Inspectorate to bring forward its planned inspection of Birmingham children's homes. She also shared the concern expressed in the Cleveland Report that the constant adverse publicity that social work was receiving was leading to demoralisation of staff.

> We are also concerned about the extent of the misplaced adverse criticism social workers have received from the media and elsewhere. There is a danger that social workers ... will be demoralised.
>
> [Butler-Sloss, 1988 (The Cleveland Report)]

She concluded that action over and above the normal management response was needed. The following month, in the context of a regular report reviewing services for children and families [Birmingham Social Services Department, 1988d], she sought the Social Services Committee's support for the establishment of a limited life project to look at services for children and families as a whole.

BACC and the management of change in the public sector

The Director had already initiated a series of actions in response to issues uncovered by investigations of abuse at the two homes [Birmingham Social Services Department, 1988b]. These included:

- a complaints procedure for children, which would always include a manager not in line management when the complaint came from a child in residential care;
- the appointment of new managers and staff for the two homes;
- guidance for staff on handling aggression;
- increased opportunities for training in the selection and recruitment of staff;
- the preparation of detailed guidance for managers on the management of children's homes;
- an improved procedure to ensure that reports from statutory visits were acted upon; and
- counselling and other support for the children affected.

The Director believed, however, that the situation needed a stronger response than this, to enable the Department to gain credibility:

not just a cosmetic credibility, but something which really reached down into the service, that had an effect on the quality of service... I really believed that we had identified the problems, and that putting them right was not just about having a list of recommendations about residential care and its management. Putting it right in my view was about changing the whole culture of the organisation, the whole management approach, [changing] the quality of practice in the child care service as a whole. It was not just about one part of it. [Adrianne Jones, Interview, 1992]

The idea of a special project was the Director's own initiative and personal decision. There had been pressure from Councillors to establish an external inquiry, but the Director believed that a typical inquiry would not only be expensive, but would address issues in residential child care on their own, issues which were already well-rehearsed. It would also keep the media spotlight on children's homes in the short term, without leading to any new solutions to fundamental problems.

The Social Services Committee accepted the Director's proposal for a major project to review the child care service as a whole. The project's director would be recruited or seconded on a fixed term contract, and would report to the Director. The project would be supported by an advisory group, drawn from a wide range of interests. The group would help safeguard the project's independence and provide support and advice for the project director. Barbara Kahan agreed to chair it and also to act as the project's consultant. The Director began to develop the idea of using a systems approach to reviewing the child care service:

It was this notion that if we were going to change fundamentally one part of the system – residential child care – we needed to understand how that would impact on all other parts. [Ibid.]

The Director was aware that morale was poor in many parts of the child care service, not just the residential sector. The needs of children were met by the service as a whole, and not just by residential care, yet communication between fieldwork and residential services was poor. Historically the Care Services section was very powerful; its managers could exercise 'the challenge to care' and refuse services to other managers. The residential care service had been managed separately from other services, and with managerial considerations, rather than the needs of children, uppermost. The process of home closures had entailed redeployment of many members of staff, some of them without the qualifications and experience necessary for their employment in other capacities. This process had undoubtedly left a demoralised service preoccupied with the needs of staff. It included a minority of staff who were unable to make the changes necessary for work in residential child care in the late 1980s. Nevertheless, the Director recognised that the residential sector was only part of the problems the Department was experiencing in its children's services. She was also increasingly concerned about the number of children in care without a social worker, and about the perceived lack of cooperation and communication between residential staff and field social workers.

A small group of staff drew up an 'outline' for the new project [Coffin, 1989], which set out the managerial context (City Council, Social Services Department and key resources), and the demographic and political contexts, in which the project would operate. Drawing on the experience of the Community Care Special Action Project (discussed in chapter 3 below) and on the literature of systems planning, the group outlined a methodology which involved wide ranging consultation, production of information, and involvement of staff at all levels and different sections of the department. The process was a key aspect of securing positive outcomes. The *Outline* stressed the importance of reviewing each part of the child care service in the context of the service as a whole. The methodology adopted by the Project is discussed more fully in chapter 3.

There were a number of factors which were held to be crucial to the project's success:

- involvement of children, young people, their carers, and foster carers;
- direct access to the management team, with 'championship' for the Project by the Director herself;
- involvement of staff at all levels in the development of ideas;
- provision of accurate information to staff and others; and
- recognition of existing good practice.

These ideas were to be refined and developed by the Project Team in its first months. There was early recognition that the Project had to work in ways which avoided repeating the mistakes of previous years, and which gave staff hope for real change and involvement in good practice. Subsequent chapters demonstrate the value of this approach to changing the culture and practice of the Social Services Department. It is argued that lessons to be learnt apply not just to management of services for children and families in a social services department but to management of change in local government generally.

The Birmingham Action on Child Care proposal came at a time when management practice was under sustained scrutiny in the public sector. During the late 1980s local government was being urged to adopt private sector management practices. It was operating in a climate of funding constraints and increased controls on expenditure by central government. There were pressures to achieve value for money, to compete with the private sector in providing public services, to involve the private sector in supplying services through competitive tendering, and to achieve comparative efficiency and effectiveness. In the personal social services a mixed economy of welfare was developing, with local government being expected to encourage diversity of provision whilst at the same time competing with other providers in price and quality. Consumer participation, customer choice, decentralisation of services, and devolution of management were all being emphasised. 'Bureaucrats and professionals' who between them decided what 'clients' needed were to be replaced by managers following the best private sector practice [Clarke and Newman, 1992]. The rationale for this change has been caricatured as follows:

> By contrast with the professional, the manager is customer focussed and is driven by the search for efficiency rather than abstract 'professional standards'. Compared to the bureaucrat, the manager is flexible and outward looking. Unlike the politician, the manager inhabits the 'real world' of 'good business practices' not the realms of doctrinaire ideology. [Ibid.]

The emphasis on management was paralleled by developments which decreased the power of local politicians, local government itself, and the professions. These included local management of schools and increased power to school governors, including parent governors; introduction of a 'lay element' into the inspection of social services; development of the National Vocational Qualification as an alternative, non-academic route into social work and other jobs; and removal of local politicians from health authorities. People from business and industry were drafted in to help manage education, training, and health.

There are, however, critical ways in which management of a public service, and specifically of local government, is different from management in the private sector. Aspects of public sector organisations which are not found in the private sector include:

> the central role of the political process and the value choices that will result; the meeting of needs with considerations of equity and within a legislative as well as a permissive framework; and the 'double obligation' of the public sector organisation towards the public as citizens as well as users of services. [Bernard, 1990]

Local government operates under financial and other constraints imposed by central government, as well as by the local political administration. With fixed budgets, improvement of a service will not necessarily result in additional resources for further development; indeed, success can impose additional strains on the authority. An improved service may simply increase demand and lead to rationing. Oversubscribed services cannot, however, usually be rationed through price, and other criteria must be found to manage their distribution. Local councillors may be reluctant to ration a popular service (for example, free travel for elderly people), and its expansion may be at the expense of other, necessary but less attractive services. At other times, success may lead to pressures on the Department's budget and then to spending cuts. As will be described later, implementation of some recommendations from Birmingham Action on Child Care was held up because of restrictions on spending. These restrictions resulted in part from the success of an initiative to fill social work vacancies and therefore ensure all child care cases were allocated to a social worker.

Social services departments' budgets are always difficult to forecast and control. Some services will be demand led, because the authority is obliged to provide them by statute (for example, child protection investigations). Others may be required by court order, even though the authority may have exhausted its budget for that item. Thus, the court may require additional services from a Guardian ad Litem – an independent social worker appointed by the court to represent the interests of children – which the authority is bound by law to fund.

Whilst a private enterprise can concentrate on meeting the needs of its customers – and usually be confident even today that if it does so its income will increase – local government may not even be able to identify clearly its customers. It is accountable to elected members, the electorate, service users and their carers. The 'customer' for children and families services could be the child, his or her parents, or mother, or father, or another carer or relative, or the family, or society in general; on whose behalf does the state intervene in the family's or the child's life? These often competing or conflicting interests mean that the management of change and the improvement of services take place in a context of contradictory and often unpredictable demands.

The management of change in local government is further complicated by timescales which are generally longer than in private enterprise. The process of setting budgets – which are the framework within which changes will occur – begins with the first representations to central government about the level of its support to local services, and may occur as long as two years ahead of the budget's actually being spent. Yet the amount which the authority will have to spend may not be known until shortly before the start of the financial year. Individual local authorities operate within nationally imposed constraints – the constraints of nationally agreed rates of pay as well as those imposed by legislation. These restrict their freedom to innovate. Decisions which on the face of it appear to be insignificant – such as to regrade one post – may have knock on effects with significant costs. Consequently, individual staff cannot usually be motivated through bonuses or pay rises.

Local government is thus faced with being required to provide quality services with limited resources, to satisfy the demands of a number of interest groups, and still motivate staff to work hard and adapt to change and new legislative requirements. One organisational solution has been to devolve decision-making as far down the line as possible, giving managers back some of their professional discretion. Birmingham, like a number of other local authorities, was gradually implementing a programme of devolved budgets and other responsibilities during the early 1990s. It should be noted, however, that this solution is not without its own problems. It is difficult to identify which management tasks can be safely devolved, since ultimately the Director and the local council remain accountable for all the Department's actions. As was noted above, a small decision, taken by a manager in the interests of improving service on 'the patch' could have significant ramifications or repercussions for the whole service. For example, a manager who disciplines a member of staff without following all the correct procedures lays the whole authority open to justifying its actions at an Industrial Relations Tribunal. Therefore, it is difficult to distinguish strategic or corporate decisions from operational ones, and operations must be guided by increasingly lengthy and complex sets of procedures, guidance and guidelines. Without these, there is also a danger that the organisation will fragment.

Performance management is one of the means of sharpening management in the public sector, ensuring organisational unity, and making the whole organisation more accountable, by setting objectives, with indicators and outcomes specified. Performance management, with contracts for chief officers, was introduced by Birmingham City Council in 1990/91. The process was valued for giving clear priorities for the council as a whole and for each Committee. The Director's contract was used within the Social Services Department as a tool for managing change.

Performance management ensured that change and development could be measured and monitored, and managers and staff held accountable for the outcomes of their actions. Its limitations included the difficulty of identifying performance indicators which actually reflect an improvement in a service experienced by the service user. It was also possible for the work of a department to become skewed to ensure that tasks in performance contracts were achieved, at the expense of core maintenance tasks. It is also, however, essentially a 'top-down' approach, and the argument of this book is that service improvements and a change in culture cannot be achieved within limited resources only through imposition from above. They require the commitment of staff at all levels to make them happen.

The chapters which follow illustrate an attempt to create a climate in which change was possible, and in which a significant improvement in services, within the constraints of limited budgets, could be achieved. BACC attempted to operate as a catalyst for change, to empower managers and staff to provide quality services, whilst operating in the real and restricted environment of a local authority. The following chapters describe a process, as well as its outcomes, and suggest that the process can be used within other public sector contexts to achieve change. Indeed, the process is shown to be inseparable from the outcomes, because the kind and scale of changes required could not be achieved without active participation of staff at all levels of the organisation.

3. BACC's philosophy and method: a framework for managing change

Birmingham Action on Child Care founded its approach to reviewing services for children on a number of key ideas, which were derived from the Director's brief to the Project, the Project *Outline*, and from its analysis of the Department's recent history. The Team started with two underlying assumptions: that the children and families services constituted a 'system' whose components could not be studied in isolation; and that a change in culture was required which could not simply be imposed from the top, but must be built up through involvement of staff at all levels. In this chapter, these two assumptions and how they were developed by the Team into its programme of work, are examined.

A systems approach to managing change

> Every problem is likely to be multi-facetted; a service is not just provided by the last link in the chain, the 'hands on' personnel or the main task group. It is inevitably provided as a result of a series of inter-related tasks, carried out by staff at different levels, with different focal concerns. Any one of them inevitably affects the end result.
>
> [Barbara Kahan: letter to Paul Sutton, 8 September 1989]

When Birmingham Action on Child Care began to look at the services for children and families provided by Birmingham Social Services Department, it was apparent that these services were not only managed separately from one another, but that the concept of them as a single service scarcely existed. BACC, however, was explicitly charged with reviewing all the services for children and families, in the context of the Director's understanding of how these related and constituted a 'system'.

In a revealing exercise, the BACC Team explored the consequences of unmanaged change. To demonstrate its hypothesis that a change in one service would have consequences for all the other services for children and families, the Team explored how the closure of a substantial number of children's homes during a relatively short period might affect other services, if the change were not managed carefully.

The first impact of the change would, of course, be felt within the service itself and related services, with extra pressure on foster carers and anxiety amongst residential workers. Pressure would soon extend to fieldwork teams – encouraged to keep children out of care; to fostering teams – seeking additional foster homes and supporting foster carers; to all kinds of day care facilities – used as alternatives to care; and to management – urged to reassure staff, give clear guidance, and find new resources.

In the longer term, without management intervention, morale amongst residential workers would plummet, and some (usually the most experienced and best qualified staff) would leave or transfer within the Department. Some foster carers, faced with caring for the most difficult children, would resign. The pressure on all the fieldwork teams would accelerate, and there would be demands for more staff and other resources. Cases would remain unallocated, as work concentrated on those children most at risk. All forms of day care would be expected to work with a higher proportion of disturbed or disruptive children. Thus, staff from all these services would start to make more demands of the support services, such as management, training and personnel. There would be increased use of the grievance and disciplinary procedures, especially in the residential sector. The remaining children's homes would be likely to be staffed by those staff least able to find work elsewhere, because of their age, lack of qualifications, or limited experience. Management would be preoccupied with the needs of workers requiring redeployment or retraining, at the expense of the service to children. The developing crisis in confidence would lead some workers to go to the newspapers, with unwelcome publicity, and ultimately to demands for an inquiry.

This series of events, sketched out as the *hypothetical* result of an unmanaged and rapid run-down of the residential sector, closely mirrors the account of events in the Department outlined in chapter 2. It is possible to see how decisions ostensibly mainly affecting children's homes can impact on staff throughout the Department, and rapidly lead to demoralisation, even without additional factors such as two unpopular reorganisations and allegations of persistent abuse in two homes. Looking back, it was felt that during the 1980s closures, managers had concentrated on needs of staff directly affected by closures, and in the process lost sight of the impact on children and the remaining homes, and on other, related, services for children and families.

This exercise helped the BACC Team to understand how the various services for children and families actually functioned as a system. They concluded that, although inevitably the work of the Department would have to be broken down into its component parts for detailed investigation and review, it was important not to finish with a string of separate and unrelated reports on different aspects of the service. Services for children and families constituted a 'system' where change in any one element would have implications for others [Birmingham Action on Child Care, 1990b]. The Team began to elaborate this conceptual framework.

Most planning is incremental. A series of small changes is planned, carried out and evaluated in the context of a set of aims and objectives for the organisation as a whole. In such an approach, each part of the organisation is only loosely related to other parts, so that consequences of changes are rarely anticipated. Constant adjustments are therefore required to keep the parts moving towards the organisation's common goals and in equilibrium with one another. Whilst the process appears rational, it is in practice haphazard, since the knock on effects are not anticipated and planned.

In contrast, a systems approach is a holistic approach. A 'system' can be defined as:

an organised or connected group of objects; a set or assemblage of things connected, associated or interdependent, so as to form a complex unity; a whole composed of parts in orderly arrangement according to some scheme or plan; ...a group, set, or aggregate of things, natural or artificial, forming a connected or complex whole. [Shorter Oxford English Dictionary]

Everything outside the system is defined as its 'environment', and the system's interaction with and adaptation to its environment becomes another area to be planned and managed. Components of the system are called 'elements' and grouped into sub-systems reflecting their closer relationship. The connectedness, interdependence, and complexity emphasised in the definition above proved to be attributes of the children and families services when the Team compiled its 'map' of the system.

In systems planning and management, each component or element is set in the context of the whole system and viewed in relation to other elements of the system or sub-system. In other words, the residential care service would be seen as only part of the Department's set of services for children and families. Managers could then take account of the ways in which change in one part of the system would have consequences, to a greater or lesser extent, for all other elements of the system. As the changes 'ripple through' the system, they can be managed and harnessed to contribute to overall aims and objectives, rather than being permitted to undermine them. Systems analysis emphasises the importance of feedback loops which ensure that there is a constant supply of information on the consequences of changes. In the context of home closures, these would include dialogue with staff, children and parents, to provide feedback about the actual effects of change. Criteria for evaluation must be established against which performance can be monitored.

The children and families 'system'

The BACC Team defined the system as services for children and families, and related services, *within the Social Services Department*. This definition was pragmatic, since any larger system would be impossible to study. It also, however, ensured that BACC's focus was clearly upon the Department's direct provision for children and families. Services provided by other city departments or by the voluntary and private sectors were not included in the system, although they would be given consideration. The Project Team also took into account other interlocking systems with which the children and families system related – systems of local and national government, and the system of relationships with and between City Departments, Chief Officers, and the Department of Health. It considered relationships with other government departments, other social services departments, voluntary organisations, and major organisations such as the Association of Metropolitan Authorities (AMA) or the Association of Directors of Social Services (ADSS).

An early analysis of the system identified just how complex it was – with over forty elements, many of these composed of a number of teams or establishments (for example, there were 33 children's homes, two Community Homes with Education, and 33 nurseries at that time). The elements of the system included services having a direct (for example, Children's Teams) or indirect (for example, Administration Teams) impact on children. Sub-systems were identified by function:

- accommodation for children;
- fieldwork services;
- day care services;
- support to staff;
- planning and monitoring;
- miscellaneous practical support to children and families.

The sub-systems are shown in Diagram 1; some elements appear in more than one sub-system, reflecting their range of functions.

Two hypothetical examples of how a change would affect the system were developed by the BACC Team and presented diagrammatically (Diagrams 2 and 3) [Birmingham Action on Child Care, 1990b]. These showed that an increase in resources could paradoxically have a negative result if consequent changes in other elements of the system were not anticipated, planned and managed. Conversely, change which results in a net reduction in resources might nevertheless have a largely positive impact if knock-on effects of change were carefully managed. It was a measure of the level of suspicion of management at the time that when Working Paper 2 was published the Unions raised as an issue with Management the plan to close day nurseries which was one of the two hypothetical scenarios sketched out in this paper. This was despite the paper's reiterated statement that the examples were 'hypothetical' and 'neither of these... changes... is planned or advocated' [Ibid.].

A systems model of the service permitted some prediction of the ramifications of change, although it required constant refining and developing as events unfolded and feedback about consequences of change was incorporated. With changes occurring simultaneously in different parts of the system and its environment, prediction was difficult, but not impossible.

Perfect management of systems is, of course, impossible. Even complete analysis of such a large system cannot be achieved. There are too many components, too many variables. Nevertheless, the concept of the children and families services as a single system was

Diagram 1: The children and families system: sub-systems

ACCOMMODATION FOR CHILDREN	FIELDWORK	DAY CARE
Foster Homes Private Fostering Children's Homes Independent Living Project Lodgings Officers Community Homes with Education Divisional Centres	Children's Teams General Services Teams Combined Teams Adoption and Fostering Teams Juvenile Justice Teams Child Protection Unit Principal Officers/Child Protection Hospital Social Work Teams Physical Disability Teams Learning Difficulty Teams Divisional Centres Parent & Child Centre	Nursery Centres Day Nurseries Child Minders Day Care Officers

MISCELLANEOUS PRACTICAL SUPPORT TO CHILDREN	SUPPORT TO STAFF	PLANNING AND MONITORING
Home Care Financial Services Property Management Trust Funds Administration	Training Management Services Policy and Performance Review Division Personnel Finance Information Court Officers Property Management Employee Welfare Service Social Services Committee Child Care Procedures Writers Administration	Policy and Performance Review Division Guardians ad Litem Adoption and Fostering Panels Social Services Committee Departmental Management Team Policy groups Birmingham Action on Child Care

Diagram 2: *A new resource, but without planned management*

- Best staff leave or transfer
- More grievances and disciplinaries
- Demand for tighter management
- Morale amongst residential staff falls
- Children's homes left with most difficult children
- Empty homes close
- Best workers leave or transfer
- Residential staff demand retraining
- Residential staff demand reassurance
- Anxiety amongst residential staff
- Empty beds in children's homes
- Reduced repairs, maintenance, supplies
- Some young children go into children's homes
- **SET UP A FEE PAID TEENAGE FOSTERING SCHEME**
- Increased workload for Adoption and Fostering Panels
- Some foster carers change from taking children to taking teenagers
- Increased numbers of foster carers
- More care orders made as care a positive option
- Increased workload for Fostering Teams
- More payments to process
- Reduced pressure on field social workers
- Fostering Teams cannot support foster carers
- Field workers drawn into supporting foster carers
- New systems to administer
- Some Fostering staff cannot cope
- More complaints
- Payments delayed or wrong
- Increased sickness levels; some staff leave
- Foster home breakdown rate rises
- **DEMAND FOR AN INQUIRY**
- Mix of young children and difficult teenagers in homes
- Children placed in residential homes again
- Problems reach the Press
- Incidents in children's homes increase

BACC's PHILOSOPHY AND METHOD   41

Diagram 3: *Managed reduction in resources*

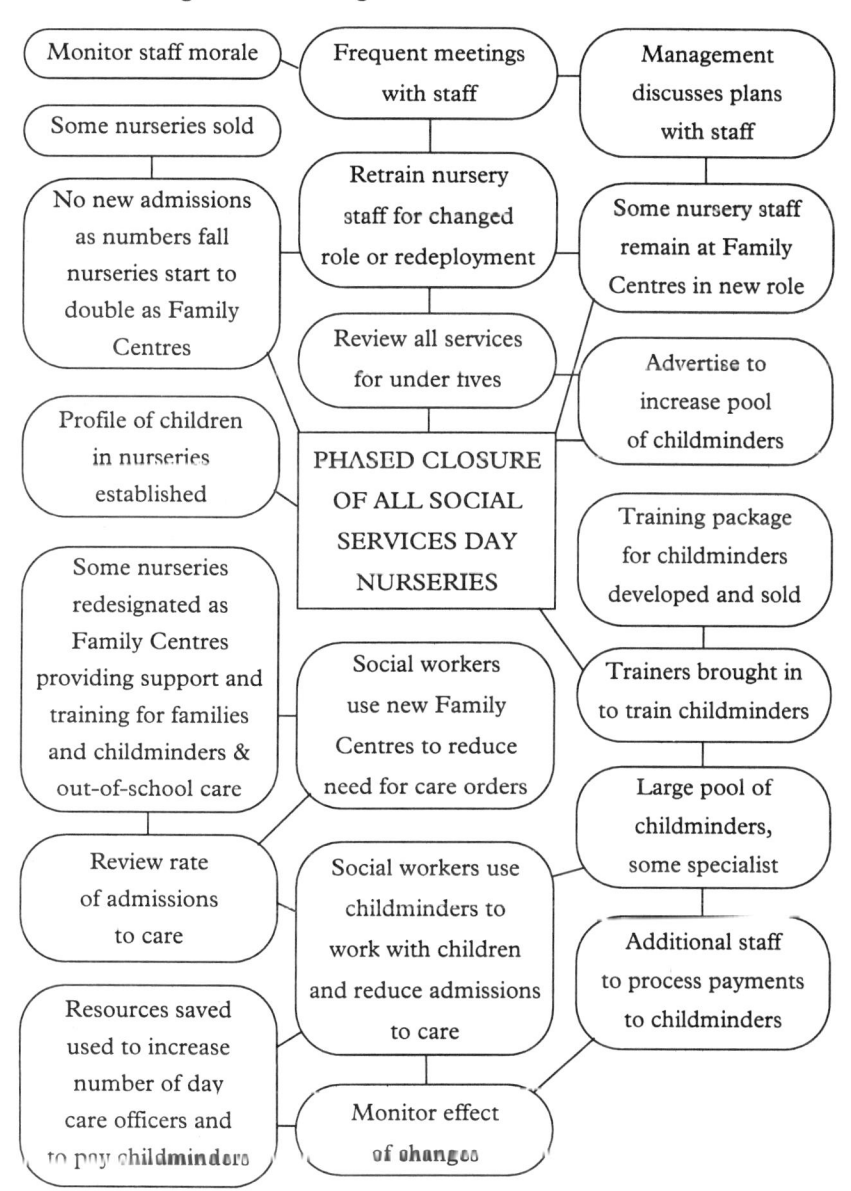

- Monitor staff morale
- Some nurseries sold
- No new admissions as numbers fall nurseries start to double as Family Centres
- Profile of children in nurseries established
- Some nurseries redesignated as Family Centres providing support and training for families and childminders & out-of-school care
- Review rate of admissions to care
- Resources saved used to increase number of day care officers and to pay childminders

- Frequent meetings with staff
- Retrain nursery staff for changed role or redeployment
- Review all services for under fives
- **PHASED CLOSURE OF ALL SOCIAL SERVICES DAY NURSERIES**
- Social workers use new Family Centres to reduce need for care orders
- Social workers use childminders to work with children and reduce admissions to care
- Monitor effect of changes

- Management discusses plans with staff
- Some nursery staff remain at Family Centres in new role
- Advertise to increase pool of childminders
- Training package for childminders developed and sold
- Trainers brought in to train childminders
- Large pool of childminders, some specialist
- Additional staff to process payments to childminders

symbolically important for BACC. It helped in understanding the consequences of change; it ensured that 'blame' for problems was shared, since no part of the system operated in isolation; and it helped to show people how they were part of the larger world of the Department. It also explained how a failure in a single part of the system could have wide ramifications.

For example, the BACC Team was not alone in experiencing frustration with the workings of the internal postal service, which in 1989 was notoriously slow and unreliable. Failings of that service undoubtedly made the work of many people more difficult. However, they also allowed people to explain away their own mistakes and missed deadlines, by laying blame on the internal postal service. The BACC Team saw the difficulties of the internal postal system as symptomatic of the difficulties of managing such a large department. Both the problems of running an efficient service and reactions of staff to the service's failings demonstrated the ways in which every part of the Department was interlinked. Birmingham Action on Child Care was determined to confront such problems directly.

Learning from history

Apart from learning from experience of closure of children's homes during the 1980s, the Project Team drew other lessons from recent departmental history, specifically from accounts it received of the Child Care Review Group (CCRG). The Team noted that this Group (whose work is summarised in chapter 4) was 'responsible for the current shape and practices of child care services in Birmingham'. In its first Working Paper, BACC described the Group's approach as follows:

This hand-picked group of Senior managers, seconded from within, literally went into retreat for determined periods of time and, deliberately fostering a hot-house think-tank approach, and by implication eschewing consultative and collaborative methods, produced the basis of the policies and procedures by which Birmingham still, by and large, operates. [Birmingham Action on Child Care, 1990a]

The Team concluded that while this approach might have been appropriate in the late 1970s it certainly would not be valid for BACC, given subsequent events and the greater emphasis on 'customer-led innovation' expected in the 1990s. BACC's working style had to exemplify the emphasis on service user consultation, choice and partnership found in the Children Act. The Team therefore stressed the need to involve staff from all levels in the Department in its work, as well as young people, foster carers, and other interested people.

The BACC Team also concluded that managers could not work in isolation, but must involve their staff:

a collaborative approach is almost certainly more time consuming and more unwieldy than a traditional detached, or 'top down' approach, but we consider that its benefits in terms of staff morale, participation and ownership far outweigh any disadvantages and will ultimately prove cost effective. [Ibid.]

The Team added that:

it is highly unlikely that the major changes [required by the Children Act] can be effected by management alone. [Ibid.]

The Community Care Special Action Project: a model for promoting change

As well as learning from recent history, Birmingham Action on Child Care learnt from another initiative with which the Department had been involved. It was not the first short-life 'special' project. As the Director noted:

we have the benefit of the experience of the Community Care Special Action Project. I believe that this is a useful model for the methodology of the child care project. [Birmingham Social Services Department, 1988d]

The Community Care Special Action Project (CCSAP), headed by Tessa Jowell, had been a pioneering initiative. Its remit was to work with people with disabilities and their carers, in the community, to gain a better appreciation of their needs and to develop services appropriately. A corporate initiative, rather than a Departmental initiative, its links with the Department were nevertheless strong. Examples of the successful introduction of new ideas and new ways of working were taken from it.

The first was its emphasis on involving users and carers. CCSAP was determined,

to ensure that services meet the needs of their users through their relevance, quality and accessibility, rather than users being simply defined in terms of existing provision or untested assumptions. [Community Care Special Action Project, n.d.]

This approach was gaining significance in the personal social services, and CCSAP demonstrated positive results to be gained from involving users and carers in thinking about the development of services. Frequently, carers made practical, low cost suggestions for the improvement of services. CCSAP also emphasised the value of networking: establishing and maintaining contacts throughout personal social services, government, and academic institutions. Such contacts were fruitful in encouraging new ideas and disseminating CCSAP's work, both formally and informally.

Chapter 4 will demonstrate how some of these ideas were translated into practice by BACC. The Team made extensive contacts with people involved in children's services, through such formal mechanisms as establishing the Advisory Group and attending conferences, as well as by ensuring that casual callers were always welcome. Topic Groups – one of BACC's primary working methods (described later in this chapter) – involved more than 100 people from inside and outside the Department with different areas of interest and expertise. BACC also made specific efforts to develop contacts with people in other organisations, and to work collaboratively with others where appropriate. Young people and foster carers were involved from the outset in the Project's work.

Part of CCSAP's success was attributed to its direct access to the City's Chief Officers, and its 'championship' by the Chief Executive. In setting up Birmingham Action on Child Care, the Director decided that the Project Director should report directly to her and should be a member of the Departmental Management Team (DMT). The Director herself acted as the Project's 'champion' throughout its life. There was, however, a danger for BACC in participating in the Management Team, that it would become drawn into the day-to-day operations. The Project *Outline* therefore specifically stated that the Project:

will not be expected to become involved in short-term pieces of work for the [Departmental Management Team] or the Social Services Committee, unless the Project's Director agrees that these are useful and relevant for the Project's objectives. [Coffin, 1989]

The Project Team was able to use its status as both an 'insider' and 'outsider'. Direct access to the Management Team was crucial to its ability to influence the direction of the Department and to make proposals for changes but its location outside the formal management structure for children and families ensured that staff came to see it as an ally, and that it could take up their concerns. The Project required 'outsider' status to protect its objectivity and allow it to be at times very critical of the Department. The Advisory Group was an important guarantor of that outsider status. Other mechanisms for reinforcing it included BACC's having its own logo and distinctive headed paper, and the Team's physical location in offices separate from the Department's headquarters.

Although it was a Departmental rather than a corporate initiative, BACC also worked directly with the Chief Officers Group when necessary. As it became clear that implementation of the Children Act would require contributions from other Departments, a Corporate Children Act Implementation Group was established as well as one-to-one links with staff in other departments. This corporate work is described in Chapter 5.

Experience with CCSAP emphasised the importance of working from 'the bottom up' as well as from 'the top down', a lesson already derived from reviewing the work of the Child Care Review Group. CCSAP was very successful at corporate level, gaining commitment to and resources for its work from Chief Officers of several departments; but at the front-line level it aroused some suspicion. Staff were anxious that commitments were being made on their behalf for a quality of response to need which they could not always deliver. Given the history of distrust, especially strong in the children's residential service, the BACC Team were keen to ensure that staff at all levels in the social services department were given an opportunity to be involved in and to contribute to the Project.

How the Team worked
The 'Birmingham experience'

In considering how to approach its work, the Team was profoundly influenced by the need to do more than make recommendations for change – 'the *way* in which BACC fulfils its brief is going to be as important as what it actually does' [Birmingham Action on Child Care, 1990a]. It is important not to lose sight of the unfavourable, even hostile, climate in which the Project began its work. Chapters 2 and 4 describe events in Birmingham and nationally in 1988 and 1989, before BACC was set up and during its early months, when the

Project's direction was established. The Team described the 'atmosphere' in 1989-1990 in strong terms:

> major components of the flavour of the 'Birmingham experience' therefore can be found in the sense of disillusion, isolation, cynicism and demoralisation affecting staff charged with front line service delivery responsibilities, and the frustration and impatience of managers anxious 'to get things done' in a relatively hostile political and social climate. Whilst these experiences are not unusual, especially in metropolitan social services departments, the size of Birmingham, the number of contributing events and some of the issues make it a particularly potent blend. [Birmingham Action on Child Care, 1990a]

The problems of 'low cloud'

The Team developed a metaphor for the problems of communication within the Department. 'Low cloud' was the shorthand reference to a situation in which the people at the top and bottom of the organisation are effectively cut off from one another. Frontline staff are likened to people living in a valley, whose view of the top of the mountain is obscured by low cloud. They know there are other people living above the cloud level, but these are mysterious and the subject of rumour about their powers and intentions. The occasional traveller between the two communities brings back stories which only reinforce the rumours. At the top of the mountain, there is another group of people, who cannot see the people living below, and who share similarly distorted ideas about their neighbours. And the few people on the middle slopes of the mountain live in a perpetual fog!

Key principles

A number of principles were adopted by the Team which underpinned its approach. These included the need to change the culture of the Department if recent history were not to be repeated. The principles therefore included:

- involving staff, service users and other interested people in thinking about the issues and developing recommendations for change;
- listening to people and valuing their contributions, without regard for formal positions in the Department's or other hierarchies;
- valuing the Department's staff and service users;

- modelling good practice itself;
- maintaining a degree of distance and objectivity in working within the Department; and
- promoting action, the key word in the Project's title.

From the beginning, the importance of gaining the commitment and co-operation of staff was highlighted. The Project *Outline* noted that:

the Project Team will need to establish mutual trust and respect with those who will carry out its recommendations,

and emphasised the need to make an early impact on the Department, for example, through regular feedback to staff and dissemination of information, 'because of the importance of gaining the co-operation of staff at all levels' [Coffin, 1989].

The Team took the view that a participative style was not just a pragmatic response to a set of problems and issues, but a desirable way of working and in line with the Department's Eight Key Principles, adopted in spring 1989 [Birmingham Action on Child Care, 1990a]. These stressed the importance of involving service users and their carers in the development of services, as well as the value of the Department's employees.

Quality care, quality service, quality people

Eight key principles which seek to guide all staff on the implementation of committee policies...
1. To recognise that the people served have rights as well as needs
2. To increase people's influence on services
3. To develop multi-racial services
4. To improve services to women
5. To deliver a high quality service
6. To make employees matter and feel valued
7. To promote innovation
8. To raise public awareness

[Birmingham Social Services Department, 1990b]

Setting up a range of Topic Groups was the Team's first major decision. The Topic Group process can be summarised as follows:

- a topic for review is selected;
- preliminary work (discussion, reading and so on) to identify the issues and problems is undertaken by the BACC Team;

- a topic group is set up; this will include Project Team members, people working in the area of work, people from related areas, consumers, and, where appropriate, members of the Advisory Group;
- the topic group meets frequently over a defined period, with work undertaken by members of the group between meetings, to produce a report or other outcome; and
- a final seminar is held to present the outcome.

The Team drew on the experience of Barbara Kahan in developing its Topic Group process. From 1970, Barbara Kahan headed the Home Office Development Group (later the Department of Health and Social Security Development Group). This Group was initially charged with promoting the development of child care services following the implementation of the Children and Young Persons Act 1969. Later, it worked in a wide range of service areas, including care of elderly people and community services. The methodology evolved included several important elements. The first was an 'open ended' approach to problem solving – questioning as a process and following where the questions led. Second was a participative style which involved a wide cross section of knowledge, skills, levels and types of responsibility both inside and outside the agency concerned. Third was a challenging attitude to preconceptions and assumed constraints, thus freeing thinking and creativity. Rather than inhibit initial energy, practical limits were only brought in to shape solutions at the end. By this method, agency participants gained an investment in change and development, creativity was stimulated by freedom of thought and external experiences, and final proposals took account of the broadest possible deliberations before they were formulated.

> While everyone admits there are problems in the child care service, these are always located 'elsewhere'; this process ensures that participants own both the problems *and* the solutions.
>
> [Birmingham Action on Child Care, minutes of planning day, 15 September 1989]

The Team agreed that the Topic Group process must allow everyone to participate on a basis of equality and with an open mind; it was essential to be receptive to new ideas. The approach was designed to break down barriers between workers at different levels and in different teams. It stressed the links between different parts of the system. It provided workers with the opportunity to reflect on their work and helped to ensure that participants 'owned' both the problems and the solutions. Work was to take place in the context of the philosophy and requirements of the Children Act 1989. All Groups were to take into account the nature of the child care system, in which each part impacts on every other part. They must pay attention to issues of gender, ethnicity, and disability, as well as to principles of good practice set out by the Department of Health [Department of Health, 1989c]. Finally, they must not ignore the political context in which BACC was working [Birmingham Action on Child Care, 1990a].

The Team decided that these Topic Groups were to constitute BACC's primary method of working, although other short term projects would also take place. The reports produced would be in the form of working papers, which BACC would draw together and integrate towards the end of the Project. It is important to note that the BACC Team was under pressure to show results quickly; some Team members had only been in post a short time when much of this thinking took place. They had little time to absorb the thinking which had taken place when BACC was first conceived, and the Project's method was developed and refined as work progressed.

Visits to operational staff and discussions with senior managers and policy and planning staff enabled the BACC Team to identify key issues by summer 1989. It noted the difficulty of knowing:

where and how to start [in looking at such a large organisation]... There are ... a number of competing interests, all of which, quite legitimately, want the project to examine their particular area of work. Some of these areas of work are very discrete and focused. Others range across several issues and even across departments or other agencies. [Birmingham Action on Child Care, 1990a]

BACC could not hope within its limited time and resources to tackle all the issues which had been identified. Criteria for selecting priority areas of work were developed. Some issues could be followed through a variety of different service areas – for example, services to Black children and their families. Others 'generated their own urgent demands on the project' – for example, residential care, adoption and fostering. The Team initially selected five areas of work:

- services to children under five (later, under eight, to reflect the provisions of the Children Act 1989);

- adoption and fostering services;
- residential care;
- planning for children; and
- positive support for children and families.

While the first three represented major service areas, the last two represented themes which would run through a number of service areas. As well as Topic Groups, four other work areas were identified:

- small scale interventions in the day-to-day life of the Department, in a trouble-shooting or consultancy role;
- promotion of training and development in specific subject areas, including the Children Act;
- encouraging innovation and initiative and helping to secure resources for trying out new ideas; and
- publicising and disseminating reports, books, and research findings.

The overview of BACC's work contained in the chronological account in Chapter 4 will show that the Topic Groups, whilst important in involving many people in thinking in depth about critical issues, were only one amongst many different approaches to reviewing the Department's children and families work. Nevertheless, the Topic Group process was BACC's preferred model for major pieces of work; in practice, other work undertaken by the Team followed wherever possible the same practice of open-ended exploration involving a cross-section of the Department's staff and other people. The Children Act Implementation Group was the most important of the other broadly based groups, and influential in its development of BACC's recommendations for the future. Its work will be discussed in more detail in Chapter 5.

There were other aspects of BACC's working methods designed to give staff a stake in changing the Department's culture. Newsletters were widely distributed – the Team aimed at reaching every workplace where staff worked with children and families – and anyone could ask to be put on the mailing list as an individual. Some of the more important issues were sent to all staff. Newsletters regularly asked people to send in their views and to volunteer to help BACC. This had the effect of bypassing line management, enabling workers at any level to feed their views in at the 'top'. Staff from a number of different locations sent ideas and comments to BACC, and others expressed their willingness to help. Some of the members of the Topic Groups were identified from people who responded in this way. All letters were acknowledged individually. Personal visits by BACC Team members to different teams and establishments were designed as much to listen to the views of staff as to inform them about the Project.

In pursuit of changes, BACC ran seminars to inform staff about the Children Bill, contributed to the training for new residential social workers, undertook trouble-shooting missions in a number of children's homes, made a major contribution to Children Act training, and provided speakers on the Children Act to assorted teams and groups. Staff from many teams and locations were involved in its work, and those who had responded positively to BACC were offered opportunities to attend national and local child care conferences. Whilst the Team was committed to valuing everyone's views, it was also prepared to confront the cynics, inviting their contributions too in changing the Department's culture. Anxieties, fears, concerns and complaints were listened to and taken seriously, but people were also expected to contribute to improving the situation.

The Team's philosophy included a commitment to 'customer care' and a courteous and helpful response to all callers. The aim was to provide a quality service, including attention to detail, presentation and style, demonstrating in its own work the message which it was trying to promote. Thus, the Team was also committed to visible efforts to work in anti-discriminatory ways, and to value different contributions by each member of the Team. The Team included Black and White members, women and men, people with disabilities, and young people who had previously been in care. The whole Team, including all administrative staff, attended and contributed to Team and Advisory Group meetings.

The Advisory Group was crucial to helping BACC to maintain its objectivity and degree of 'distance' from the Department and its management structure. It supported the Project credibility in the Department and nationally, and provided a critical forum and a 'sounding board' for discussion of BACC's key ideas and major reports. Members of the Group contributed individually to the Topic Groups and acted as consultants for specific pieces of work. They also helped disseminate the work of the Project to other agencies. Involvement of trade unions and professional social work organisations in the Advisory Group ensured that these groups had the opportunity to contribute to BACC's development from an early stage. The Advisory Group members brought their own areas of expertise to BACC, and the BACC Team itself read widely and drew on social policy and social work research and accounts of best practice.

As consultant to the Project, Barbara Kahan was involved with the Team in a variety of ways. She met with the staff group at intervals throughout BACC's life, and was involved at the earliest opportunity with the Team's thinking on how it would work, and what its relationship with the Advisory Group should be. Both the Project Director and the Director of Social Services had individual discussions with her from time to time. She assisted with work on the review of community homes with education; examined the record keeping systems of one social work team and discussed supervision with them; and she looked at workload issues with another team. She made a very helpful contribution to BACC's work on unallocated cases, attending the Departmental Management Team when the first presentation of the issues was made, and advising the House of Commons Health Committee of the work which Birmingham Social Services Department had undertaken. Draft papers were read and commented upon. She chaired the joint meeting held between the Management Teams of the Education and Social Services Departments, and spoke at both the Birmingham Child Care Conferences. Her contribution helped the BACC Team to maintain its morale and enthusiasm, and provided a source of external validation.

BACC was committed to 'action' – the key word in its title. Much of the work described in chapter 4 led to action during the life of the Project. To ensure that the Project would continue to result in action, it was initially proposed that BACC would be tied more tightly into the management structure in its final phase by involving senior managers in an implementation group. By this means, it was hoped that the momentum would not be lost when the Project ended. Revision to the Department's structure, which came about partly as a result of BACC's work, made this unnecessary, however, as the new management structure for services to children and families became the focus for change. This revision is described more fully in chapter 5.

The Topic Group process was even more time-consuming than BACC had originally expected. Only four of the five groups proposed were established, and a second series, which was at first considered, was never started. The Groups were large and their discussions often discursive and sometimes heated; new ideas were generated, and difficulties and differences of view made explicit. The BACC Team needed to provide leadership to ensure that the main issues were identified and given priority. Lack of a clear agenda left some of the Groups unable to sort out crucial issues from the detail needed to improve services. An open-ended exploration of issues was an integral part of the process, and essential to its success, but it consumed substantial amounts of staff time and other resources. Seminars were not held when the Topic Groups completed their work — there were too many other issues competing for the Team's time by then — although two of them were given all day sessions by the Advisory Group. The Advisory Group helped to evaluate and finish off the work of the Residential Services and the Foster Care Topic Groups, before their reports were finalised for presentation to the Departmental Management Team. Nevertheless, as a method it achieved a great deal, not only in the products of each Topic Group, but also in the overall communication, openness to change, and better understanding between different parts of the service.

As the Project neared its end, there were still issues which it had not tackled, or which were unfinished. Issues of ethnicity, religion, language and culture, were likely to be topics which the Department would continue to explore and refine over many years. Others, like the changes required by the Criminal Justice Act 1991, were relatively new concerns, which BACC had just begun to address. Many of BACC's recommendations were being put into practice and were beginning to raise new issues. Some areas of work — for example, child protection, adoption and juvenile justice — had received almost no consideration at all by BACC. It was clear that the new management team and the Children and Families Unit in the Strategic Policy and Review Section would have to develop means to tackle all these and many other issues. Because BACC was working in the ever-changing environment of local government, its work could never be 'finished', although the Project had to end. Whilst the emphasis was on 'action', with many initiatives starting to show results during the Project's lifetime, some of its later work existed only on paper: it would form the starting point for the new Children and Families Management Team.

Conclusion

At its final meetings the BACC Team found time to reflect on its experience. The list of work undertaken – whether completed or still in progress – was impressive, as will be apparent from the chronological account in Chapter 4. At the final Advisory Group meeting, a wallchart and verbal presentations summarised the range of work which had been undertaken. At the same time, the Team were aware of very real problems and pressures generated by its methods of work. These included the costs of success – for example, expectations that staff would be available to give advice and support and to answer queries. The Topic Group process had been more time-consuming than anticipated, although the results were – in the end – very satisfactory, not just in the content of the reports and their recommendations, but because there were staff throughout the Department with an investment in the outcome. BACC had suffered, as all limited-life projects do, from a sense of disappointment during the middle phase of the Project, when there were as yet few clear results. The pressure generated by the Children Act 1989, the NHS and Community Care Act 1990, and later the Criminal Justice Act 1991, together with the changes occurring in the Department itself, created an accelerating pace of change with Team members experiencing considerable fatigue.

BACC's approach was expensive in staff time – not just the time of the Project's own staff, but the time of staff and others involved in all its working groups, training events, and consultations. For example, over 100 people participated in the Topic Groups; 400 staff attended the first series of Children Act seminars, and 2,500 staff were involved in the Children Act Training Programme. The costs of this style of managing change were undoubtedly high. The alternatives were, however, likely to be still more costly. The consequences of imposed solutions to problems, without consultation, and without thought for the management of change throughout the system, were presented at the start of this chapter. The costs of disaffection, of additional staff sickness and absenteeism, of loss of experienced staff, of extra management time, and of grievance and disciplinary investigations is enormous, if difficult to quantify. For example, the cost of suspending and eventually dismissing one member of staff comprises:

- salary of staff member whilst suspended;

- time of a manager and others in undertaking an investigation;
- time of senior managers and other staff preparing for and attending the disciplinary hearing;
- time of senior managers, other staff, councillors, and legal staff preparing for and attending any appeal;
- time spent by union officers throughout this process; and
- time spent in counselling those involved.

This does not take into account the adverse publicity, the impact on other staff, and the impact on service users, which are much less easy to assess. Thus the cost of one dismissal is potentially very high; and increased resort to the disciplinary procedure is only one result of poorly managed change.

The expense of BACC can, however, only be justified if it led to improvements in the service to children and families. The next four chapters focus more closely on BACC's work and examine its outcomes.

4. The history of BACC

BACC clearly has made significant achievements over its lifetime... the programme of work embarked upon is quite remarkable.
David Berridge (letter to Paul Sutton, 1992)

This chapter sets out a brief descriptive and mainly chronological account of Birmingham Action on Child Care, from its beginnings in 1988, to its winding up in 1992. It shows how the method and philosophy described in chapter 3 were put into practice on a month by month basis, and provides a context for more detailed accounts of the Project's work in implementing the Children Act and improving services for children. The importance of the process as well as the outcomes is emphasised. It describes the Project's development over three years, indicating the achievements which will be drawn together in chapter 8. Key themes emerge from this chronological account which are developed in later chapters:

- BACC's response to the Children Act 1989 (chapter 5);
- The development of a sense of direction for services for children and families (chapter 5);
- BACC's focus on **action** for children (chapters 6 and 7); and
- The Project's increasingly high profile locally and nationally (chapter 8).

The life cycle of a project

The theme which permeates this chapter is BACC's life cycle, characteristic of limited life projects. Typically, the earliest phase is one of excitement at the potential, with many approaches to the work discussed and examined. This is closely followed by the necessity to choose priorities amongst options, develop a programme of work, allocate responsibilities and set a timetable. The start of work 'in earnest' is exhilarating for a short time, but the project soon moves into its middle phase of unremitting labour with few results for some time.

At this stage both insiders and outsiders begin to question whether the objectives will be achieved. Successful completion of the project may depend on commitment from individuals and the ethos of the team. Some protection against loss of morale and team members may spring from pieces of work which have immediate results, and support from outsiders who understand the process may be valuable.

The penultimate phase, when project work is complete and results begin to be evident, is usually again a time of excitement (and hard work). (If the project has been unable to complete its work, or if its results are disappointing, this period may instead be one of disillusionment.) The final phase when the project is decommissioned will be a time of loss and sadness, especially if the team has been mutually supportive, successful and creative.

BACC's project career fits this model. During early 1989, the Team was being recruited and examining possibilities for its work. It met as a Team and with Barbara Kahan as consultant to the Project and future chair of the Advisory Group. The second half of the year was mainly a time of planning, when the methodology underpinning the work programme was worked out in detail, and priorities were decided. Early 1990 saw the first meetings of Topic Groups focusing on key issues, as well as the start of many other initiatives. Almost all BACC's work had its foundations in this period.

The next year, however, from mid 1990 to mid 1991, was the critical middle phase. There were a number of mechanisms which helped to ensure that the Project survived this period. The Team was sustained by working relationships which had been developed in the early months, and by encouragement from members of its Advisory Group and the Director of Social Services. Its method of working ensured that the Team was seen as helpful and accessible and there was positive feedback from providing advice and assistance. In addition, some short term pieces of work showed results.

From about July 1991, the pace of work accelerated, with many reports presented to the Departmental Management Team and subsequently to Councillors. The first Birmingham Child Care Conference represented the peak point in the Project's life, when its achievements and method of working were in the public eye. Its work was not yet complete, however, and the last nine months of its life were also a time of hard work and excitement, as earlier initiatives were completed and others launched. The Project Director, Paul Sutton, was successful in his application for the post of General Manager, Children and Families, which carried responsibility for all the Department's resources for children, and thus secured the continuation of BACC's work. Some staff, however, were leaving BACC as they found new posts elsewhere, and in its last months many people, not just the Project's staff, were expressing their sense of loss. These stages of BACC's life provide a structure for the chronological account given in this chapter.

BACC's development is parallelled by an account of the continued public interest in child care shown by the press and other media, which focused on various national and local 'scandals' during this period. The existing role of local government was also under sustained scrutiny by central government and by the media. Central government was imposing funding constraints and expenditure controls on local councils, and placing great emphasis on value for money, competitiveness, efficiency and effectiveness. In children's as well as community care services, the development of a mixed economy of care was advocated. Local authorities were to help to develop and manage that 'market', as well as being direct providers of welfare. Consumer participation and consultation reinforced the impetus towards higher expectations and higher standards. Women, people with disabilities, and Black and minority ethnic people were increasingly central to demands for services to meet their needs.

BACC's review of the Department's services for children and families took place therefore at a time of major change in the personal social services. The Children Act 1989 and the National Health Service and Community Care Act 1990 became law during this period and their combined impact led to change in the shape of the Department and also in the way individual workers provided services to the public. A major review of adoption law was commenced during the period. The Criminal Justice Act 1991 was passed, with profound implications for social services departments, not yet fully realised. Changes in personal social services were mirrored by changes in education services. The Education Reform Act, Local Management of Schools, Grant Maintained Status and the 1992 Education White Paper have major implications for all children and families, but especially for children looked after by local authorities.

The establishment of BACC and its Advisory Group: January – June 1989

It was in October 1988 that the Social Services Committee decided to set up a major project to review its child care services. A small team of experienced managers and social workers were to spend two years looking not just at residential care, but at the whole range of child care services. The Project Team would be supported by other Departmental staff, and assisted by an independent Advisory Group. The Project Director was accountable directly to the Director of Social Services. The Project's aims and objectives were:

to establish new objectives, priorities and resources which will enable the child care service to make a clear and positive response to future demands:

(a) to analyse the needs of children and families who require the assistance of the statutory child care services and to draw up general principles for the development of the services;

(b) to review and develop child care policies, practices and resources in the light of the redefined needs and principles;

(c) to propose an overall implementation strategy with specific plans and a timetable of action to put into effect the changes required.

[Birmingham Social Services Department, 1988d]

These objectives were to be met within existing and projected financial constraints, with no necessity for major reorganisation of the Department and with the likely impact of the Children Bill – which was published the following month – taken into account [Coffin, 1989].

The Director hoped to establish the Project as rapidly as possible by recruiting staff on secondment from within the Department as well as from outside. The Project director and deputy were to be recruited from outside the Department, to help to ensure BACC's credibility. Ben Brown, seconded from the Social Services Inspectorate, became Deputy Project Director in February 1989, and joined a small Team of staff already seconded to BACC for two days. Barbara Kahan, the Chair of the National Children's Bureau, had agreed to head the Advisory Group and act as consultant to the Project. The post of Project Director was advertised, and Paul

Sutton, from Bradford Social Services Department, was recruited and began work at the end of June 1989.

During 1989, Birmingham's children's homes featured regularly in the local press. Reports included alleged improper child care practices and sexual relationships between staff and girls in care, as well as children running riot. Some good news was highlighted – extra resources to refurbish children's homes, and the launch of a remand and teenage fostering project in South Birmingham.

Nationally, social workers were blamed for the death of a Southwark child, Doreen Mason. Transracial adoption of children was a topic debated energetically and inconclusively. In Birmingham, a decision was made towards the end of 1989 to remove a two-year-old child of Asian origin from White foster carers for placement for adoption by Black carers. It was reported on the national news, and attracted strong opinions, with managers in the Department receiving abusive letters. Against this background, many social workers were cynical about the possibility of change, and saw BACC as another 'cosmetic exercise', where any recommendations would simply be lost.

1989 was a critical year for social services: the Children Bill was debated in Parliament and received the Royal Assent in November 1989, and Ministers stated that it would be implemented in 1991 and in its entirety (unlike previous legislation). The long-awaited White Paper on community care [Department of Health, 1989b] was published in November, promising a key role for local authorities in organising care in the community for elderly people and those with disabilities.

From the start, the Project Team had emphasised the importance of involving staff and listening to their views. By the time the Project Director arrived, this work had already begun. The first three Newsletters had been sent out by the Team to tell staff about BACC and invite them to contribute. Staff were beginning to respond and a database was being built up which included names of staff and others wanting to be kept informed or to contribute. The Newsletters also provided early information about key aspects of the Children Bill. These Newsletters, issued throughout the Project's life, were widely distributed and important in ensuring that large numbers of staff were aware of BACC and how it worked.

The initial Team had spent time trying to map the child care system – producing a working definition of it and identifying and classifying its components. They had also met and discussed with Barbara Kahan ideas about the role and composition of the Advisory Group, and other planning issues.

The Group needed to be large enough to include people from the many organisations and interest groups concerned with children's welfare, but small enough to work well together. Discussions between the Team and Barbara Kahan identified over twenty names, amongst them people from health, education, housing, children's rights, professional associations, trade unions, research, foster carers, the police, the probation service, social work training, staff from different parts of the Department's child care service, young people in care, the Social Services Inspectorate, the voluntary child care sector, and the Director herself.

Laying the foundations: July – December 1989

A Newsletter was only a first step to ensuring that the Project was accessible. Once senior staff were in post, they made personal contacts throughout the Department by visits and telephone calls. Ben Brown used the first few months visiting children's homes, talking to senior staff about BACC and listening to their anxieties. He picked up a number of specific complaints from children, particularly Black children, and visited establishments where management had expressed concern. Paul Sutton visited social work teams, day nurseries and residential homes, and by the end of the year they had made over 80 visits throughout the Department.

In September 1989 the Team held several planning meetings, some with Barbara Kahan, the Project consultant. These set the direction for BACC and identified its methodology. They were critical to the development of the Project, building on the approach set out in the *Outline* [Coffin, 1989], and refining the method of work already discussed in detail in Chapter 3. The meetings also identified priority areas of work, as set out in Chapter 3, the main focus of BACC for the next two years.

To provide an introduction to the Children Bill, staff from throughout the child care service and from all levels were invited to attend a series of seminars. Participants were deliberately mixed in small group sessions to ensure that staff acquired a better sense of each other's contribution. The Team planned four seminars for October 1989, each for 80 staff, but the response was so overwhelming that another two had to be held in December. These seminars gave Birmingham Social Services staff an early opportunity to learn about the Children Act, and each participant returned to the workplace with a folder of basic information.

In September, the Director, Barbara Kahan and Paul Sutton gave presentations to a multidisciplinary, invitation-only conference, attended by key people from many services. This was a valuable opportunity for BACC to make many contacts and to raise awareness of its existence nationally. Paul Sutton was already a member of the Advisory Group set up by the Social Services Inspectorate and chaired by Jane Rowe to produce *The Care of Children: Principles and Practice in Regulations and Guidance* [Department of Health, 1989c]. This guide to the principles of good child care practice was published at the end of that year (1989). It aimed to assist practitioners and their managers to relate law to practice and to understand the context in which regulations and guidance under the Children Act would be issued.

At the request of the Director, the Social Services Inspectorate (SSI) brought forward its inspection of the City's children's homes, following the revelations of 1987 and 1988. The BACC Team monitored the Department's response to the inspection report [Social Services Inspectorate, 1989]. The report indicated that children's homes were operating with little sense of purpose or direction, with residential workers feeling isolated and undervalued. Staff were working hard to meet children's immediate needs, but there was no proper planning process to enable both children and staff to understand why children were in care and what was likely to happen to them. The isolation of staff and their poor morale were potentially dangerous, and the SSI made a number of recommendations with the objective of moving the service from 'providing well intentioned accommodation to offering creative intervention' [ibid.].

The Advisory Group held its first meeting in December 1989 at the Birmingham Council House. The meeting was well-attended and the programme was designed to ensure that members from a variety of backgrounds shared a common view of the history of the service and current concerns in child care. The Chair of the Child Care Sub Committee and the Director of Social Services both made presentations. Subsequently, whole day meetings were planned at a venue with facilities for seminar type work and with the active involvement of the whole BACC Team. Members of the Advisory

Group showed great commitment to BACC's work, coming from considerable distances for meetings. This support was important to the Project throughout its life.

Getting underway: key initiatives commence, January – June 1990

The flood of press reports of incidents in Birmingham's children's homes continued during the early months of 1990. So too did controversy about fostering of Black children of mixed parentage. Birmingham was praised by the Commission for Racial Equality for the efforts made by its fostering and adoption services to place Black and minority ethnic children appropriately. In addition, a series of stories about bogus social workers and health visitors attempting to examine children prompted fears of child abuse and abduction. The Department took the opportunity presented by these fears to publicise its services to parents through the local press and schools.

Abuse hit squad set to check homes

An abuse watchdog team is to be set up to check Birmingham children's and old folk's homes.

A £30,000-a-year 'inspector general' will head the team, which will tour homes to ensure residents are not being abused and facilities are up to scratch.

They will also check private schools and nurseries.

The body will take on new duties arising from Government legislation, due to be implemented next year.

The NHS and Community Care Bill requires the council to inspect its own, private and voluntary residential care homes.

And the Children Act means councils must register and inspect private and voluntary children's homes, day nurseries and boarding schools.

Councils must also set up complaints procedures for children, parents, guardians and foster parents. Until now, social services departments have had no duty to inspect their own homes.

The watchdog team would be directly responsible to the director of social services. An appointment is expected to be made before October.

Members of the city's social services committee were expected to approve the position today.

[Birmingham Evening Mail, 13 June 1990.]

The local press also reported completion of the first induction training course for residential child care workers, a BACC initiative which was instrumental in helping to raise morale and standards in the Department's children's homes. Other staff were also involved in training initiated by BACC, with a training event for middle managers on the Children Act 1989 run in March 1990.

Towards the end of 1989, the existence of Pindown – a punitive regime in children's homes in Staffordshire – became public knowledge; public concern was to grow during the next few months, culminating in June 1990 in the establishment of an independent Inquiry to be carried out by Allan Levy, QC, and Barbara Kahan. The Inquiry began its work in July 1990, and reported in May 1991, heightening media interest in child care issues. The hysteria surrounding residential homes at this time was such that the local press in June 1990 headlined the proposal to establish an Inspection Division under the NHS and Community Care Act as 'Abuse hit squad set to check homes' [Birmingham Evening Mail, 13 June 1990].

In 1990 the Project began work on its main programme, with Topic Groups meeting to examine key issues. Each Topic Group brought together people from within and outside the Department, including Advisory Group members, with a direct or indirect interest in the topic to be discussed. Four Topic Groups began work in 1990 – Residential Care, Foster Care, Services to Children under Eight, and Planning for Children. Another large and very influential group was also set up, the Children Act Implementation Group. The participative methodology and systems approach developed by the Project Team were recorded in some detail during this period [Birmingham Action on Child Care, 1990a, 1990b], and laid the foundation for the work of these groups. Links were made with the Open University, and agreement reached that BACC's progress would be followed by staff from the University and the Project used as a case study for students.

The Advisory Group met again in March and June 1990, to receive progress reports on BACC's work, to consider the methodology and systems approach, and to look at aspects of the implementation of the Children Act. The BACC Team found these events challenging but rewarding. Careful preparation was required, but meetings were an opportunity to explore ideas in a non-threatening and stimulating forum. The Advisory Group was already proving its use in bringing a fresh perspective to bear on the Team's work, as well as giving it encouragement in facing the task.

At this time, the Departmental Management Team began a series of meetings designed to prepare itself for the future – for the 'major changes' which the Children Act 1989 and the National Health Service and Community Care Act 1990 would bring. Tensions and common elements between the two Acts were identified, and the BACC Team played a key role in ensuring that the excitement created by opportunities in the Community Care Act did not overshadow the need to address issues in the Children Act. The Project Director presented BACC to the City Council's Chief Officers Group, paving the way for further corporate work on child care issues, and in particular a corporate response to the Children Act.

Two members of the BACC Team attended one of a series of child care seminars organised by the Dartington Social Research Unit (part of the University of Bristol). The seminar, *Evaluating Child Care Services*, gave them an opportunity to discuss BACC's approach to seeing the child care system as a whole and trying to map the effects of changes. Through contacts made at the Seminar, Paul Sutton agreed in principle to participation by Birmingham in a new approach to assessing outcomes in child care, funded by the Department of Health [later published as Parker et al, 1991]. This study, reported more fully in Chapter 7, proposed measures to evaluate regularly the development of children in care and the quality of that care.

At meetings with a major charitable foundation, BACC staff agreed the basis for an innovative programme of work with sexually abused girls, described in Chapter 6. This eventually came to fruition with the signing of a Service Level Agreement (a contract for the provision of services on the Department's behalf) with the foundation in March 1991. BACC's involvement with this project was an example of how lack of a dedicated management structure for children's services led to pressure on BACC to be involved in operational matters. Its role as an objective reviewer of the Department's services was thus potentially compromised whenever such pressure was not resisted.

The first of the Children Act Consultation Papers was received in May 1990; there were to be 24 of these, with the last being published in July 1991, less than three months before the Act's implementation in October 1991. These Papers consisted of draft Guidance and Regulations sent out for comment to various agencies and people who had an interest in the issues. BACC coordinated the Department's responses, through wide distribution of the Papers to interested people, and through meetings and summary papers. This work helped to inform social workers throughout the Department about the changes on the horizon, and gave them opportunities to be involved in the development of legislation. Such involvement contributed positively to morale.

By August 1991, the Department had sent in detailed comments on 15 of the 24 Papers, and had contributed to achieving changes in some of them. For example, submissions from BACC and others in the Department helped to ensure that the volume on Family Placements included guidance on arrangements for repeated short placements for respite care of children with disabilities [Department of Health, 1991e]. Coordination and production of responses on the Consultation Papers involved extensive administrative work and was undertaken to tighter and tighter deadlines set by the Department of Health, as the date for the Act's implementation grew nearer.

Work also began in April 1990 on two separate but related topics – management information and unallocated child care cases. Management information (statistical information about service provision) available in mid 1990 was generally inaccurate and out-of-date. It did however indicate that numbers of children who were the subject of care or supervision orders were apparently without an allocated social worker. In common with other social services departments, the Department was experiencing difficulties in recruiting and retaining sufficient qualified social workers, and this was clearly one but not the only factor involved. A small group was set up to look at the problem. Management information, however, needed to be improved, in terms of what was collected, how it was presented, and its reliability, so that it would become a useful tool for managers. A small group was also set up to look at this involving administrative staff and people from the Information Systems Section.

In common with other authorities, the Department was behind schedule in implementing fully the Boarding Out of Children (Foster Parent) Regulations 1988, which came into force on 1st June 1989. These Regulations ensured that proper agreements were made with foster carers and provided for the supervision of children placed with foster carers. At 31 March 1990, nearly 900 children were placed with foster carers, so the scale of the task was considerable. Staff were resistant to undertaking additional duties when teams were short staffed. Whilst undoubtedly the problem of implementation was exacerbated by staff shortages, it was compounded by lack of a centralised and comprehensive list of foster carers. As short and long term foster carers related to different teams in the Department's decentralised structure, information about fostering came from many different sources. A member of the BACC Team spent many frustrating hours reconciling the records and assembling a complete list which could be used to trigger reviews at appropriate times.

The Departmental Management Team gave support to a proposal from BACC to set up a pilot fee paid foster care service, to provide short term foster care initially for children under 12 years. In Birmingham foster carers were paid expenses only for taking in children for the Department. Although rates paid by Birmingham Social Services Department were relatively generous (and could sometimes be quite high in special cases), the sums paid were not intended to replace wages or salaries. It was increasingly difficult to recruit sufficient carers since women were more often involved in paid work outside the home; and it was especially difficult to recruit foster carers from a wide variety of backgrounds, including Black and minority ethnic carers. The task of fostering was also becoming more demanding, as children were now placed in foster care who previously would have been in children's homes or other residential units. Moreover, the requirements of the Children Act 1989 would make further demands on foster carers. BACC argued that a fee paid service (that is, including a 'reward' element) with good training and support would meet these requirements more effectively in the future.

Finally, the initiatives started in this fertile six months included a proposal to hold an annual Child Care Conference in Birmingham. The proposal was given approval in principle by the Departmental Management Team and the Social Services Committee, and the first was planned for October 1991, when the Project would be moving into its last phase and the implementation of the Children Act would be commencing. The Conference was designed to spread information about work in Birmingham to improve child care services; to provide training and networking opportunities for Birmingham social workers; and to raise awareness nationally about the complexity of the task of local authority child care in the 1990s.

Continuing hard work – deferred results: the middle phase, July 1990 – June 1991

In the second half of 1990, public attention through the press and other media was focused on foster care as well as residential care for children. In Birmingham a single man was convicted of a serious sexual assault on a child in care. It emerged that not only had he befriended the boy whilst he was in care, but that he had also been recommended as a potential foster carer. There were predictable demands that only couples be permitted to foster, and that increased vigilance should be exercised in selecting foster carers. Further reports of incidents in Birmingham's children's homes followed, this time mainly focusing on unruly behaviour. The Department's concern over unallocated cases, and consequent risk to children, was also reported. Elsewhere, allegations of organised or ritual sexual abuse of children in Rochdale were disputed in the courts and the media during the autumn.

> Britain's children's homes are 'failing a generation of young people who deserve better', says a Midland social services director.
>
> Mr Peter Smallridge, of Warwickshire County Council, told a conference in Birmingham that the important job of caring for children and teenagers in homes usually went to a council's least trained staff.
>
> [Birmingham Post, 12 October 1990]

A national conference arranged by the National Children's Bureau reported the initial findings of a research study of the outcomes of Warwickshire County Council's decision to close all its residential homes [Cliffe, 1992]. The research (which is discussed again in Chapter 5) demonstrated that the range of children and young people for whom foster homes were found was broadened, and very few children and young people were placed in residential care. Some saw this as demonstrating that 'children's homes are "failing a generation"' [Birmingham Post, 12 October 1990]. This view did not, however, take account of other findings from the research study, which also examined the quality of the fostering experience for the children and young people. Although almost all children and young people were placed in foster homes, there was frequently only a limited choice of placements available, and therefore no ability to take account of individual needs. The amount of movement of children in care was above the national average, and minority ethnic children were rarely found foster homes of a similar culture. The researchers assessed some placements and moves of children as unacceptable. Certainly the research did not suggest that there was no role for residential care. Others pointed out the specific work which children's homes could undertake with children and stressed, following the imprisonment of a Derbyshire foster carer for indecent assault and manslaughter, that foster care could also be dangerous for children [*The Guardian*, 20 October 1990].

At BACC, the Topic Groups continued to meet. First responses to Children Act Consultation Papers were written and sent in, work continued on unallocated cases (with structured interviews with all the relevant Team Managers), and a review of the Department's two Community Homes with Education was set up. The Government announced that it would be reviewing adoption law, and a meeting was called by BACC to prepare a detailed response to the first of the lengthy consultation papers sent out [Department of Health, 1990; France, 1990; Thoburn, 1990]. The Advisory Group met in October and reviewed BACC's work in detail, discussing specific questions which had exercised the Team.

**The Children Act 1989
Basic Training Lectures
Five key components:**

- the welfare principle
- parental responsibility
- court orders affecting a child's upbringing
- children in need and children looked after by the local authority
- child protection

The Children Act Training Plan was received and approved by the Departmental Management Team. It involved almost 2,500 workers attending a series of five lectures introducing them to key concepts in the Children Act. Lectures were followed by workplace training adapted to the needs of specific groups of staff, and the third phase of the programme was specialist training for key groups of workers. BACC worked with the Training Section and Child Care Procedures Writers to develop training packages, and members of the Team contributed to all the early lectures.

Public interest in child care issues continued into 1991, with local press reports in the first half of the year about the behaviour of children and young people in the city's homes. In the national press there were further reports of cases of alleged ritual child sexual abuse in Rochdale and Orkney, and of abuse and indiscipline in children's homes in Wales and Southwark. Debate about the existence or otherwise of organised, ritual abuse of children continued. In May, the Pindown Inquiry report [Levy and Kahan, 1991] was published. It revealed an illegal and harsh regime involving solitary confinement and deprivation in some Staffordshire children's homes, which had continued for almost six years. The report, nevertheless, stressed the positive role for residential care, a message few chose to hear.

The Department of Health in response asked the retiring head of the Social Services Inspectorate, Sir William Utting, to undertake a review of residential care for children [Utting, 1991], and all social services departments were required to carry out an immediate check on care in their own homes, to ensure that nothing resembling Pindown was in operation. The follow up inspection of Birmingham's children's homes by the Social Services Inspectorate showed considerable improvements had taken place in practice and in conditions [Social Services Inspectorate, 1990]. Thus, the checks made after the publication of the Pindown Report [Levy and Kahan, 1991] on procedures and practice in all the Department's homes revealed only minor deviation from correct procedures.

A broad interpretation of 'children in need' (discussed in Chapter 5) was agreed by the Departmental Management Team (and subsequently the Child Care Sub-Committee [Birmingham Social Services Department, 1991c]). It set the pattern for implementation of the Children Act. The first volumes of Guidance and Regulations were issued by the Department of Health in March and April [Department of Health, 1991c, 1991d, 1991e, 1991g], although Consultation Papers were still being issued on other aspects of the Children Act's implementation.

The Residential Topic Group produced an early draft of its report, which was discussed and amended on the advice of the Advisory Group when it met in April 1991. It met again in June to give similar concentrated attention to the report of the Fostering Topic Group.

Some earlier work began to show results. The fee paid fostering project started recruitment of carers in January 1991, Children Act Training commenced with lectures in February, and *The Children*

Act 1989 and Children in Need [In Need Implementation Group, 1991] and *Partnership in Prospect?* [BACC/NCVCCO, 1991] were published in March and May 1991. Members of the BACC Team, who had been trained during 1990 on the use of the Open University's Children Act Training Package [Open University, 1991], ran sessions to train trainers from several West Midlands Social Services Departments in its use.

The Corporate Children Act Steering Group, involving staff from the Social Services, Central Executive, Education, Recreation and Community Services, Housing and Libraries Departments began to meet in January 1991, and proved essential to ensuring contributions from other departments to the implementation of the Act. Birmingham City Council's commitment to developing personal social services was demonstrated by its Budget for 1991/92, which gave £3 million growth money to the Social Services Committee, to be spent on children's services and community care services equally. In June 1991, corporate working produced a joint approach with the Housing Department to the housing needs of young people leaving care.

Partly in response to conclusions which the BACC Team was beginning to draw from its work, the Departmental Management Team began to consider the future 'shape' of the Department. Although initially reluctant to consider any kind of reorganisation, the Management Team recognised that the generic structure of the Department, with specialised teams and managers only at the lowest level, would not meet the need for clear lines of accountability and lead responsibility required by the Children Act; and that the differences in emphasis between the prescriptive Children Act and more loosely drawn Community Care Act would require separate management up to the highest level. In anticipation, the Social Services Committee [Birmingham Social Services Department, 1990i] had given agreement in December 1990 to the principle that separate, dedicated management was required for community care services for adults and services for children and families.

BACC's work had revealed the flaws in the generic structure that would make implementation of the Children Act problematic. The group set up by the Departmental Management Team to examine the issues utilised the successful BACC model – inviting and responding to contributions from teams and individuals throughout the Department, as well as from other Departments and agencies. The

Departmental Management Team then discussed the options and issued a draft report for consultation. The outcome of this work was later to prove crucial to the implementation of BACC's recommendations.

The first Birmingham Child Care Conference and the Implementation of the Children Act: July – October 1991

In the months preceding the first Birmingham Child Care Conference and the implementation of the Children Act in October 1991, local and national newspapers continued to report the inquiry into events in Orkney, where social workers had removed children from homes following allegations of sexual abuse. In addition, the trial of Frank Beck, a senior social worker in Leicestershire, revealed a catalogue of abuse of children in residential care over many years. Concurrently, the Local Government Management Board published a report of a survey which showed continuing shortages of qualified social workers [Local Government Management Board, 1991].

Sir William Utting's report [Utting, 1991] was published in August, with recommendations for the protection of children in

---

Unwanted

Birmingham's children's homes have become the dumping grounds for the city's most troubled youngsters. In the first of a two day investigation, Keith Kendrick visits the home that houses the city's most violent young people.

Hope for the wild children

Handling teenagers who have got out of control must be one of the most difficult jobs facing social workers.

They have to pick up the broken pieces of those on whom society has turned its back, and try to rebuild them into acceptable men and women. It is a thankless task...

Children's homes can easily become the breeding grounds for rebellion rather than a replacement for the loving care missing from the child's life.

It is the job of social workers to redirect the pent-up energies being wasted on crime, violence, and drug abuse into building decent lives.

And there is some hope they are succeeding.

[Birmingham Evening Mail, 28 August 1991]

residential care, and for training for residential social workers. In response, the Department of Health announced a special training initiative for officers in charge of children's homes. Volume 4 of Guidance and Regulations under the Children Act, *Residential Care* [Department of Health, 1991f], issued at the same time, therefore attracted considerable attention. It brought together existing good practice and research findings and also incorporated recommendations from the Pindown Inquiry.

Following approaches by BACC, the local press carried a feature article focusing on three Birmingham children's homes, which set the difficulty of the task in context.

The remaining four volumes of Guidance and Regulations [Department of Health, 1991h, 1991i, 1991j, 1991k] supporting the Children Act were published in the summer and autumn, the last three not being received until October 1991. Clearly, their late arrival affected local authoritics' ability to prepare for implementation. Nevertheless, it must be acknowledged that the Department of Health had set itself – and nearly achieved – a punishing schedule for the production of these volumes. Together they represented a central government initiative, unprecedented in scale, to assist local authorities.

By this time, much of the work of the Topic Groups and the Children Act Implementation Group was reaching the Departmental Management Team in the form of reports with recommendations attached.

The Children Act Strategy Report set out the implications of key 'messages' of the Act for development of the Department's services. It established the need:

- to resource work which provides positive support for children and families;
- to work corporately across departments and jointly with the health authorities;
- to provide a consistent service throughout the city;
- to set standards and monitor outcomes;
- to provide information and encourage active participation by consumers; and
- to consider the child's religious persuasion, ethnic origin, and cultural and linguistic background when providing services.

> **During July 1991, the Departmental Management Team considered:**
> - services for children under eight
> - Day Care Officers' roles and responsibilities
> - the appointment of additional Day Care Officers
> - guidance for Managers of Residential and Day Care Establishments
> - allocation of the Family Support Budget (Children Act 1989, Section 17)
> - a Children Act Strategy
> - fees and charges under the Children Act
> - participation in research into the Act's implementation

This was followed in September by a further key report prepared by the BACC Team, *Looking After Birmingham's Children: a five year strategy for change* [Birmingham Social Services Department, 1991e]. This report, agreed by the Management Team in September 1991 and the Social Services Committee in October, set out a new role for residential care, stressing the positive uses of children's homes and proposing changes in balance between the use of residential and foster care. It recommended that over a five year period the fostering service should be expanded by recruitment of more foster carers, so that foster care became a choice for children and young people of all ages. The residential sector would also provide choice for children and young people, and increasingly fulfil a more specialised role, with eventually fewer homes with better staffing ratios and more trained staff. Each home would have a clear statement of its purpose. This was not a cheap option, and initially would require injection of additional resources, as children's homes would need to be maintained and improved to meet the requirements of the Children Act, whilst foster carers were being recruited and trained. The training, support and level of fees required to maintain a foster care service capable of meeting a wider range of children's needs would itself be costly. Eventually, with fewer children's homes, some savings might accrue, but these would not be significant. The whole process would be managed in such a way that staff and children were informed and involved. The overall objective was to provide a quality service geared to individual children's needs.

Strategies for the retention and recruitment of social workers, which were part of BACC's recommended programme for dealing with unallocated child care cases, resulted in the Department's

Children's and General Services Teams being virtually fully staffed. Birmingham's work on this issue was praised by the House of Commons Select Committee in its report on the issue in July 1991. The Project Director, Paul Sutton, and Rita Webb of the Central Executive Department, gave verbal evidence to the Select Committee as well as providing the Committee with a copy of the BACC report on unallocated cases [Birmingham Action on Child Care, 1990d]. The Committee concluded:

We were impressed with the thoroughness of the analysis contained in that report both in respect of the difficulties it identified and also the potential solutions advanced. [House of Commons: Health Committee, 1991]

The first Birmingham Child Care Conference

The first Birmingham Annual Child Care Conference, held at the new International Convention Centre, in October 1991, was in many ways the high spot for BACC. It was attended by over 400 people from throughout the United Kingdom, although a significant number of places were reserved for Birmingham Social Services Department staff. Representatives from every team delivering services to children attended, gaining a new view of the size and variety of their Department, and a fresh sense of its identity. The focus of the Conference, 'Crisis and Change: culture and child care in the '90s', attracted local and national media interest. Speakers included Beverly Anderson, broadcaster and educational consultant; Adele Jones, from the National Institute for Social Work; Rupert Hughes, Assistant Secretary, Department of Health, and a key figure in the development of the Children Act; Jeff Rooker MP; Baroness Faithfull; the City's Chief Executive, Roger Taylor; and several contributors from the National Children's Bureau, including Barbara Kahan herself.

The following week, on 14 October 1991, the Children Act came into force in its entirety. The BACC Team assisted by the Child Care Procedures Writers staffed a helpline for a fortnight to deal with social workers' and others' initial problems. 119 calls were received; encouragingly, the majority of the queries were made by people with a grounding in the Act's main provisions. The Children Act training had given staff in the Department a good start. There were, of course, some difficulties; late arrival of Guidance and Regulations meant new forms for use under the Act were not available for some time. Draft internal Departmental Child Care Procedures were, however, issued in time for the Act's implementation, a considerable achievement considering the rapidity with which such a major and complex piece of legislation had been implemented.

The final months: November 1991 – July 1992

Throughout this period, both the national and local press continued to report abuse and incidents in children's homes, including further revelations of abuse in homes in North Wales. A full inquiry was set up into the circumstances which allowed abuse in children's homes in Leicestershire to go undetected over a long period. A well-publicised trial of family members accused of ritual abuse collapsed because of its dependence on the unsatisfactory evidence of the children alleged to have been abused. A report from the National Children's Home showed that children and young people were the perpetrators in significant numbers of cases of child sexual abuse, within families, in residential and foster care, and in other situations [National Children's Home, 1992].

Much of the work of BACC at this stage represented the continuation, development or completion of earlier work. Members of BACC gave further presentations on the Children Act to various groups. Work continued on the appropriate use of day nurseries. Following presentation of its survey of day nurseries to the Departmental Management Team in November 1991, the BACC Team organised a consultation exercise on the options for the future use of nurseries, and also considered the appropriate structure and level of fees for nursery users. Monitoring of the incidence of unallocated cases was combined with work on initiatives designed to deal with the problem, with a further report to the Management Team in February 1992. The Management Team agreed to a small research project to look at procedures for dealing with allegations of abuse against foster carers. It also reviewed its response to the involvement of young people, especially girls, in prostitution, and it discussed new formats for assessment.

In November 1991, a joint meeting of the Departmental Management Teams between education and social services considered a number of aspects of joint working, in particular the education of children in care. The implications of local management of schools and grant-maintained status for the education of children with social problems were identified.

In November 1991, after national advertisement, the Project Director, Paul Sutton, was appointed General Manager, Children and

Families. As one of the Director's two deputies, he took up his appointment from 1 April 1992, with managerial responsibility for all the Department's services for children and families. The new structure for the Department which became operational from that date also included establishment of a Children and Families Unit within the Planning and Review Section (Policy and Performance Review Division). A number of members of the BACC Team joined this Unit when the Project's funding ceased. These managerial changes in the Department came about partly as a result of recommendations made by BACC, and were designed to ensure that the work of BACC was integrated into the Department and able to continue when the Project ended.

Both the Departmental Management Team and the Child Care Sub-Committee received a series of reports which represented the outcome of work undertaken by BACC. The Team worked on planning for the 1992 Conference, which the Social Services Committee had agreed could go ahead. It was involved in the City Council's submission to City Challenge – a special initiative by the Department of the Environment which aimed to bring together local and national government departments and Urban Programme funds to tackle deprivation in selected areas. The Project Director undertook work for the 'Child in the City' Sub-Commission of the Eurocities Network, and visited Lyon in France in March and May (1992).

At its meetings in December 1991 and February 1992 the Social Services Child Care Sub-Committee discussed reports from Birmingham Action on Child Care on:

- a quality foster care service for the 1990s (based on the Foster Care Topic Group's report)
- aftercare for children looked after by the Department
- joint work with the Library Service on the Children Act
- policy guidelines for the registration and inspection of day care
- a proposal for a second child care conference
- the Department's response to the Social Services Inspectorate's follow up inspection of Birmingham's children's homes
- a quality residential care service for the 1990s (based on the Residential Care Services Topic Group's report)
- an evaluation and proposal to extend the fee paid fostering project
- joint work with the Education Department

The BACC Team with members of the Advisory Group met for two days at the end of January 1992 to review its work and consider how to record it. The idea of a book, which Barbara Kahan, as Project consultant, had tentatively suggested at the outset, was considered and recommended to the Director.

The final meeting of the Advisory Group was held in April 1992, when some of the Project's key work was presented to the Group. The first meeting of the Editorial Group for this book was held in May, and it continued to meet as required until January 1993. The final few months were, of course, a time for looking forward to new opportunities as well as for taking leave of colleagues. Many people expressed their sadness at the ending of the Project; and some, their anxiety about coping without it!

After BACC, what?

By the time the Project ended, managerial structures had been designed to ensure that BACC's work in improving services would not be quickly eroded. The generic structure of the Department had been replaced with a largely specialist managerial structure (set out in Chapter 5) which ensured dedicated management for children and families services from the grassroots up to the Director. Within this structure, lead responsibilities for specific aspects of service were assigned to senior managers, with support from both operational managers and the Children and Families Unit in the Policy and Performance Review Division. When BACC was established there had been no unified children's service, but a variety of services for children and families. From 1992, the new management structure created a single service. There was a new sense that senior managers understood how the parts of the service interrelated and impacted upon one another.

Integrating BACC into the management structure in this manner could ensure that its recommendations for change were put into practice. It was more difficult to see how the unique BACC approach could continue after the Project ended. Involvement of staff from across the Department in the work of the Project; the Project's accessibility; BACC's semi-independence of the Department; its privileged position as a critical observer – these aspects of the Project's work would be difficult if not impossible to continue or replicate from within a formal management structure.

In the few months following the end of the Project, the difficulty of protecting the gains made by BACC quickly became apparent.

Although the Department received a growth budget for 1992/93, it was also required to make 'efficiency savings' as a condition of receiving that growth. Politically, this was important, since other departments were contributing their efficiency savings to pay for growth in Education and Social Services Departments' budgets. Amongst a number of factors which made the achievement of sufficient savings difficult for the Department were some of BACC's successful pieces of work. The Department's employee budget was not fully funded by Birmingham City Council since it was assumed that at any one time a percentage of posts would be vacant. With the success of the recruitment and retention strategies, which had been part of the response to the problem of unallocated cases, the Social Services Department's level of vacancies was very low. It soon became clear that it was heading for an overspend on the employee budget for 1992/93. The success of the fee paid fostering scheme, which had recruited more carers than had been anticipated, also contributed to the potential overspending. Consequently, the spending of all the Department's growth money was delayed whilst efforts were made to find additional savings elsewhere and balance the strictly cash-limited budget. Growth money was released gradually, in line with Departmental priorities, and the resources allocated to the implementation of the Children Act were therefore protected. How this happened is discussed in chapter 5.

The Project came to an end in July 1992, but the second Birmingham Child Care Conference was held in October 1992, at the International Convention Centre. It attracted speakers and delegates from all over Britain and Europe. The theme was *The Child in the City*, and presentations looked at the ways in which various services and agencies could work together to create a 'child-friendly city', which would be safe, hospitable and nurturing for children.

What is remarkable from the account given above is the range of work undertaken by a small team, never numbering more than the equivalent of ten full time people. Without the participative approach adopted by the Team, such a range of work could not have been achieved. The impact of BACC's work on the Department, underpinned by the philosophy and methods adopted by the Team, is the subject matter of the following chapters. Whilst the next three chapters concentrate primarily on the outcomes of BACC's work, the contribution of process to outcomes is included, and will be looked at again in the final chapter, chapter 8.

5. A strategy for child care

Even without BACC, Birmingham Social Services Department, in common with others in England and Wales, would have faced the necessity of reviewing its operations and making major changes, because of the challenges of the Children Act 1989 and the National Health Service and Community Care Act 1990. The Department maximised the value of its investment in BACC by using the Project to lead its approach to implementing the Children Act. This was added to its remit shortly after the proposal for BACC was approved. BACC, of course, benefited from the impetus for change created by the Children Act: staff recognised that change was inevitable and therefore welcomed opportunities to help shape the future.

BACC was also able to contribute to the development of an explicit strategic framework for children's services. It played a key role in revision of the Department's management structure which was necessary for implementation of its recommendations and of the two Acts of Parliament. This chapter sets out the work that BACC undertook on the implementation of the Children Act and the development of strategy, while chapters 6 and 7 provide more detail of individual pieces of work.

Implementation of the Children Act

It was recognised from the start that the newly published Children Bill would influence the work of BACC. The extent to which the Children Bill (later the Children Act 1989) would structure and dominate its work was not, however, at first realised. Every aspect of BACC's work was to a greater or lesser extent affected by the Children Act and its philosophy. The Act was both an advantage to the Project – because it carried with it a requirement for change – and a disadvantage – because of the time spent on its interpretation and implementation, and on responding to the consultation process organised by the Department of Health.

The Children Act 1989

The Children Act became law on 16 November 1989 and was implemented in full on 14 October 1991. It is unprecedented in size and scope, combining both public and private child care arrangements; it deals with the consequences for children of parental separation and divorce as well as with issues of child welfare and protection. The Act is based on a set of interlinked principles, the expression of an underlying philosophy which holds that while the child's welfare is the paramount consideration, the family is the best setting for the child's upbringing. Families are free to bring up their children in a variety of ways, and the local authority must offer a range of services to parents and others caring for children to help them fulfil their parental responsibilities. Where the authority intervenes to safeguard a child's welfare, it must still seek to work in partnership with parents. Parental responsibility can only be transferred through adoption; thus, the local authority shares parental responsibility for a child in statutory care with his or her natural parents (or other long-term carers).

Other important provisions in the Act include the concept of choice for service users (both parents and children); and rights to be consulted, to make representations, and to complain. Services must be publicised and some, such as day care services, must undergo a public review every three years. For the first time, stress is given in an Act of Parliament to the local authority's duty to take account of a child's 'religious persuasion, racial origin and cultural and linguistic background' (Section 22 (5)(c)) in any decisions made about a child it is looking after.

The Children Act Implementation Group

The main vehicle for implementing the Children Act in Birmingham was the Children Act Implementation Group, led by BACC. This large group, which first met in April 1990, included staff from children's homes, area offices and head office – managers at all levels as well as basic grade workers. There were representatives of fieldwork, adoption and fostering, residential care, child protection, and services for people with learning difficulties; BACC Team members, administrative staff, and staff working in training and policy development. Amongst these were staff responsible for policy and practice development for service delivery to Black and minority ethnic people. The child care procedures writers and a city council solicitor were also members of the Group.

The Group met twice a month at first, and subsequently monthly, between April 1990 and October 1991. It established a number of sub-groups, five at first, but ultimately seven. These included additional people, who were not members of the Implementation Group, thus widening the numbers of staff and others involved in development of policy and practice. Links were constructed to the BACC Topic Groups, especially the Services for Children Under Eight Group, and to the Task Groups set up for implementation of the NHS and Community Care Act 1990. There were specific links with inspection and quality assurance and with management development and training, especially in relation to the Children Act Training Strategy. The Children Act Implementation Group's seven topic areas were:

- protection of children;
- partnership with parents;
- court and legal processes;
- services for children looked after by the local authority;
- information for the Children Act;
- day care for children under eight;
- aftercare/leaving care.

The Implementation Group initiated work on the use of language in social work, which would identify and define key terms, ready for translation into the main minority languages used in Birmingham. It concerned itself with interpretation of 'children in need'; with local implementation of aspects of the Children Act in advance of October 1991; and with Education Supervision Orders. In September 1992, the Group was superseded by the Children Act Development Group, which was to follow up implementation issues systematically during 1992-3.

The Children Act Implementation Group epitomised the way in which BACC worked. Its membership was from different levels in the Department's structure, and comprised people with different interests. It was open to ideas from all its members, and had interlocking membership with other key groups. Through its

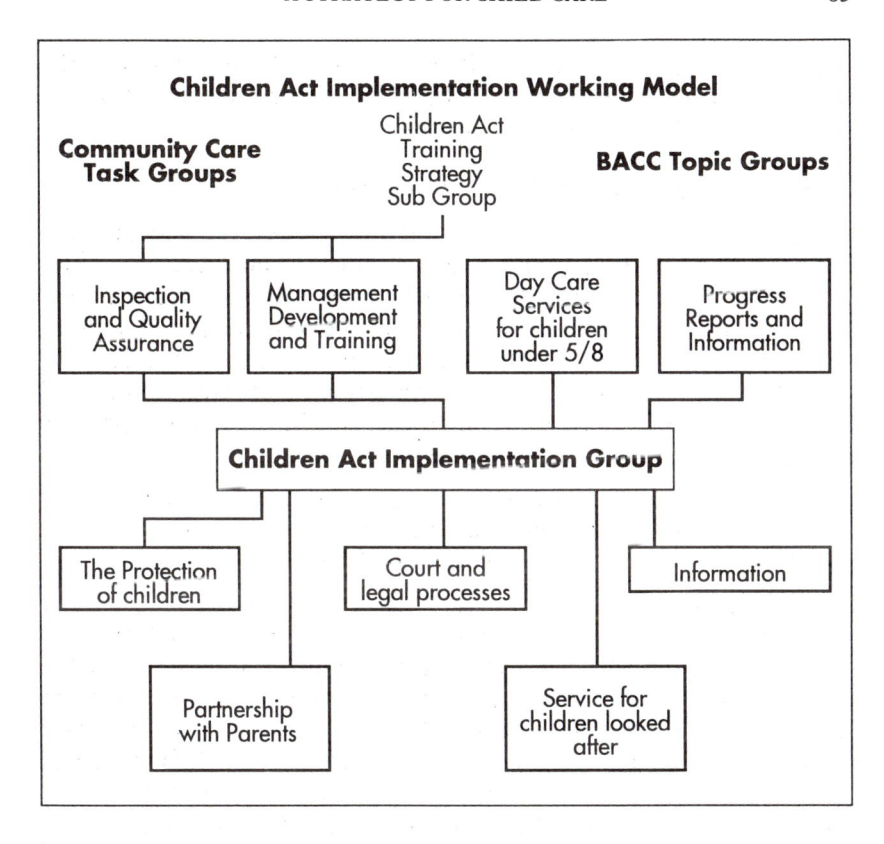

Children Act Implementation Working Model

Community Care Task Groups — Children Act Training Strategy Sub Group — **BACC Topic Groups**

- Inspection and Quality Assurance
- Management Development and Training
- Day Care Services for children under 5/8
- Progress Reports and Information

Children Act Implementation Group

- The Protection of children
- Court and legal processes
- Information
- Partnership with Parents
- Service for children looked after

sub-groups and other links, the number of people involved directly or indirectly was increased, helping to create a climate for change in the Department. Like most groups, its vitality varied during its life, with interest at times dying away and then reviving. Attendance at meetings fluctuated, sometimes falling off to no more than BACC Team members and one or two others, then increasing again. The commitment of the BACC Team ensured its survival. It was, however, an important vehicle for development of policy and practice in relation to the Children Act. It received and refined reports and other papers produced by individuals and its sub-groups, and these were not solely inspired or written by the BACC Team. It was, therefore, an arena in which staff at all levels and from all areas of work could make a contribution if they wished. New ideas and approaches were raised at its meetings, and the majority of the formative reports produced by BACC were first discussed at the Children Act Implementation Group.

A corporate response to the Children Act

In early 1990, Councillors led an initiative to develop and improve day care for children under five and out-of-school care for older children. Known as the City-Wide Child Care Strategy, it was launched in April 1990 and at first involved Economic Development, Education, and Social Services Departments. Later, the Library Services Department and the Department of Recreation and Community Services were to contribute. Its objective was to provide quality child care to meet the needs of:

young children, working parents, particularly women who wish to work, employers and local communities and their voluntary organisations. [Birmingham Social Services Department, 1990c]

Its first proposals evolved without reference to BACC, and the Project's reservations about potential confusion involved in using 'childcare' or 'child care' (apparently interchangeably) to mean day care were overruled. According to the first report, the initiative was driven by a number of social and economic concerns – to assist women to participate in the labour market; to raise the incomes of and spring the poverty trap for single parents; and to enable Birmingham City Council to take the lead in coordinating provision of day and out-of-school care for children. Social, developmental and educational needs of children were not identified as a concern at this stage. The requirements of the Children Act for local authorities to review provision of day care, to provide information on its availability, and to provide services for children in need which included day and out-of-school care were not referred to in this first report. Despite the absence of these references, the Group was concerned to develop services which local authorities were empowered by the Children Act to provide to children in need and other children.

The City-Wide Child Care Strategy required resources from all three originating Committees (Economic Development, Education and Social Services), and the report identified pilot schemes to promote day care for children to be set up in three deprived inner city areas as a first step. BACC became involved soon after this, and helped the Strategy Steering Group to take account of requirements of the Children Act. By late summer 1990, training for childminders had begun in one area and was in preparation in others; three pilot holiday schemes (to look after the children of council employees) had been run; partnerships with other major employers for the provision of 'child care' were being explored; and sites for new nurseries were being identified. In October 1990, a 'Child Care Matters' conference was held to try to involve businesses in providing day care for their employees. In addition, a Child Care Company was proposed, to undertake consultancy work, but this did not prove feasible.

> Child care is a classic example where the City Council needs to assume its new role as a strategic, enabling authority. ...The Council has a major opportunity here as a catalyst to plan and pull together child care services to the benefit of the electorate.
>
> [Birmingham City Council, Corporate Child Care Steering Group, 1991]

The Social Services Department's Management Team agreed in May 1990 to offer 60 places at day nurseries to the Training Enterprise Council (TEC) for use by the children of trainees. (Although this proposition was accepted, it brought to the fore issues surrounding the use and purpose of day nursery provision which are discussed briefly in chapter 6. Some Team members felt that day nursery places were essentially a social work resource, and should not be used to meet what were primarily economic objectives. Others recognised that these developments would create a better social mix in nurseries.) The funds raised would be used to create a pool of nursery staff to provide cover for sickness and holidays.

By October 1991, a review of this initiative showed that take up of the places by TEC trainees had been slow, possibly because of changes in the TEC programme, but it was also likely that many parents did not consider a short-term nursery place satisfactory and preferred to make their own, more reliable arrangements. The scheme was to proceed during 1992/93 on a reduced scale (20 places). Other developments were more successful. Four community nurseries had been opened, and four others were planned. 95 places for childminder training had been provided, and of 68 people completing the course 55 had become registered as childminders. A subsidised childminding scheme had been set up to support parents undertaking training, and equipment was available for lending to childminders. Four schemes gave holiday care to the children of employees of Birmingham Council and three other large local employers. Local initiatives for after school care provided nearly 200 new places for primary school children, and equipment to support other schemes was purchased.

These developments were the result of cooperation between staff at local level, facilitated by the personal interest of the Chief Executive and political interests of elected members. The strategy's role in economic regeneration was crucial to this support. In other areas of work, cooperation between Birmingham City Council departments to give priority to the needs of children and young people was more problematic. BACC argued that implementation of the Children Act required contributions from several different departments, and the Children Act Corporate Steering Group became the primary vehicle for securing cooperation.

The Children Act Corporate Steering Group was set up in January 1991 to maximise contributions by other departments to implementation of the Children Act and to ensure that cross-departmental liaison and assistance required by the Act (especially under Section 27) was achieved. Its active membership included representation from Social Services, Education, Housing, Libraries, Recreation and Community Services, and Central Executive Departments. Since the focus for the Group was to be development of a whole-authority response to the Act, health authorities and voluntary organisations were not involved.

A small steering group of middle and senior managers was established. Short-life working groups with a wider membership to consider specific issues, including children in need (see below), child protection, aftercare, Education Supervision Orders, and liaison and notification were set up. (There were many references in the Act to liaison and notification across departmental boundaries, for example, in relation to educational needs of children looked after by a social services department.) The Corporate Steering Group helped to create a cooperative atmosphere which had not previously existed amongst senior staff from the departments involved. They were enabled to understand each other's work, and to appreciate the potential for and constraints on mutual assistance. One result was recognition of the need for corporate responses to a range of children's issues, apart from implementation of the Act.

Outcomes of the Children Act Corporate Steering Groups' work included

- a joint strategy with the Housing Department for provision of housing for young people ceasing to be looked after by the local authority;
- a three-year agreement with a local voluntary organisation to prevent youth homelessness;
- regular meetings between senior staff in the Housing and Social Services Departments to discuss matters of mutual concern;
- a joint day seminar with the Education Department, which resulted in a commitment to further cooperation on a range of issues;
- a joint policy with the Education Department on Education Supervision Orders;
- establishment of an information service by the Library Service for childminders, parents and others;
- cooperation with the Department of Recreation and Community Services on registration and inspection of services for children under eight, and cooperation on development of out-of-school provision; and
- greater understanding by Chief Officers of children's issues.

After the implementation of the Children Act in October 1991, the Group's remit gradually changed to a wider focus on children's issues. There were no other explicit mechanisms in the city to resolve problems of corporate working between departments at that time. It was therefore proposed that the Children Act Implementation Group be superseded by The Child in the City Corporate Group. Its terms of reference were to promote the welfare of children, by coordinating activity and resolving policy conflicts between departments, promoting joint initiatives, and seeking to attract new resources. This Group had still not met by the end of January 1993, however.

The Children Act Corporate Steering Group was a first step towards dealing with problems which the Group identified as impeding corporate responses to the needs of children and families within the city. The Group provided the first opportunity for issues of coordination and development of corporate policy and procedures to be discussed between Departments. While there were many instances of cooperation between staff locally and in an ad hoc manner, there was a vacuum in cooperative working at management team level. The Steering Group filled this vacuum, identified and developed corporate strategies and budget proposals, and provided leadership on child care matters.

The difficulty of this undertaking should not be underestimated. BACC and the Corporate Group tried to ensure that Birmingham's successful City Challenge Bid in 1992 explicitly addressed children's needs in its proposals for the regeneration of Newtown (in Birmingham's inner city area). Because of the overriding priority given to economic concerns, however, the Group, despite its wide membership, was not able to introduce these changes into the Bid. The slow progress in setting up its successor, the Child in the City Corporate Group, underlined these difficulties. Nevertheless, these Groups were the best means available to raise the profile of children's issues at corporate level.

A key concept: the interpretation of 'children in need'

The concept of 'children in need' was fundamental to an implementation strategy for the Children Act 1989. It was the cornerstone of Part III of the Act, *Local Authority Support for Children and Families*, which itself represented one of the major crucial differences between this Act and previous legislation. Chapter 2 described the tension which has existed since 1948 between the *duty* of the local authority to protect children, and *powers* to prevent their admission to care. While local authorities could provide a range of preventive services, they were not required to do so, and resources for child protection took priority over preventive work. The 1989 Act was the first to *require* local authorities to provide a range of supportive services for children and families and for children 'in need' (Part III of the Act), while Schedule 2 set out the services the authority was empowered to provide. Section 17 deals particularly with children 'in need':

It shall be the general duty of every Local Authority (in addition to other duties imposed on them by this Part [Part III])
   (a) to safeguard and promote the welfare of children within their area who are in need; and
   (b) so far as is consistent with that duty promote the upbringing of such children by their families,
by providing a range and level of services appropriate to those children's needs.
[Children Act 1989, Section 17 (1)]

The Act also stated, however, that:

every local authority shall take reasonable steps, through the provision of services under Part III of this Act, to prevent children within their area suffering ill-treatment or neglect. [Children Act 1989, Schedule 2 (4)(1)]

This did not imply that only children at risk of neglect or ill-treatment were in need. The Act defined 'in need' as follows:

... a child shall be taken to be in need if –
(a) he is unlikely to achieve or maintain, or to have the opportunity of achieving or maintaining, a reasonable standard of health or development without the provision for him of services by a local authority under this Part;
(b) his health or development is likely to be significantly impaired, or further impaired, without the provision for him of such services; or
(c) he is disabled...
[Children Act 1989, Section 17 (10)]

This definition at first sight was very wide – with the potential for generating a massive increase in demand for services. Local authorities were expected to take 'reasonable steps' to identify the extent to which there were children in need within their area [Children Act 1989, Schedule 2, Section 1(1)]. The way in which a local authority interpreted the definition of 'in need' for this purpose therefore determined the range and scope of services it provided, and the extent to which these were seen as stigmatised. A wide interpretation enabled an authority to provide services to children not 'at risk', but where help was nevertheless needed. Its very broadness could, however, raise hopes of support for families who then could not be assisted because of limited resources. At the other extreme, a very narrow interpretation, restricting services to children 'at risk', would lead to stigmatised services, undermining the ability to support families.

Most authorities were, inevitably, seeking ways of clearly prioritising services. The requirement to publicise services provided for children and families [Children Act 1989, Schedule 2, Section 1(2)] ruled out containing demand by ensuring that it was mainly professionals who knew what was available. (Chapter 6 outlines the work undertaken in Birmingham to provide information under the Children Act.) Therefore, the way in which a local authority interpreted the definition of 'children in need' contained in the Children Act and the Regulations and Guidance was a critical decision with political implications. Elected members had to balance an apparently unlimited demand by families for preventive and supportive services against the reality of limited resources.

Some local authorities, subject to severe financial restraints, expressed considerable anxiety and sought ways to restrict demand. The absence of a conjunction – 'and' or 'or' – between (a) and (b) in Section 17 (10) (above) initially led some authorities to assume – and even to add to their own guidance – an 'or' between the two. Choosing Section 17 (10) (b) as their definition of need had the effect of restricting services to those children whose health or development was at risk of being 'significantly impaired' [Gardner, 1991]. Such a definition would have further contained demand because of the potential stigma for parents virtually admitting that children were at risk of harm or neglect. Moreover, the authority could refuse to provide a service to any family where a child or children were not 'at risk'. A letter from the Department of Health in January 1991, reiterated later in the Guidance and Regulations, reflected central government concern at narrow interpretations:

The definition of need in the Act is deliberately wide to reinforce the emphasis on preventive support and services to families... A local authority cannot lawfully substitute any other definition. [Department of Health, 1991d].

The difference between 'in need' and 'at risk' was crucial for service users. If they are not distinguished, receiving a service might not only carry a stigma but might imply that the parent was guilty of neglect or harm to the child. Nevertheless, despite the Guidance from the Department of Health, local interpretation and the adoption of priorities are required by the Act. How these were developed could reinforce or blur the distinction between 'in need' and 'at risk'.

In Birmingham, the Children Act Implementation Group first began to consider the importance of this concept in August 1990. The Information Sub-Group had noted the legal requirement to publicise services available to 'children in need'. Clearly, the interpretation adopted would affect not only who received a service but the nature and amount of service provided. Following a Family Rights Group seminar on 'children in need' in December 1990, BACC's Project Director joined the national In Need Implementation Group. This Group produced a publication, *The Children Act 1989 and children's needs – make it the answer not the problem* [In Need Implementation Group, 1991], which argued strongly for a broad and inclusive definition of 'in need'. In Birmingham, the Departmental Management Team discussed the concept and a draft interpretation of its meaning in February 1991 and the Social Services Committee finally endorsed the interpretation recommended by BACC in September 1991. The 18 categories of children included in the interpretation are set out in Appendix 3.

The BACC Team argued for the adoption by Birmingham City Council of an inclusive understanding of 'in need' firmly based on the Guidance and Regulations: the Act was not the sole responsibility of the Social Services Department, nor could the needs of 'children in need' be met by social services alone. If there were effective corporate commitment to the Act's implementation, then the requirements of Part III of the Act would be manageable.

> The Act provides opportunities to widen the base from which services are delivered by providing for and indeed requiring cross-Departmental collaboration....
>
> [Birmingham Social Services Department, 1991c].

BACC noted that:

the Act potentially affects large numbers of children, not simply those who might traditionally be the recipients of personal social services provided by the Social Services Department. [Birmingham Social Services Department, 1991c]

It pointed out that 'children in need' are not a discrete or static population – all children may potentially be 'in need' at some points during their childhoods. The Department of Health noted that:

parenting capacity may be limited temporarily or permanently by poverty, racism, poor housing or unemployment or by personal or marital problems, sensory or physical disability, mental illness or past life experiences. Lack of parenting skills or inability to provide adequate care should not be equated with lack of affection or with irresponsibility. [Department of Health, 1989c]

The Report produced by BACC for the Social Services Committee and Chief Officers recommended that each service department should adopt a broad interpretation of 'in need', and then identify

> Some children may need services continuously, for example, as a result of a substantial disability or long term illness, perhaps of a parent. Other children's circumstances will change over time and they may move in and out of being 'in need'.
>
> [Birmingham Social Services Department, 1991c]

the priority needs for which it could make provision. It recommended that service departments link their Children Act strategies into the City's Anti-Poverty Strategy, which was working to identify where those children most affected by poverty in all its manifestations were most concentrated. The interpretation of 'children in need' recommended by the social services department for city-wide adoption recognised children suffering from various structural forms of deprivation – for example, the impact of unemployment or of living in a deprived area – as well as individual circumstances. The full definition is set out in Appendix 3.

It is important to note that the Act laid on local authorities a *general* duty to provide services to children in need. It did not confer on the families of children in need a right to receive a service, only to be considered for a service. The Social Services Department or other departments of the local authority could provide a service in many different ways. It could simply give information, advice or counselling; it could provide or facilitate support groups and self-help groups; or it could offer intensive support including the provision of a social worker, help in the home, respite care, and accommodation away from home.

The inclusive interpretation of children in need adopted by the Social Services Department committed it to developing its services to support children and families, under Part III and Schedule 2 of the Children Act. In the short term such an approach was likely to cause problems of unmet demand from families, but it provided the impetus for a future shift of resources away from 'child rescue' and into preventive work in its broadest sense. The support of other departments of the local authority was likely to be crucial in achieving such a shift, and at the time of writing it is not yet clear whether this will be attainable, given continuing pressures on local government finance. The next section examines resources available to the Social Services Department for implementation of the Children Act.

Resources for work with children and families

During the period 1988 to 1993, the Department's budget was increasing faster than inflation; a growing elderly population and care of people with disabilities in the community rather than in hospitals and other institutions led Birmingham City Council to allocate more resources to personal social services annually. The proportion of the Department's budget allocated to children and families had, however, fallen quite substantially during the 1980s, as the percentage of children in the population reduced and the number of children in residential care also declined. It was clear by 1989 that this trend could not continue. With specific concerns about conditions in residential care and unallocated social work cases, after 1989 the children and families budget (including fieldwork, administration, training and other support services) levelled at about 32 per cent of the total budget. Implementation of the NHS and Community Care Act, however, ensured that high priority continued to be given to expenditure on elderly people and people with disabilities. By 1992, the Social Services Department's budget could only be increased to meet the growing demands upon it at the expense of some other departments' budgets. Before looking at the consequences of these growing financial pressures, the allocation of the additional money for children and families services each year is set out below.

The 1989/90 budget included an addition of £177,000 for children and families services, which was to be spent on reducing unallocated child care cases, provision of short-term foster care for Black and minority ethnic children, and raising boarding out allowances for foster children. A saving of £50,000 from the budget for children's residential care was also earmarked for increasing fostering allowances, to the level recommended by the National Foster Care Association. By 1990/91, concern about staffing in children's homes, implementation of the new Boarding Out and Charge and Control Regulations 1988, and implementation of the Children Act 1989 increased the children and families budget again, by £650,000. The full impact of implementing the Children Act was not, however, incorporated into the Department's budget until 1991/92, when £1,243,000 out of a social services growth budget of £3 million was allocated to children's services.

This additional money was allocated as follows:

- £700,000 for social work with children – the family support budget, work on unallocated cases, incentives for retention of qualified staff, and a centre for sexually abused girls;
- £240,000 for children looked after by the department – night staff in children's homes, recruitment and payment of foster carers, and an after care service;
- £155,000 broadly classified as protecting children's rights – for establishing a system of children's reviews in line with the Act (including Independent Reviewing Officers, additional Assistant Team Managers and review clerks), for the children's rights service, fees for Guardians ad Litem (independent social workers appointed by the courts), and expenses for independent visitors (for children in the Department's care who have lost contact with their families);
- £120,000 for services for children under eight – additional day care officers to promote, register and inspect day care provision, and staff to undertake a review of day care.

The budget for 1992/93 also included additional expenditure for children's services, of £1.3 million, most of it for developing the foster care service (£0.75 million), but with a substantial sum allocated for improvement of services for children under eight (£0.3 million), and provision for expenditure on residential care, the complaints procedure, and independent reviews.

By 1992/93, however, Birmingham City Council was under increasing financial pressure. Growth in education and social services budgets was to be funded by savings made by other departments. All departments were given strictly cash limited budgets, and the Social Services Department was also expected to make efficiency savings to assist in the development of its services. These requirements proved difficult to meet. The most significant factor preventing the Department from keeping within its cash limited budget was a projected overspend on the employee budget. Like other departmental budgets, the Department's employee budget was funded on the assumption that a percentage of posts would always be vacant, due to staff turnover. In the case of the Social Services Department this percentage was relatively high, since historically there had always been difficulties in recruiting sufficient numbers of qualified social workers, and there was a high turnover of manual or domestic staff. Success in the recruitment and retention strategies developed by BACC to tackle the problem of unallocated cases, combined with the impact of the recession (which reduced staff turnover), resulted in 1992 in there being few vacancies in the Department, and the employee budget thus heading for an overspend. In addition, another successful initiative, the Fee Paid Fostering Scheme, exceeded its targets, so that more money was being spent on foster care than had been anticipated. To remain within the cash-limited budget, the Director had to delay the release of the growth money. Whilst the majority of the developments went ahead during 1992, the expansion of the Fee Paid Fostering Scheme to cover all short-term foster homes regrettably had to be delayed until April 1993.

Close cooperation with other departments, through the Children Act Corporate Steering Group and through individual contacts, facilitated contributions from other departments to the implementation of the Children Act. The Housing Department accepted a strategic role in providing or enabling the provision of housing for young people who ceased to be looked after by the local authority, and joined with a local voluntary organisation in obtaining £300,000 from the Department of Health for a three-year project to tackle youth homelessness. The Library Service was in the process of establishing a child care bureau at its central Children's Library where teachers, other professionals, parents, carers and foster carers, childminders, children and young people could gain easy access to information about available services. Within the Children's Library, a Centre for the Child in the City was planned, supported by £50,000 from the Social Services Department. This Centre was to house the child care bureau, provide a logical location for the Children's Rights Officer, and a place for the Young People's Forum to meet.

This corporate acceptance of responsibility for implementation of the Children Act represented a new development in Birmingham, where corporate and joint working had historically been difficult to develop and sustain. The new commitment to supporting families, to recognising that parents requesting help from the local authority were not failing in their duties, but acting responsibly, led to acceptance of the concept of the 'child-friendly city', which was highlighted at the second Birmingham Child Care Conference in October 1992.

Training for the Children Act 1989

Training was essential if staff at all levels were going to make the conceptual shift and practical changes necessary for the Act's implementation. The impact of new Regulations and Guidance, new procedures, and new resources would be considerably lessened without a change in the way in which staff approached their work. In visiting teams throughout the Department, the BACC Team encountered many who were excited by the possibilities the Act offered. But they also met those who felt the Act was impossible to implement without extensive new resources; and at the other extreme those who said, 'we're Doing All That Already'. This second response – the DATA syndrome – was not a reflection of the reality, but was as likely to inhibit change and development as the first [Marsh, 1990]. Both these extremes would make implementation of the Act in the true spirit of its philosophy problematic.

Apart from a needed change in attitude, there were many new terms and concepts to learn. The Act brought together public and private law, abolished some powers open to the local authority, and substituted others. The Regulations and Guidance were changed. Workers needed to revise their basic legal knowledge, and to start to use a set of new terms.

Initially, there was widespread disquiet and uneasiness about the provisions of the Children Bill. One of BACC's first public actions was therefore to run seminars to inform staff of the general direction of the new legislation, explaining its background, general philosophy, and key concepts. Each identical seminar gave only a basic outline of the nature of the new legislation, but staff had opportunities to discuss with one another a fundamental concept in the Bill – partnership with parents – and consider its implications for their own practice. These first seminars were well received, but represented only a tentative first step in the massive undertaking of training all the Department's 2,500 workers involved with children and families.

In considering the next stage, the BACC Team, in consultation with the Training Section and the Child Care Procedures writers, took the view that training was required for all workers who dealt with children and families. All staff, including administrative staff, needed to be familiar with the new terminology and with the basic concepts in the legislation. Different teams and staff at different levels would then need training packages to suit their needs.

A three-stage training programme was devised and written in house, bringing together the knowledge acquired by the BACC Team, the Training Section, and the Procedure Writers, with material from the Open University and other sources. The first stage of the programme was a set of five lectures, which all children and families workers, including the Director and her senior managers, attended. These five lectures covered the key components of the Act, as set out in chapter 3. Each worker was issued with a training plan and a record was maintained of the work he or she had undertaken. The Children Act Training Team ran sessions to train or brief managers on using the training package devised for their teams. There were 25 different versions of the training package, each including core modules and additional material developed for the specific needs of different workers. Workplace training was then carried out by managers using this material which had been designed by the Children Act Training Team. The programme continued until early 1992, and was followed by further, more specialist training materials provided for individual workers and teams to meet their specific needs.

The Children Act Training Team provided support to managers carrying out this ambitious programme, including acting as co-trainers if required. In addition, training was provided for Adoption and Fostering Panels and some foster carers. Shortage of staff in 1992, when vacancies in the Training Team could not be filled for a period because of pressures on the departmental budget, held up the rolling programme of child care training which was planned, and which would have included newly appointed social workers, and staff changing specialisms.

Two members of the BACC Team attended an Open University Course designed to prepare them to train trainers to use the Open University's Children Act Training Package. They went on later to run two courses to enable trainers from other West Midlands social services departments to use the package.

Further work was undertaken to ensure that a range of other groups had some understanding of the Children Act. Members of the BACC Team spoke to groups as diverse as social work and educational psychology students; health visitors and school nurses; trade union personnel; managers in the Libraries Department, the Education Department and the Recreation and Community Services Department; health authorities; local Members of Parliament, and magistrates. This willingness to inform others was a prerequisite to the corporate and cooperative working which the Act was to require.

A strategic direction and policy framework

A crucial report, first received by the Children Act Implementation Group and subsequently discussed at the Departmental Management Team, was a paper prepared by Paul Sutton setting out the broad direction which the service for children and families should take in the future. Presented to the Departmental Management Team in July 1991, only four months before the implementation date for the Children Act, it nevertheless predated some of the Regulations and Guidance issued to implement the Children Act (at the beginning of July 1991, only four out of nine volumes had been published). Because of this, and because the Act represented such a major shift in child care law, the Report noted that at this stage it was only possible to construct a basic framework for strategic planning. The more detailed level of planning would be developed over the next five years, 'as the changes introduced by the Act start to "bed down"' [Birmingham Action on Child Care, 1991c].

The Report, entitled *Directions for Strategic Planning in Work with Children and Families*, took eight principles from the Children Act and examined their consequences for the Department's services. These were:

- that requesting assistance in bringing up children was the act of a responsible parent, and therefore services should be widely publicised and accessible;
- that children should be supported and maintained in their own families, with statutory intervention as a last resort;
- that the Social Services Department should work in partnership
  – with parents and children;
  – with other departments of the authority;
  – with the health authorities; and
  – with voluntary organisations;
- that services should be integrated and consistent across the authority;
- that children looked after by the local authority should be accommodated wherever possible and appropriate in a family setting, near to home, with their siblings, and with their ethnic

and linguistic origins, and religious and cultural background taken into account; that these arrangements must be monitored and reviewed regularly; and that services must be provided to support young people who have been looked after by the local authority until they are 21-years-old;
- that service users must be consulted on service provision, and participate in planning and decision making, with written agreements defining obligations; and that they are entitled to make representations and complaints;
- that the courts and local authorities should consider a child's 'religious persuasion, racial origin and cultural and linguistic background' [Children Act 1989, Section 22 (5)(c)] when making any decision; and that local authorities will take account of the different ethnic groups in the area when arranging day care and recruiting foster carers [Ibid., Schedule 2 (11)(a) & (b)], and, by extension, developing other services for children and families;
- and that the local authority will facilitate the provision of a range of services for children and families, identifying gaps in provision and either making provision itself or working in partnership with others to do so.

The Report set out the direction in which the Department should move in consequence of these principles:

- **towards a needs-led, consumer orientated service**, through good publicity for services, multiple access points for a service, including non-social services department premises, consumer orientation in the reception of callers and the provision of services, and the regular, routine reporting, recording and measuring of unmet need;
- **towards a range of positive support services for children and families** and reducing the emphasis on child rescue and child protection, through the devolution of budgets as far down the line as possible, to enable imaginative responses to need, with a gradual shift in resources to the provision of services to children under Part III of the Act; and with the development of a range of services to meet the needs of families from different ethnic and cultural groups;

> The value of the family as its own resource will require the authority to adopt much greater flexibility in the range of resources it deploys to meet need ...validating expressions of need and meeting them rather than providing services which tend to focus on parental shortcomings.
>
> [Birmingham Action on Child Care, 1991c]

- **towards the Social Services Department taking the lead** not just in 'working together ... for the protection of children from abuse' [Home Office et al., 1991], but for the provision of services to children in need by the whole local authority, the health authorities, and the voluntary sector;
- **towards integrated, coordinated services provided on a city-wide basis** and with common standards, criteria for service and levels of provision;
- **towards a high quality service for children looked after**, where centralised, detailed monitoring will ensure adherence to prescribed methods and quality standards and evaluate outcomes, thus ensuring that being looked after by the Department would be a positive option for children. Strong professional leadership from senior management would insist on high standards and professional practice. In consequence, there should be a movement of resources into family-based care, but a smaller residential sector would undertake a specialised role; there would be a corporate commitment to providing services and support for young people leaving care until they were 21;
- **towards user participation and empowerment**, with children, young people and their families involved in decision-making, with well-publicised rights to challenge decisions and make complaints;
- **towards a social services department which works appropriately and in partnership with *all* families**, taking into account their ethnic origins, religious persuasion, language, and culture, through the evaluation and development of existing and future services, and reassessment of recruitment, staffing and training strategies;
- **towards the promotion of a mixed economy of welfare**, in which the Social Services Department would be both provider and enabler of service provision, working with other agencies,

particularly the voluntary sector and community groups, to identify and fill gaps in service provision.

This Report brought together the work of many of the individuals and groups reporting to BACC or to the Children Act Implementation Group. It set their recommendations in a strategic framework which implicitly acknowledged the interconnectedness of the children and families services. This Report, and a subsequent report, examined below, *Looking after Birmingham's Children*, both tried to take a systems approach to planning the future directions of the children and families services.

The principles and their consequences set out above were reflected in the development of policy in a number of ways. Ten Basic Policy Statements, put forward by BACC, encapsulated the principles and were presented to and approved by the Social Services (Child Care Sub-) Committee in September 1991 [Birmingham Social Services Department, 1991d]. These were later issued as a leaflet for social workers. The work on the implementation of the Children Act (described above) took these principles forward, for example through the interpretation of 'in need', and the work of the Corporate Steering Group. The budget bids for the children and families service were designed to provide the resources for the developments which flowed from the principles. *Looking After Birmingham's Children* worked through some of the principles and directions to present a more detailed proposal for the development of the children's placements system, and this is described in the next section. Chapters 6 and 7 set out other detailed work undertaken by BACC, and show how these principles and strategic directions were dealt with in practical recommendations and service developments.

Looking After Birmingham's Children

Looking After Birmingham's Children: a five year outline plan for change to the system of children's placements [Birmingham Social Services Department, 1991e] was a key report which showed the way forward for the Department. It was presented to the Social Services Committee in October 1991. It drew together the work of the Fostering and Residential Care Topic Groups to set out the direction in which the children's placements system should move in the future. This Report specifically sought to plan for the development of the service to meet the requirements of the Children Act using a systems approach.

> [The residential care service] is distracted by ... having to act as a safety-net for the inadequacies of the foster-care [service], by meeting the needs of small children for safety and protection sometimes in the same building where the needs of teenagers for boundaries and controls on their behaviour are also being addressed.
>
> [Birmingham Social Services Department, 1991e]

It noted that:

the success of any one part of the placement system will depend crucially on the success or failure of the other part [Ibid.],

and went on to examine some of the internal and external factors which affected the functioning of the placements sub-system. It noted that efforts to create a residential care service which clearly met the needs of its target population – teenagers – were vitiated by children's homes also being required to deal with inadequacies of the foster care service, and to care for younger children who could not be looked after in foster homes. The numbers of children looked after by the Department would also depend on the effectiveness of the services designed to support children and young people in the community. External factors which might affect the amount of provision required and the cost of the resources included demographic change, unemployment levels and other socio-economic factors. The use of residential care and foster care was also subject to the vagaries of public opinion – heightened concern about, for example, under-age sexual activity might lead to more care orders. New legislation such as the Criminal Justice Bill (at that time still in Parliament) could place additional demands on the placements system, with young offenders being remanded into the care of the local authority.

The BACC Team concluded that both residential care and foster care were required. Warwickshire County Council, which had closed all its children's homes, had been able to accommodate the majority of children requiring placements in foster care at least partly because demographic trends had reduced the numbers of children looked after by local authorities. Nevertheless, research [Cliffe, 1992] showed that there were then difficulties in providing a choice of foster placement for children and young people, especially in ensuring that they could be accommodated near to home and school, and with carers from an appropriate ethnic, cultural and linguistic background. There were also real difficulties in recruiting sufficient numbers of foster carers, especially for older children, so that there were concerns about the quality and stability of provision available for older children and young people. It would not be possible for Birmingham to rely on falling numbers of children requiring accommodation to facilitate a shift of emphasis towards foster care, since demographic and other factors were more likely to lead to increased demand for placements.

There were, however, positive reasons for retaining children's homes. The BACC Team, supported by the majority of senior managers in the Department, considered that there was a specific role for residential care for some children and young people, and that it would be foolhardy to attempt to meet their needs without a range of children's homes as well as foster care.

> ... the best Local Authorities have pursued policies to capture both the increased potential of offering the possibilities of family placements to all children aged under 12 and to many teenagers, whilst preserving residential care as a highly focussed form of care in its own right.
>
> [Birmingham Social Services Department, 1991e]

The Report set out a carefully researched and reasoned argument for its recommendations. It noted the requirement of the Children Act for children, young people and their families to be consulted about placement options: 'for this consultation to have meaning, a real choice of placements must be available in practice' [Ibid.] Moreover, the local authority must take into account the child's ethnic origins, religion, language and culture, as well as endeavouring, where this was consistent with the child's welfare, to place him or her near to home and without separating siblings. It stressed that, although the use of foster care had grown at the expense of residential care during the 1980s, and although most professional opinion was agreed that family placement was usually preferable to group care in a residential setting, there was a clear role for residential care for some children and young people. Both forms of care were likely to be most successful when used in a specific planned way for clear purposes. It set out the circumstances in which residential care was likely to be the preferred option. These were ranked as follows:

For children under 12:

- as the preferred option:
  - for keeping parents and children together;
  - for containment or secure placement
- as an equal choice in some circumstances:
  - for addressing issues of emotional or psychological health;
  - for post-placement breakdown;
  - for some assessments
- as a second choice:
  - for respite care for some children with disabilities;
  - for some remands in care

For children over 12, there was a much greater role for residential care, where residential care may be an option offered to the young person and his or her parents in all circumstances except where permanent placement was contemplated.

The specific functions which residential care might meet had been described by Berridge [1985] and reiterated by Wagner [1988] and Utting [1991]. They were summarised in chapter 2.

The Report then outlined the likely demand for foster care and residential care in Birmingham if foster care were available for all children aged under 12 requiring it, and as a realistic choice for young people aged over 12. The calculations suggested that up to 300 additional foster places (in addition to the existing 900) were needed to ensure adequate choice. As a consequence, the number of places in residential care could then be reduced by over 50 per cent to 200. It was this scale of reduction in the residential sector during the 1980s which was one of the factors leading to the crisis in residential care which preceded the establishment of BACC. The Report did not refer to these events, but it stressed the importance of positive planning for further changes.

Reduction in residential facilities could not take place until expansion of foster care was well underway. Recruitment of new foster carers would require a lead-in time of approximately twelve months from the start of a campaign to the point where new placements were available. Thus the first two of the five years for which the Report planned would require additional resources while new staff established new fostering schemes, including supported lodgings for older teenagers and remand fostering. During the second year the number of children accommodated in children's homes might begin to fall, but expenditure would have to be maintained in order to achieve the higher standards of care that a real choice between residential and foster care demanded. The Report concluded that unit costs in children's homes would rise as the homes worked to greater purpose with fewer children. Some compensatory savings might be anticipated in the third and fourth years, with closure of some homes, but the placements service as a whole would remain more expensive, in order to meet the requirements of the Children Act. Thus, the implications of the strategy were that considerable additional resources for children's placements would be required for at least two out of the five years, and overall expenditure on children looked after by Birmingham would remain high at the end of the period.

The Report was the foundation for the Department's work for the next five years, and therefore of crucial importance. With hindsight, it is clear that it laid insufficient emphasis on the positive aspects of the plan for residential care. Although it referred to the manner in which children's homes would be freed from performing unintended and inappropriate tasks, and be allocated 'a clear set of tasks and dedicated resources', it did not spell out the benefits for the sector sufficiently clearly. Despite its statement of the positive role for residential care, residential care was still portrayed as second best to foster care. It also failed to pay attention to the futures of staff employed in residential care. Although morale in children's homes remained high, there were misunderstandings, so that trade unions asked during 1992 which homes were to be closed.

To avoid the problems which beset the residential sector in the late 1980s, a systems approach suggests that it is necessary not just to consider appropriate timing for change, but the manner in which existing staff may be retained, trained (or retrained), redeployed or given early retirement. Staff morale in residential care is undoubtedly improved by clarification and recognition of the role and functions of residential care. Some staff, however, were likely to find the requirement to provide a quality, professional service to some of the most demanding children and young people a daunting prospect. Staff whom the Department wished to retain in residential work needed to know early that there was still a realistic career in residential care; the others needed opportunities to make alternative plans, if morale was not to plummet.

The Report also gave insufficient weight to difficulties in attempting to find 300 new foster places. Development of a fee-paid service (described in chapter 7) was seen as part of the answer, but it was by no means certain that the target could be achieved. Evidence suggests that higher payments will not necessarily improve recruitment. Despite high remuneration, the fostering service in Warwickshire was in many cases unable to provide a choice of foster homes, and the closure of the county's children's homes was enabled not through building up the numbers of foster carers so much as through the reduction in the numbers of children received into care [Cliffe, 1992]. Birmingham was starting from a relatively low level of fostering, and there was, therefore, some scope for increasing numbers of foster carers, and the Report suggested that development of a fee-paid service together with a dedicated teenage fostering service could begin to reach the target.

Nevertheless, despite these criticisms, the Report broke new ground in its use of research and examples of best practice, and in its interpretation of Departmental statistics. It attempted to show realistically how requirements of the Children Act for a children's placements service would impact on the Department over a five-year period. It did not avoid the resource implications of these requirements. It also stressed the need to monitor and review the plan to take account of changes occurring elsewhere in the child care system and its environment. Implementation of the strategy was reflected in developments started or proposed during 1991 and 1992, which are examined in chapter 7.

Preparing the organisation for change

> If mismanaged, restructuring can all too easily make people feel helpless, anxious, startled, embarrassed, dumb, overworked, cynical, hostile, or hurt.
>
> [Kanter, 1990]

In 1989, when BACC was established, the Social Services Department was still feeling the aftershocks of two reorganisations, in 1982 and 1987. The Project *Outline* therefore specifically required BACC to develop its recommendations without necessity for further major reorganisation [Coffin, 1989]. Nevertheless, many people in the children and families services were already dissatisfied with the Department's 1987 management structure, in which the majority of managers above team manager level were generic and responsible for services for all client groups.

At the top of the structure, it was often difficult to identify a single senior manager, other than the Director herself, with lead responsibility *and the authority*, to implement action or create change.

The reorganisation in 1987 referred to in chapter 2 was led by a drive to facilitate delivery of services at local level, through neighbourhood and constituency based offices. Key objectives included availability of a wide range of services locally; management of operational and support services locally wherever possible; and taking decisions as close to the consumer as possible. The structure was based on the principle of providing services close to where people lived whilst at the same time retaining the ability to provide specialist services covering larger areas. This reorganisation led to improvements in services and allowed local innovation, achieving 'flexibility

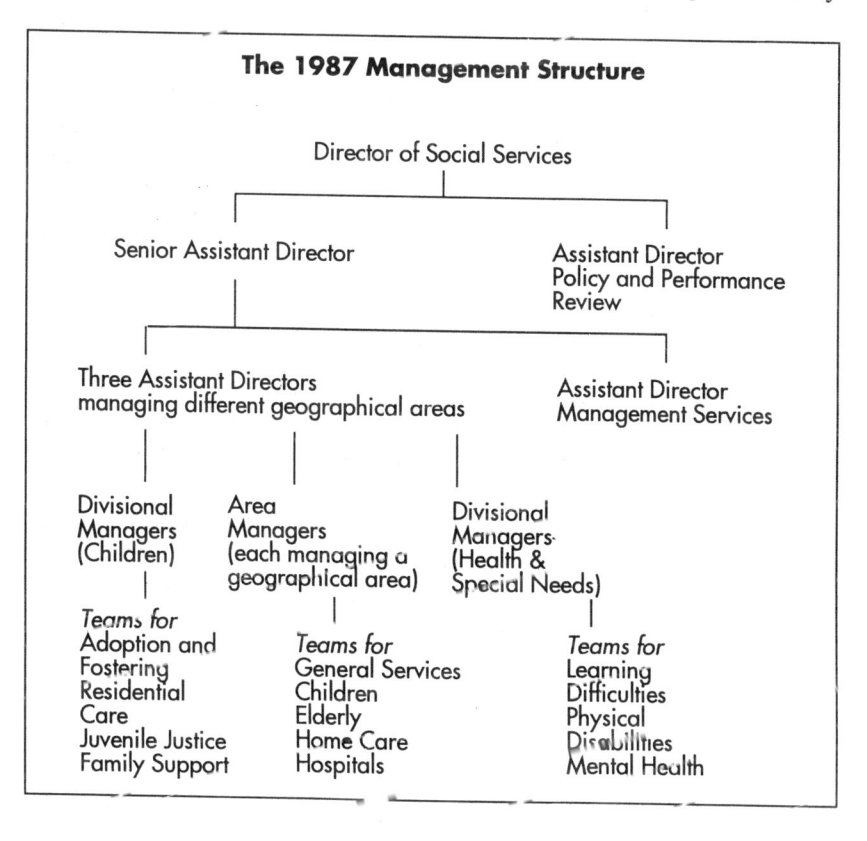

The 1987 Management Structure

Director of Social Services

- Senior Assistant Director
- Assistant Director Policy and Performance Review

- Three Assistant Directors managing different geographical areas
- Assistant Director Management Services

Divisional Managers (Children)
- Teams for Adoption and Fostering
- Residential Care
- Juvenile Justice
- Family Support

Area Managers (each managing a geographical area)
- Teams for General Services
- Children
- Elderly
- Home Care
- Hospitals

Divisional Managers (Health & Special Needs)
- Teams for Learning Difficulties
- Physical Disabilities
- Mental Health

within consistency'. By 1990, however, the need was emerging to modify this structure to take account of the Children Act 1989, the NHS and Community Care Act 1990, and issues being highlighted by BACC. The Director decided not to precipitate major changes, preferring to await development of policy and guidance by the Department of Health, and a considered departmental response. It was therefore some time before the Management Team formulated new proposals. When they did so, they were responding as much to reiterated questions of managers and other staff, as to their own observations. Rather than change being imposed from above, as had been the case with the two previous reorganisations, the necessity for some kind of organisational response to new legislation was being expressed at all levels in the department. Much of this impetus came from the work of BACC in articulating the needs of the children and families services. Equally, the development of assessment and care management, and the requirement to establish systems for purchase of services, led to consideration of the appropriate form for community care services for adults.

A report to the Social Services Committee in December 1990 set out principles and constraints which would shape any new developments, and sought approval for a consultation process. The Report noted:

the need to develop an integrated, professional child care service in response to the increasing complexity of child care issues. [Birmingham Social Services Department, 1990i]

It stated that BACC had concluded:

the Department's structure should ensure that services for children and families form an integrated whole, with clear lines of accountability at the most senior level and throughout the organisation... [At present], there are inherent difficulties in coordinating services for children. [Ibid.]

The Report's proposal that 'provision of social care for adults [be] managed separately from services for children and families' [Ibid.] was accepted by elected members, and a wide-ranging consultation process was begun both inside and outside the Department.

> Restructuring threatens to disempower large numbers of people, illuminating and enhancing the power of 'commanders' and making other people feel more dependent and less valued in the process.
> [Kanter, 1990]

A consultation document was prepared, outlining the reasons for change, principles already agreed, and issues to be addressed. A Task Group was set up to produce an options paper for the Departmental Management Team. It circulated the consultation document widely within the Department, to other departments, to the District Health Authority, Family Health Services Authority, Probation Service, Police, professional associations, trade unions and to local voluntary organisations. The senior managers leading the consultation met with some of these organisations and agencies, and with a number of area and divisional teams, to discuss the issues. Over 80 written responses were received and considered by the Task Group. This process was important in gaining acceptance for the need for modifications to the Department's structure. It ensured that staff throughout the Department were aware of the reasons for considering change, and enabled to submit their views. It increased the numbers of workers who recognised that change was inevitable. Although the process of consulting and involving staff represented a massive undertaking, it ultimately saved time and resources at a later date, and helped to avoid the demoralisation that followed the previous reorganisation.

The Departmental Management Team met for two days in April 1991 and considered the options paper prepared by the Task Group. It produced recommendations which were accepted by the Social Services Committee in July [Birmingham Social Services Department, 1991b]. These effectively separated management of services for children and families from management of community care services at the highest level. Whilst teams at area and divisional level remained together, there were significant changes for middle and senior managers, who were required to opt for either community care or children's work. The Director's two deputies – General Managers (adopting health service terminology) – would head the two major service areas.

The process of recruiting these two managers was begun immediately, with national advertisements attracting a wide and enthusiastic response for both posts. Both posts were filled, with

BACC's Project Director obtaining the Children and Families post. This clearly strengthened the potential for ensuring that BACC's work could continue when the Project ended. The Project *Outline* had envisaged involving senior managers in BACC during its final year, so that they would be committed to taking forward any new developments, but this was unnecessary. The new management structure created clear lines of accountability for work with children and families throughout the Department. It also provided a strong focal point for implementation of new policies and procedures in response to BACC's work and the Children Act.

Management of children and families services after April 1992

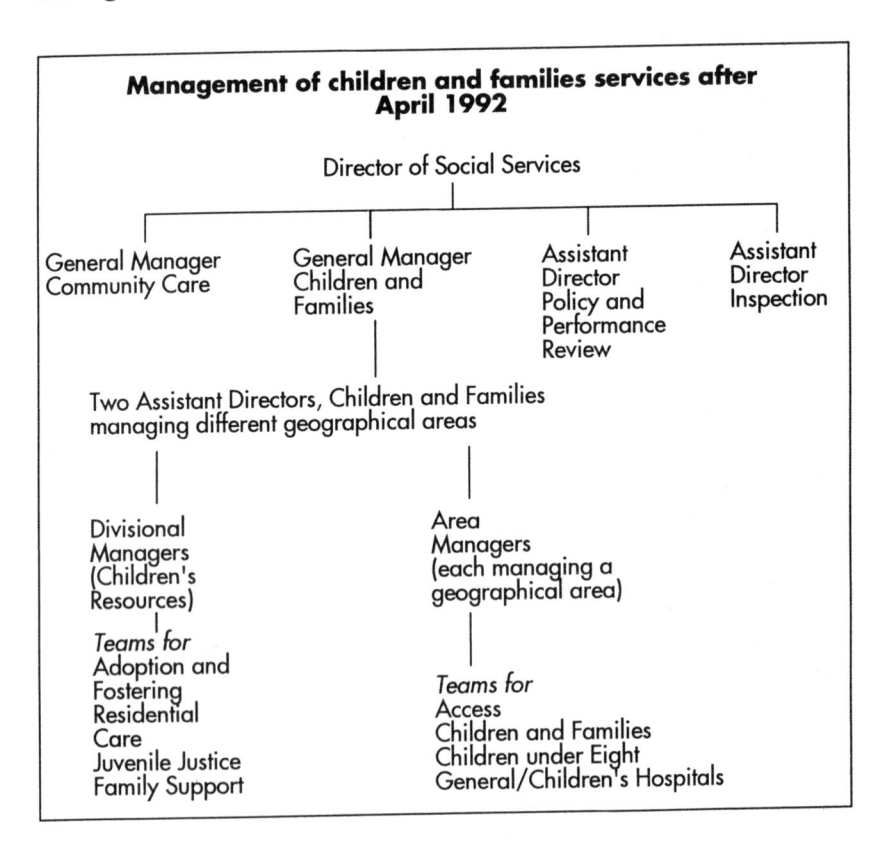

```
           Management of children and families services after
                              April 1992

                        Director of Social Services
         ┌──────────────────┬──────────────┬──────────────┐
    General Manager    General Manager   Assistant      Assistant
    Community Care     Children and      Director       Director
                       Families          Policy and     Inspection
                                         Performance
                                         Review

         Two Assistant Directors, Children and Families
         managing different geographical areas

              │                         │
         Divisional                 Area
         Managers                   Managers
         (Children's                (each managing a
         Resources)                 geographical area)
              │
         Teams for
         Adoption and
         Fostering                  Teams for
         Residential                Access
         Care                       Children and Families
         Juvenile Justice           Children under Eight
         Family Support             General/Children's Hospitals
```

Structural development of the operational management of the Department was mirrored by changes in the Policy and Performance Review Division. Units were created within the Strategic Planning Section to deal with community care and children's issues. Several new posts were created in the Division to strengthen its capacity to respond to and initiate work on children and families services. These posts were funded from growth and from resources released by the conclusion of BACC. The unit was led by an Assistant Principal Officer and initially included a Planning Officer and a Coordinator, a Day Care Adviser, and the Child Care Procedures writer. Other posts were to be added when resources became available in April 1993. In addition, a member of staff was seconded for a year (from August 1992) to promote the development of out-of-school activities, in cooperation with the Department of Recreation and Community Services.

The new operational management structure and the Children and Families Unit in the Policy and Performance Review Division held the potential for development of a strong policy, planning and monitoring capacity in the Department as a whole. The Policy and Performance Review Division was responsible for establishing and monitoring performance targets and indicators which were key components in the Department's approach to management. Within the new structure, there were sufficient senior managers, coordinators, planners, and advisers whose primary area of interest was children's services to enable clear leadership to develop. The Children and Families Unit, which included staff who had worked for BACC, developed a strong identity almost immediately. Its members worked closely with the General Manager, Children and Families, and his two Assistant Directors, each of whom took lead responsibility for different aspects of the children and familics services. BACC's work effectively formed the agenda for the new children and families service as it started its work in 1992.

Conclusion

Birmingham Action on Child Care was responsible for a wide range of initiatives during its three-year life. Interpretation of the Children Act and articulation of a strategic direction for the Department were crucial to ensuring that all these took place within a coherent policy framework. BACC provided a focus for innovative thinking, within the Social Services Department and for other departments, laying the foundations for new developments. The Project worked on policy and practice within the Department and at corporate level simultaneously, so that there was a sense of continuous activity on a number of fronts. In the process, the Project was able to secure cooperation from people throughout the Department on the details of the implementation of the Children Act. The results of this work in service developments are described in the following chapters, Chapters 6 and 7. The Team made a contribution to day care for children under five by its assistance to the City-Wide Child Care Strategy. The Children Act Corporate Steering Group led to cooperation between departments, to additional services for children and young people, and to the establishment of a forum to ensure that children's needs gained recognition in the policies of the City Council. Its work on the interpretation of 'children in need' was crucial to implementation of the Children Act in line with the philosophy behind the legislation. BACC succeeded in gaining commitment of Councillors to a generous interpretation of 'in need' which would facilitate the development of new services. Resources as well as the cooperation required by the Act were evinced by Birmingham City Council's allocation of growth money to the Social Services Department and the practical contributions made by other departments. An ambitious training programme was launched to ensure that the Children Act was implemented and, while it could not be completed exactly as planned, it was clear that most staff had an understanding of both the spirit of the legislation and its detailed application.

In its report *Directions for Strategic Planning*, BACC established clear directions for Birmingham's children and families services in responding to the Children Act and the report's key principles were widely disseminated. *Looking after Birmingham's Children* similarly set the direction for the residential and foster care services. As a result of these initiatives, the sense that there was a single children and families service, rather than a number of loosely related services, began to emerge. It was given reality by modifications to the Department's management structure which were also a direct result of work done by BACC. The new structure provided dedicated management and planning personnel for the children's services, giving the managerial and professional leadership which the Director had envisioned as necessary to revitalise the service.

6. Services for children in need

This chapter and chapter 7 set out the work undertaken by BACC in more detail than was possible in earlier chapters. The chronological account of the Project given in chapter 4 and the strategic framework presented in chapter 5 are filled out. Some of the importance of these descriptions is in the amount that was achieved in three years by such a small Team (see Appendix 5), although the detail of changes achieved will be of great interest to many managers and practitioners. Taken together, the Project's work transformed Birmingham's children and families services from a low point in 1988 to the high point in 1991, when Birmingham's social workers felt they could legitimately celebrate their achievements at the first Birmingham Child Care Conference.

The context for these achievements was not encouraging. The City's Anti-Poverty Unit estimated that in 1992 half the population of Birmingham lived in or on the margins of poverty [Birmingham City Council, 1992]. This estimate is borne out by early results from the 1991 Census, which showed that 30 per cent of men of working age (16 to 64), and 40 per cent of women (16 to 60), excluding students, were either unemployed or not economically active, a substantial increase since 1981 [OPCS, 1992]. The Census for the first time also provided statistics of the proportion of the population with a 'limiting long-term illness', which stood at 14 per cent for Birmingham.

Preliminary results from the 1991 census also showed that over 20 per cent of the population of Birmingham was Black and/or from a minority ethnic group [OPCS, 1992]. These figures have major consequences for the delivery of social services to children and families. Every aspect of the service requires examination to ensure that it is accessible to Black and minority ethnic children and their parents and carers. Every social worker and all other staff - even those who do not come into contact with the public – need to review their working practices to ensure that the Department can meet the needs of all children who require its services.

Meeting the needs of Black and minority ethnic children and families

The Children Act required that:

before making any decision with respect to a child whom they are looking after, or proposing to look after, a local authority shall ... give due consideration ... to the child's religious persuasion, racial origin and cultural and linguistic background. [Children Act 1989, Part III, Section 22 (5)(c)]

A group of BACC staff undertook to produce a paper setting out some of the issues involved in this approach, and the steps which the Department needed to take to meet the Act's requirements [Birmingham Action on Child Care, 1992f]. The paper did not provide an exhaustive account of all the issues; nor was it a manual for practice. It attempted to provide a basis for discussion from which individual staff and teams could develop good practice; and to provide tangible indicators of acceptable and unacceptable practice. It insisted that anti-racist, anti-oppressive and multicultural practice is achievable, and firmly located the responsibility to achieve it with managers, workers, and carers. Finally, it set the issues in the context of the Children Act and the rights of service users. The paper noted that the changing international situation – such as the resurgence of racism in Europe and the influx of refugees – presented new challenges; it was, therefore, part of a process, in which 'there will never be an absolutely certain or correct position to take', and in which new ways of thinking will emerge [Ibid.].

The paper set out requirements of the Children Act 1989 and Race Relations Act 1976, and their implications for management of social services – for example, setting standards and developing policy, monitoring the recruitment and composition of the workforce, and monitoring the use of services. It presented, with examples, the impact of discrimination and racism on access to services, assessment, information, consultation, representation and complaints procedures, the quality of services, and their monitoring and review. It gave guidance on questions to be considered in developing anti-discriminatory practice in all these fields. It looked at care environments and ways in which they can be welcoming and appropriate for children and families from a variety of ethnic, religious, linguistic, and cultural groups. By the end of the Project, work on assembling a glossary with definitions of common social work terms and jargon had been completed. Funding was being sought to translate these into the five most used minority languages, for publication and distribution [Birmingham Social Services Department, 1993b].

Social Services Committee policy recognised that the interests of each Black child were paramount, and that the child's best interests were likely to be achieved by placing him or her with foster carers or prospective adoptive parents of his or her own ethnic group wherever possible. Although the Commission for Racial Equality had praised Birmingham in 1990 for its efforts in recruiting Black and minority ethnic foster carers, people in the Department were aware that this was a continuing priority. The success of the pilot fee-paid foster care project in 1991/92 (see chapter 7) in recruiting new carers from Black and minority ethnic communities was welcomed – two thirds of the newly approved places were in Black or minority ethnic homes [Birmingham Social Services Department, 1992b]. It was hoped that the planned expansion of the scheme would meet with similar results. A proposal from a number of Black social workers of mixed parentage for an advice and support service for work with Black children of mixed parentage was welcomed by the Director. These children were considered to be over-represented amongst children looked after by the Department, and this was a cause for concern. The scheme involved Black social workers of mixed parentage acting as a resource for other social workers, who were expected to consult them about their work with children of mixed heritage. It went ahead in 1992.

The Department was also committed to increasing the proportion of Black and minority ethnic staff, especially amongst qualified social workers and in management. Targets were established for recruitment, and training was provided for prospective managers and staff in their first management positions. Specific efforts were made to ensure Black staff received training and support for applying for management positions. A training course was designed to meet their needs. The Department's recruitment initiatives – the bursary and sponsorship schemes aimed at recruiting newly qualified social workers directly from universities and colleges – were targeted at Black and minority ethnic students. Its secondment programme also gave priority to providing qualifying training for staff able to meet the needs of Black and minority ethnic service users, in practice mainly Black and minority ethnic people themselves.

These initiatives were recognised as only a beginning in providing services which were genuinely accessible and appropriate to parents and children from all Birmingham's communities. A continuing commitment was required, and action on a number of fronts – training, support, recruitment, resources. Policy and practice would need constant revision to ensure their relevance to changing circumstances.

Empowering children

> We all knew what it was like in care; what we also knew was we had no voice in it, no rights in it. When we left, who cared anyway.
>
> [Moss, 1990]

Listening to staff and children

Some of BACC's earliest work involved listening to staff and children in residential care. Ben Brown, the Project's Deputy Director, spent his first few months with BACC visiting children's homes and other establishments and meeting managers and their senior staff to inform them about BACC. He also met a number of other staff groups. At the same time, he made other visits where he focused on asking staff what they thought was happening, listening to their concerns and feelings, and sharing their understanding of the events of 1988. Some visits were specifically concerned with practice or management. He found that he was asked to look at complaints from children and young people, particularly from Black children in care, as well as discussing issues concerning Black staff. This work was important in establishing links with staff, children and young people, especially those in residential care where the heaviest criticisms from the press and elsewhere had been directed.

A complaints procedure for children

> [The events in children's homes in 1987 and 1988] raise particular questions ... about the handling of complaints and allegations of abuse and there are undoubtedly lessons to be learned.... One mechanism to protect the rights and interests of children and staff is a well-publicised and credible complaints procedure.
> [Birmingham Social Services Department, 1988b]

Following the revelations of the difficulties which both children and staff in children's homes had experienced in gaining attention when they complained about abuse and ill-treatment, the Director undertook to review the operation of the Department's complaints procedure [Birmingham Social Services Department, 1988b]. A new general complaints procedure had been circulated for consultation in January 1988, and this was brought into operation in October 1988, together with two booklets, one for the public in general (*Comments, Suggestions, Complaints*) and one specifically designed for children in care. The latter, *Questions and Answers*, set out basic information for children in care, and included both a direct, confidential telephone line to the Director and a form for notifying the Director of a complaint. To ensure staff were properly informed, child care procedures were produced which stressed the right of children to complain and gave advice on how to handle their complaints [Birmingham Social Services Department, 1988c]. The process for dealing with complaints and other enquiries made by or to Councillors was also reviewed, and a procedure established to ensure that the reports sent in by Members following their visits to children's homes and other establishments were acted upon [Birmingham Social Services Department, 1988e]. These developments had preceded the establishment of Birmingham Action on Child Care, but were part of the context in which it began work.

Because of the sensitivity of the whole issue of children's complaints, the Director did not allow the matter to rest, and kept the procedures under constant review herself. During 1989, BACC staff were extensively involved in talking to children, young people and staff, and concluded that the complaints procedure needed to be part of a wider approach to consumer rights. Reviewing the operation of the children's complaints procedure a year later, the Director found that the right to complain directly to her had been exercised by children 20 times since the booklet was distributed. She concluded that:

our experience of operating a complaints procedure for children in care has highlighted ... the importance of seeing a complaints procedure as part of a broad spectrum of activity which includes information; participation; choice; consumer rights; explanations/clarifications of policies etc. [Birmingham Social Services Department, 1989a]

She then sought agreement in principle to the establishment of a children's rights service, and asked BACC to take the necessary action.

There were still some problems, however, with the general complaints procedure, with staff perceiving it as:

a negative process rather than as one which seeks to make our services more relevant and sensitive to consumer needs. [Birmingham Social Services Department, 1989b]

There were difficulties of definition (what is a complaint? what is the distinction between a serious and a minor complaint?) and it was not clear what action should result from a complaint and from the experience of complaints cumulatively. Following consultation with staff, the procedure was revised again and re-introduced in May 1990. A programme was then established to ensure that all managers received training in how to carry out investigations.

The Children Act 1989 and the NHS and Community Care Act 1990 both required local authorities to establish complaints procedures, although there were differences in their requirements. As a result, the Departmental Complaints Procedure was revised yet again, and two procedures were introduced – for adult services, and for services for children and young people – both coming into operation in July 1992 [Birmingham Social Services Department, 1992c, 1992d]. The two sets of procedures were explained in short booklets for consumers. BACC and young people in care (or formerly in care) who worked with the Project contributed to the writing and design of the children's booklet. The new procedures included provision for children to be supported by the newly appointed Children's Rights Officer, and for independent people to review complaints. The importance of ensuring that Black and minority ethnic children were supported by people from their own cultural background was stressed.

> Every local authority shall establish a procedure for considering any representations (including any complaint) made to them by any child who is being looked after by them or who ... is in need...
> [Children Act 1989, Part III, Section 26(3)]

A children's rights service

During 1989 and 1990 BACC was involved in plans for a children's rights service. The Team considered various models for development, and discussions were held with Leicestershire Social Services Department, the first local authority to appoint a Children's Rights Officer. The role of a Children's Rights Officer was primarily to act as an advocate for children and young people, listening to their concerns, supporting them if they had complaints to make, and ensuring that their perspective was taken into account in the development of policy and practice.

The potential for conflict between a children's rights service and service departments was recognised. It would need to be as independent as possible of service delivery, but close enough to be able to work with managers to improve services. The need was clearly not confined to social services; the possibility of a children's rights service being located in the Central Executive Department or of its being run by another agency for Birmingham City Council was considered. Initially, however, it was critical to establish support for the concept within the Social Services Department, and to proceed with a project which could be achieved within the Department. The Social Services Committee approved the appointment of a Children's Rights Officer in principle in October 1989 [Birmingham Social Services Department, 1989a], but at this stage both funding and an appropriate location for the officer were still to be found.

By June 1990, Birmingham Social Services Department [Birmingham Social Services Department, 1990g] was also committed to establishing a division to undertake the inspection and registration functions required by the Children Act and the NHS and Community Care Act 1990. The Child Care Sub-Committee confirmed the decision to locate a Children's Rights Officer within this new Division in June 1990 [Birmingham Social Services Department, 1990f]. Funding for a single officer with administrative support was made available for part of 1991/92 from that year's growth money.

The post of Children's Rights Officer (CRO) was finally advertised in December 1991 and the appointee took up her post in February 1992. A large part of her work was dealing with complaints from children. The new children's complaints procedure came into operation from 1 July 1992, and, as part of the process, all complaints made by children were seen by the CRO. The procedure was widely publicised, and during its first two months – July and August 1992 – 29 complaints were received directly by the CRO and a further 28 at other offices, compared with only two complaints from children received centrally during the same period in 1991. Nevertheless, the CRO felt that further publicity was needed, including translation into other languages and Braille, and presentation on video and audio tape. It was thought that these complaints might only be the 'tip of the iceberg'.

One role of the CRO was to ensure that children or young people had access to support in making their complaint if they required it. As a member of the User Consultation and Complaints Section in the Inspection Division, she was also occasionally asked to undertake complaints investigations. A second aspect of her work was to act as an advocate on behalf of the children accommodated by the Department – some 1,800 children. One young person, previously in care and working with BACC, helped to set up a Young People's Forum. Initially, this was a small but diverse group of young people, but plans were in progress to set up a system of representatives from all the children's homes, with groups meeting from the two Departmental Divisions, North and South. It was more difficult to draw in children and young people in foster care, but the group looked for ways to publicise their existence. A feature in *The Birmingham Voice* – Birmingham City Council free newspaper – was started in October 1992 by members of the group. The group hoped to challenge the stereotypes of young people in care by interviewing celebrities who had themselves been brought up in care. Its first article was an interview with Olympic athlete Kriss Akabusi [*Birmingham Voice*, 1 October 1992]. The CRO hoped eventually that young people involved in the Forum would be able to join a panel of advocates to act on behalf of children, although she was conscious of the need to avoid exploiting their willingness.

The CRO was also asked to provide advice to parents, children, foster carers, social workers, voluntary organisations, schools, youth workers and others on various issues related to children's rights – for example, on confidentiality, support from social services, financial support, or housing. She was able to present the views of young people to the Child Care Sub-Committee when it was considering whether to close the home they lived in. She was consulted on new policies, procedures, and training programmes, by the Department and other agencies, and herself actively contributed to training programmes.

As this account indicates, one issue immediately apparent was the size of the workload for one person. Within the first few months, the CRO was already working jointly with her counterpart in Education, exploring the possibility of setting up a corporate children's rights service in the future, which would deal with work arising from both departments, and from the Youth Service, recreational and community facilities, and the Libraries and Housing Departments. It was hoped it might even be possible to cover the National Health Service. Such a joint service would go some way to resolving another dilemma faced by the CRO, which was that some children and young people did not perceive her as independent. Her employment by the Department and physical location in a departmental building occupied by the Inspection Division led some young people to question whether the service could be truly impartial. She herself acknowledged potential conflicts of interest when called upon to undertake investigations, as well as to support children making complaints.

Some of the problems which accompany the process of developing complaints and representations procedures and establishing a credible children's rights service will be apparent. It is difficult to devise complaints procedures which are accessible and easy to use. They must distinguish clearly between a complaint and issues which might be dealt with more informally, and must be clearly differentiated from other procedures such as disciplinary and grievance procedures. It is essential to devise a procedure which protects consumers' rights, which is recognised by staff as fair, and which they can accept as contributing to a better service. Complaints can be time-consuming and their investigation may take managers away from other essential work – hence the importance of guidance in the early stages to help staff and consumers resolve a difficulty without resort to the formal procedure. Nevertheless, good records of complaints have to be kept to help managers to identify shortcomings in the service. All staff involved with a complaints procedure need to have training in its operation, and the managers responsible for investigations need to understand what kind of actions can and should result from a successful complaint. There is always potential for some consumers to abuse complaints procedures or to pursue a hopeless grievance. This may cause staff to become cynical about the value of the procedure.

There is inevitably likely to be some conflict of interest between staff and consumers in the operation of a complaints procedure, however committed staff are to using it as a means to ensure that services are appropriate and responsive. Without strong commitment from management, complaints procedures and development of children's rights may receive low priority, especially where they compete for scarce resources. Because of the timing – shortly after allegations of abuse in Birmingham's children's homes – staff were anxious about the possible impact on them of the complaints procedure when it was first introduced in 1988.

A successful complaints procedure and children's rights service inevitably generate some bad publicity for the responsible authority, especially in the first phase of operation, when a backlog of complaints may be picked up. The more open atmosphere which followed the events of 1987/88 led to a series of press and other reports of incidents and abuse in Birmingham children's homes. Managers are likely to regard a complaints procedure as a mixed blessing. Councillors too may be ambivalent about the introduction of complaints procedures and children's rights services, despite often construing their *own* role as champions of the electorate against 'bureaucrats'. In Birmingham, Councillors required assurances that the increase in complaints was a sign of a more healthy department, where children, parents, and carers were aware of their rights and believed they would be heard. Absence of complaints could be a sign not that all was well but of a repressive atmosphere. Staff came to realise that a children's rights service and an accessible complaints procedure are essential to ensure that the abuses of power epitomised by the 'Pindown' phenomenon cannot persist unchecked. They safeguard the position of children, parents and carers, and also that of the majority of staff who are trying to do their jobs well.

Involving young people

Although the Wagner Committee report on residential care had been overshadowed by the Cleveland Report which was published at about the same time, the concerns it articulated about conditions in children's homes were taken forward from 1989 onwards by the Wagner Development Group. During 1991 and 1992, one of the young people employed by BACC was a member of the Wagner Children's Group, and was able to offer the Group the perspective of her own experiences in care and the views of the Young People's Forum.

The Young People's Forum, which BACC initiated, was such a simple idea that it is difficult to know why it was not established earlier. By 1991, the concepts of consulting service users, partnership with service users, and the rights of children and young people to be heard, were firmly established by the Children Act. Such concepts too were congruent with the approach of both BACC and the Community Care Special Action Project which preceded it. The Young People's Forum was a low cost approach to dealing with some of the concerns of young people looked after by the Department. It proved to be responsible and articulate, and surprisingly willing to work within the Department, rather than taking its complaints to the Press. The continuation of this cooperative stance will depend as much on the response of the Department to the young people's concerns as on the personalities of those involved.

Developing quality services – inspection and review of services

In April 1990, the Director proposed the setting up of an Inspection Division, which was eventually established the following year. Establishment of an 'arms' length' inspection unit, able to inspect both the independent sector's and the local authority's community care provision 'even-handedly' was a requirement of the National Health Service and Community Care Act 1990. The new division encompassed not just the inspection and registration functions required by that Act, but also registration and inspection functions under the Children Act. It was proposed that, later, the inspection of day services for adults and field social work services, which there was no statutory duty to register or inspect, should also be undertaken. The new Division included registration of private and voluntary children's homes and inspection of all children's homes and boarding schools. In developing standards for these inspections, it drew on the work of BACC and the Department's Care Audit Team. In 1992, agreement with the Education Department for joint inspections of residential special schools was reached [Birmingham Social Services Department, 1992e]. Registration and inspection of day care for children under eight remained the responsibility of Day Care Officers (discussed later in this chapter). Childminding, day nurseries, and play groups were felt to benefit from the local knowledge of these officers, as well as from their expertise and support, especially when they were first starting. Similarly, selection and registration of foster carers remained with Adoption and Fostering Teams, but the new Division managed the Children's Rights Officer, the Panel of Guardians ad Litem and Reporting Officers, and User Consultation and Complaints.

Reviews for children and young people looked after by the Department
Regulations under the Children Act 1989, Section 26, required the Department to review the case of every child looked after or accommodated by the authority up to three times a year [Department of Health, 1991e]. Guidance added that these reviews should usually be chaired by a manager senior to a team manager. Under the Regulations, these reviews had to be monitored by the Department, to ensure that Section 26 and the Regulations and Guidance were complied with. The BACC Topic Group, Planning for Children, set up early in 1990, recognised that the Department's practice in relation to reviewing regularly and making plans for all the children in its care was not always satisfactory or consistent. The Group developed a format for reviewing children which incorporated draft Children Act Regulations and Guidance. Taking this work further, BACC was able to ensure that the 1991/92 budget included provision for establishing a system of reviews. Resources were included for the appointment of Independent Reviewing Officers to assist in ensuring reviews were carried out and to chair a proportion of them; and for an Independent Reviews Monitoring Officer, based in the Inspection Division, to monitor the reviews system.

As the BACC Topic Group commented in 1991, the system of reviews was no mere bureaucratic procedure:

reviews of children looked after are a major mechanism to ensure that planning for children is proactive and purposeful, that the child's welfare is promoted vigorously and that individuals involved in the child's life are charged with clear responsibilities with timescales attached in order to meet those responsibilities. [Birmingham Action on Child Care, 1991a]

In July 1992, 1,726 children and young people were being looked after by the Social Services Department. Independent Reviewing

Officers estimated that there would be approximately 4,000 reviews a year, which they characterised as 'a basic building block for quality planning for children' [Birmingham Social Services Department, 1992h]. Their investigations indicated that the Department was not at that time fulfilling its statutory obligations. They therefore put forward a system to ensure that every child was properly reviewed. The three elements of the system – a Basic Facts record, a Care Plan, and a Review Form – were designed as an integrated set, which would ensure that a Plan was produced for each child aiming at permanency, and which could only be changed by a statutory review. The series of steps involved in producing the Care Plan and reviewing it regularly were intended to reduce the need for other meetings, and improve the quality of record keeping. As a corollary, an administrative system was recommended to support social workers and managers in operating the procedure. The Independent Reviewing Officers would chair a proportion of reviews each year. The Independent Reviews Monitoring Officer would receive details of the numbers of reviews required and conducted, and attend a selection of reviews to assess their quality. The monitoring system was expected to assist the Department in assessing performance and identifying areas of concern. Training for managers, field social workers and residential workers was planned, to familiarise them with the system and its documentation, ensure that they were aware of the statutory basis of reviews, and emphasise the importance of active participation by children and parents [Ibid.].

Independent visitors

The Children Act 1989 placed a duty on local authorities to appoint an independent visitor for any child they are looking after if the child has, in effect, lost touch with his or her parents (or other person with parental responsibility). A child may refuse to agree to appointment of an independent visitor, and that refusal will be accepted if the local authority is satisfied that she or he has made an informed decision. The local authority itself may decide not to appoint an independent visitor if it considers an appointment would not be in the child's best interests. Independent visitors are an important safeguard for children in care, especially those in foster care, who may have restricted access to the Children's Rights Officer and the Departmental Complaints Procedure. They may also play other parts in a young person's life:

For example, a teenager being prepared for independence may like someone to act as an older brother or sister (particularly someone who has themselves been a part of the care system). A young child might require a substitute grandparent or aunt or uncle... Some children would benefit from contact with a person from the same culture, religion, race or linguistic group. [Birmingham Social Services Department, 1991f]

The main demand for independent visitors was likely to be from children in long-term foster care, but the report produced for BACC concluded that it was difficult to estimate how many children were eligible. Visitors receive out-of-pocket expense only, and act as a befriender to the children, but cannot take them to the visitor's home without prior knowledge and agreement. Nevertheless, for the protection of the children and young people, the Department required a thorough assessment and a search of criminal records for each independent visitor. The Management Team decided to look for a voluntary organisation to provide independent visitors through a service agreement, and to consult Black and minority ethnic organisations about the recruitment of visitors from their communities [Ibid.].

Services for children in the community

> Every local authority shall provide such day care for children in need within their area who are —
> (a) aged five or under; and
> (b) not yet attending schools,
> as is appropriate.
>
> Every local authority shall provide for children in need within their area who are attending any school such care or supervised activities as is appropriate —
>
> (a) outside school hours; or
> (b) during school holidays.
>
> [Children Act 1989, Section 18(1) & (5)]

The Children Act ensured that day care for children would no longer be seen as a Cinderella service, provided almost as a sideline by social services departments, to support their mainstream social work activities. Under Part III of the Act, day care, after school and holiday care, were amongst services which local authorities should provide for children in need and could provide for other children. Section 19 required the authority to review both its own services and day care for children under eight provided by the voluntary and private sectors, and to publish the results. A further impetus to review and reconsider day care services in Birmingham was provided by the City-Wide Child Care Strategy (considered in chapter 5), which was concerned to promote the availability of day care services for working parents and those joining training courses.

> A local authority may provide day care for children within their area ... even though they are not in need... A local authority may provide ... care and supervised activities for children within their area who are attending any school even though those children are not in need.
>
> [Children Act 1989, Section 18(2) & (6)]

Early in 1990, when the City Wide Strategy was getting under way, the Department had 33 day nurseries or nursery centres, providing day care places for up to 1,500 children a day, with approximately 2,000 children able to receive a service in any one week. Private and voluntary day nurseries provided a further 2,500 places and registered childminders over 3,000 places for children under five. Excluding the contribution made informally by relatives, the largest amount of pre-school provision was made by pre-school playgroups, with places for 6,000 children [Birmingham Social Services Department, 1990a, 1991a]. The Department employed 18 Day Care Officers, whose job was to promote, register and inspect non-statutory day care provision for children under five.

> Although many aspects of the department's child care provision have been reviewed and have changed since 1979 (when the first large-scale review of services to children took place), day nurseries have never received equivalent attention or subsequent strategic direction.
>
> [Birmingham Action on Child Care, 1991f]

Management of services for children under five was fragmented, both between Departmental Divisions and within each Division, where day nurseries were managed separately from the Day Care Officers. Services lacked a clear policy direction, and staff felt that they were marginal to the Department. There was no mechanism for coordination and cooperation with other city departments concerned with under fives provision. Despite the existence of waiting lists, some day nurseries were under-occupied. Thus, during the period October to December 1989, for 1,468 places available per session, only an average of 1,106 children were registered, and the average attendance was still lower, at 857 children – an occupancy level of only 58 per cent of total places available. Low numbers were explained partly by staffing shortages, especially by difficulties in recruiting nursery nurses. Despite these problems, there were many examples of good practice, a core of dedicated staff, and a willingness to learn and participate in developing the services [Birmingham Social Services Department, 1990d, 1990e; Birmingham Action on Child Care, 1992d].

BACC responded to these issues by becoming involved with the City-Wide Child Care Strategy, by setting up a Services for Children Under Eight Topic Group, by including day care for children under eight amongst the topics specifically addressed by the Children Act Implementation Group, and by its contribution to the consultation on the Department's management structure. The outcome of the City Wide Child Care Strategy was described in chapter 5.

A survey of the Department's day nurseries: what is day care for?

An early and important action by the Services for Children under Eight Topic Group was to carry out a comprehensive survey of the Department's day nurseries. It examined some characteristics of the children using the nurseries and some aspects of the nurseries' work. Two questionnaires were used, one collecting information about the Department's nurseries, and the other about a sample (697) of the children attending them. They were designed to gather factual information to support decision-making and to assess a number of assumptions about day nurseries – for example, that they were regularly used as a 'social work resource', by working with numbers of children 'at risk', but were not well equipped to deal with such children.

The survey results were presented to the Departmental Management Team in October 1991. The draft report indicated that while nurseries were used as part of a social work plan in a minority of cases, the majority of children were referred because of 'generalised concern' about them, because parents were in employment, or because of developmental delay. Only 7.5 per cent were on the Child Protection Register and fewer than one in ten (9.5 per cent) were the subject of any court order. A quarter of the children had an identified social worker, but the volume and frequency of contact between the nurseries and social workers was low. More than half the children at the nurseries were from single parent families, and very few were in foster or residential care (2.8 per cent). The report indicated that Black and minority ethnic children were over-represented in nurseries, and that a significant number of them were bi-lingual, speaking English at nursery and another language at home.

Only five out of the 32 nurseries included in the survey were fully staffed. The majority of non-manual staff had an appropriate qualification (79 per cent) or were about to commence training, and more than half had attended short courses during the previous 12 months. Black and minority ethnic people were under-represented amongst managerial staff, although well represented amongst nursery officers. Nevertheless, there were two nurseries where all the staff were White European and another two where the only Black member of staff was a domestic worker. Given the high percentage of Black and minority ethnic children attending the nurseries, these figures were a cause for concern. The statistics suggested a considerable divergence between nurseries in the way they were working. For example, the most commonly cited reason for children leaving nurseries was age; however, one nursery reported that 21 out of 22 children had left because work objectives had been achieved, a reason rarely given by other nurseries. [Birmingham Action on Child Care, 1991f]

A report to the Departmental Management Team in October 1991 concluded that it would be possible to provide an open access nursery service combined with a specialised, intensive service for a minority of children, without disadvantaging any existing user group.

> [There was] a lack of clarity about how day nursery provision fitted alongside the range of other resources for children and families. In turn, this led to confusion and disputes about who the nurseries were serving and for what reason(s). As a result, discussions about the possible re-targeting of the service were impaired because of doubts about what this would mean for current and potential users.
>
> [Birmingham Action on Child Care, 1991f]

The Departmental Management Team asked for further consultation to take place on the options for future nursery provision, but in the meantime provided some guidelines on appropriate relationships between social workers and nurseries. It asked for further work to discover the reasons for over-representation of Black and minority ethnic children, and for action to ensure that children's needs in relation to their ethnic origins, religion, language and culture were met.

Consultations identified five possible options for provision of a nursery service, ranging from no Departmental provision at all, with the Department taking an enabling role in relation to the private and voluntary sectors, and purchasing places for children in need where necessary; to providing only specialist units to be used for children (and their parents) as part of a social work plan – that is, the family centre/child protection unit model. BACC recommended a middle position – the development of a service capable of meeting a variety of needs, from the simple need for day care itself (for example, to enable a parent to go out to work or training) to the more complex need for specific work with children and their families in a day care setting. Effectively, this was the kind of service already being provided by the Department's day nurseries, although not in the context of a set of objectives or strategic plan which acknowledged that the nurseries could and should provide such a range of services.

If this option was accepted, there were two further options – to provide for a specialist service to children and their parents at all nurseries, or to centralise this service at a few sites (which might be renamed 'family centres'). The majority of nurseries would then be designated as neighbourhood day nurseries, providing places for children in need, children with parents at work or in training, and others on a 'first come, first served' basis. This second option was the preferred outcome, since it removed the stigma from local authority day nurseries and opened them to a wider range of families. It also enabled the Department to contribute to the City-Wide Child Care Strategy.

No clear consensus emerged from the consultation. Respondents were concerned to develop a service which did not stigmatise children, was responsive to local need, and which made the best use of a scarce resource, but they were divided about the best model for achieving this outcome [Birmingham Action on Child Care, 1992e]. By September 1992, concern expressed by the Social Services

Committee at continuing high levels of vacancies in day nurseries, its commitment to the City-Wide Child Care Strategy and anxiety about the Departmental budget, combined to produce a scheme providing places for working parents [Birmingham Social Services Department, 1992g]. Up to 200 places were allocated to the children of City Council employees, at a flat fee comparable with that charged by the less expensive end of the private and voluntary sector. Children in need continued to receive a free service. The Department was prohibited by the Children Act from charging parents on income support or family credit for nursery places, and had thus lost an estimated £200,000 in income. The scheme would more than replace this loss. It proved controversial, however, with some staff concluding that this was the wrong use for Departmental nurseries. It did not, of course, pre-empt the decision still to be made about the best future model for nursery provision.

Management of services for children under eight

In order to deal with the lack of coordination between managers of day nurseries and day care officers, and the heavy workload for some Children's Team managers responsible for a number of nurseries, BACC proposed the establishment of team managers for services to children under eight as part of the new managerial structure of the Department [Birmingham Social Services Department, 1991b]. This recommendation was accepted in principle, but could not be implemented until early 1993, since the necessary resources were not available. The new structure facilitated better coordination and planning of services to children under eight. Managerial responsibility for them was given to specific Area Managers and lead responsibility to one Assistant Director. On BACC's advice, a new post of Day Care Review Adviser was established in the Policy and Performance Review Division, specifically to ensure that the local authority's duty to review day care services for children (Children Act 1989, Section 19) was carried out thoroughly.

Standards for registration

The Children Act gave local authorities new duties in respect of registration and inspection of all day care facilities for children aged under eight — day nurseries, childminders, playgroups, playschemes, and after or out-of-school projects. The BACC Team worked closely with Day Care Officers to produce Departmental standards. These included new ratios of staff to children, but also qualitative requirements in relation to care of children, including some designed to ensure that ethnic origins, religion, language and culture were respected and promoted. Time was allowed for childminders and other day care facilities to meet the new standards. The additional workload for Day Care Officers was considerable, and appointment of additional Officers was agreed by the Departmental Management Team in July 1991.

All facilities were to be re-registered during the first year after the Act's implementation, a task which Birmingham Social Services Department was not alone in finding almost impossible. Registration and inspection of day nurseries proved to be an area of considerable controversy. The Department's right to set its own standards for registration was challenged by private nursery owners, and negotiations with their organisation were set up. Before these could be completed, it became known that the Department of Health was concerned that the way in which local authorities were interpreting the new standards set out in Volume 2 of the Children Act Guidance and Regulations [Department of Health, 1991d] might lead to a decrease in the number of day care places for children under five. New Guidance was eventually issued in January 1993 [Department of Health, 1993], which set out the principle that registration should be granted unless there was specific evidence that either the building or the provider was seriously unfit.

Out-of-school provision

On the initiative of BACC, joint working with the Department of Recreation and Community Services produced a commitment from that Department to raising the quality of its out-of-school provision – holiday schemes and after school (latchkey) clubs – as soon as resources were available [Department of Recreation and Community Services, 1992]. That Department adopted the broad interpretation of 'children in need', which included both a wide definition of possible needs, and a list of categories of children who might be in need, and accepted its duty to assist in the provision of services for them. It was in a position to make a significant contribution to their welfare, since it ran playschemes in parks during the major school holidays, provided all year round staffed play facilities at playcentres and adventure playgrounds, and funded voluntary and community groups to provide similar facilities. The importance of ensuring that these facilities could be used with confidence by working parents was understood and accepted. A new staff member was appointed (for a year from July 1992) in the Social Services Department, to promote development of out-of-school provision of all kinds. There were links between these initiatives to provide out-of-school provision for children in need, and other children, and the City-Wide Child Care Strategy.

Social work services for children and families
Unallocated cases
During 1990, the problem of children in the care of the Social Services Department who were without a social worker was a source of considerable concern, and BACC was asked to examine the extent of the problems and propose some solutions. The first difficulty encountered by BACC was that management information systems were not sufficiently well developed to provide even crude data about the number of children in care who did not have a social worker. For example, although it could reveal how long children had been in care, it could not produce figures indicating how long they had remained unallocated. The child protection register also at that time did not reveal whether each child on its records had a social worker. These deficiencies in management information may have explained why the system was known be to highly inaccurate. Low priority was given to bringing the database up to date, since no one was likely to use the results!

BACC's first analysis of available information [Birmingham Action on Child Care, 1990d], combined with interviews with team managers, suggested that 14 per cent of children in care – 247 out of 1,788 children – did not have a social worker at 31st March 1990. There was an uneven distribution between areas of the city and in the length of time these children had been in care. Unallocated cases were held by team managers. A few managers had so many unallocated cases that they had no clear idea of the current circumstances of the child and family. If these cases were thought to require social work input, they were normally given as discrete pieces of work to a social worker. Although guidance for team managers on core tasks had been issued, it was apparently either not consulted or not seen as relevant. Workloads between teams and individual social workers varied enormously. There were problems of transfer of cases from General Services Teams (who worked with new cases in the short term) to Children's Teams (who provided ongoing work and support). It was at this point that a case could become unallocated. There was evidence that reviews of both allocated and unallocated cases were not always undertaken, or were conducted inappropriately. The absence of care planning in these circumstances had serious consequences for the work of others throughout the children and families services, and for the children themselves. The priority BACC gave to reviews and care planning was discussed earlier in this chapter.

The level of vacancies in social work teams, and especially the shortage of experienced social workers, contributed to the problem. Team managers were concerned about vacancies on their teams, but generally were not asking for additional posts, above the number already established. When social workers left, time taken to recruit a new worker often meant that the team manager felt he or she would never catch up with the workload. They also complained that lack of administrative support made their work more difficult. Some managers felt that workloads were made unacceptably heavy by responsibility for day nurseries. Managerial responsibility for day nurseries was removed from managers of Children's Teams in 1993.

The October 1990 report on unallocated cases [Birmingham Action on Child Care, 1990d] made a number of recommendations which were then monitored every three months for the next two years. The recommendations included:

- introduction of a workload management scheme;
- guidance to team managers on priorities for allocation;
- prohibition on transferring a case between teams or areas if the result was that it became unallocated;
- recruitment and retention of staff initiatives, which included new approaches to advertising as well as financial and other incentives for applicants;
- examination of the justification for the division in the Department's structure between General Services and Children's Teams;
- review of the management of day nurseries;
- appointment of assistant team managers and of additional social work assistants;
- appointment of team clerks to assist with the administrative burden; and
- to continue with, and monitor, 'case busters' teams which were targeted at areas with high numbers of unallocated cases.

This analysis is impressive in its range and comprehensiveness. Despite the shortage of reliable information, BACC had accepted that the problem of unallocated cases was unlikely to have a single cause – such as high vacancy rates – and that therefore it needed to be tackled in a number of different ways. These included ways of managing better within the existing staffing levels as well as initiatives which it was hoped would bring teams up to establishment.

Following BACC's analysis, work was undertaken immediately on recruitment of social workers, and recruitment and retention incentives were developed and offered to Children's Teams during the next year. These included a subsidised car leasing scheme, and bursaries and sponsorships for students on Diploma in social work courses. The Department's advertising material was improved, and managers attended recruitment fairs to promote the Department. A survey was commissioned to examine the reasons why social workers left the department. Action was started on all BACC's other recommendations within three months of the October 1990 Management Team discussion.

**Unallocated child care cases
Birmingham 1989-92**

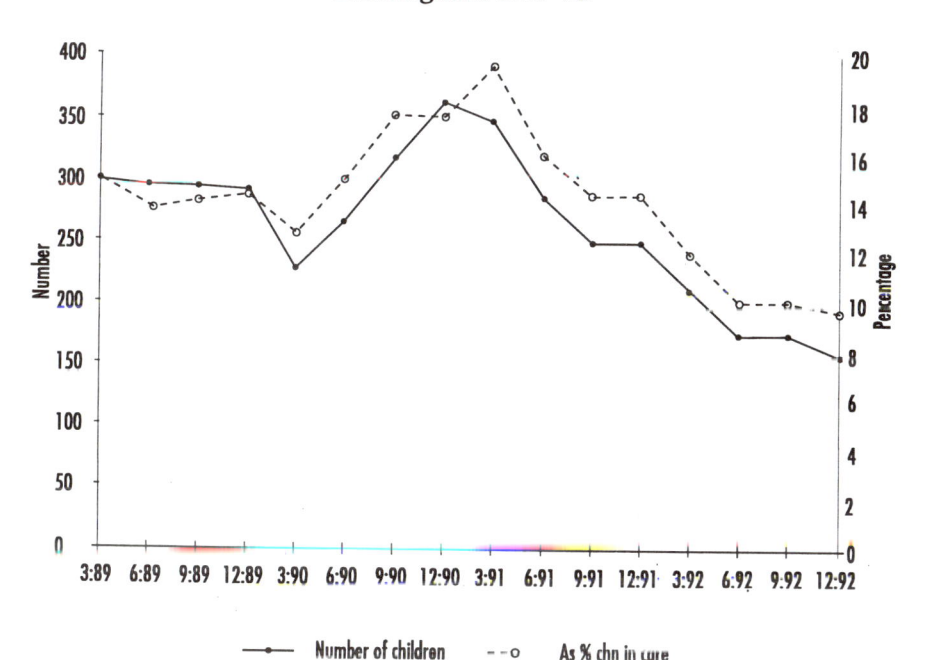

It took some months for these initiatives to make an impact. Both numbers of children in care and numbers without an allocated social worker fell during 1991 and 1992, until the percentage of children in care without a social worker, after an initial increase, fell to 10 per cent in September 1992. There were, however, considerable differences between areas; some teams were apparently very successful in tackling the problem and others failed to make an impact on it. Recruitment and retention of staff initiatives were having an effect by early 1992 [Birmingham Action on Child Care, 1992c], and a workload management system was being introduced for all children's teams. The 'case busters' project had been successful and was being introduced into additional areas. Accuracy of the management information systems was still doubtful, however, particularly as there were apparently different definitions of 'unallocated' and of 'case' in existence amongst team managers!

During 1991, BACC also undertook an examination of the very high rate of unallocated cases reported for one area children's team, where the level of staffing and workload appeared similar to other teams. A number of possible factors were identified, including the isolated location of the team; a build up in unallocated cases over a long period, so that it was impossible to catch up; high levels of staff sickness; and lack of social work assistants to support social workers. Specific recommendations were made to try to help this team, including the introduction of a 'case busters' team to deal with the backlog, which were beginning to show results by early 1993.

BACC's work on monitoring and dealing with the issue of unallocated cases was commended by the House of Commons Health Committee and subsequently the Department of Health introduced monitoring of the level of unallocated cases of all social services departments.

Success of recruitment and retention initiatives, combined with slowing of staff turnover with the onset of the recession resulted in very high staffing levels in the Department by 1992. As has been described, this had implications for the Department's budget.

Local authority support for children and families (Children Act 1989, Section 17)

Under Section 17 of the Children Act 1989 local authorities have a general duty:

to safeguard and promote the welfare of children within their area who are in need, by promoting their upbringing by their own families wherever possible. The services which local authorities should provide are set out in Part III and Schedule 2 of the Act. Chapter 5 considered the definition of 'children in need' and potential implications of the Act's requirements for their welfare. In Birmingham, specific support to children and families was already being developed through day care for pre-school children and out-of-school provision for older children.

£244,000 was allocated from the 1991/92 growth budget towards the further implementation of Section 17. This augmented the £90,000 previously spent under Section 1 of the Child Care Act 1980, to support the Department's duty to provide 'advice, guidance and assistance' to diminish 'the need to receive children into or keep them in care' [Child Care Act, 1980, Section 1 (1)]. This budget was allocated to social work teams and spent by them on supporting children in their own homes. Although there were departmental guidelines on the use of the Section 1 budget, in practice much of it was spent on income maintenance (food, clothing, equipment, furniture etc).

Guidelines set out by BACC and agreed by the Departmental Management Team in July 1991 [Birmingham Action on Child Care, 1991b] emphasised the use of the new Section 17 budget for packages of support services for families. These included activities or holidays for the child or parent/other carer, group work, development of babysitting circles or out-of-school care, paying for playgroup or playscheme places, purchase of practical help such as cleaning, home care, or respite care, and food, fares or equipment, where these were part of a rehabilitation plan. Part of the Section 17 budget for 1992/93 was held back to pay for the one-year appointment to develop out-of-school care which was discussed above. The remainder of the budget was allocated to social work teams to develop imaginative responses to children in need, in line with the guidance given.

Response to child sexual abuse

In 1990, BACC began discussions with a national charitable foundation about facilities for girls who had been sexually abused. The foundation worked with young offenders, homeless young people, and others at risk, and its projects included services for adolescent survivors of sexual abuse, female and male. BACC staff visited some of these and concluded that a facility was required in Birmingham which would be able to provide support, counselling and advice to young women who had been sexually abused, and training and consultation for professionals working with them. The Team also identified a specific need to ensure that such a facility could meet the needs of Black and minority ethnic women. A service agreement to provide a project in an inner city area of Birmingham was drawn up with the foundation. Funding for the project proved difficult to find, however, and subsequent problems over planning permission for premises held up the new venture. In 1993, its future was still uncertain.

Since 1989 the Social Services Department had worked with young people, primarily young men, thought to be involved in prostitution, with funding from the Department of Health. Research carried out in 1991 studied the involvement in prostitution of young women in the care of the Department. Methodological problems not surprisingly prevented even an estimate of how many had been involved in prostitution. (Apart from difficulties of definition and of establishing a base line 'population' of young women in care – given the movement in and out of care, young women were naturally reluctant to discuss this aspect of their lives.) Only 20 young women were identified who were thought to have been involved in prostitution. For some their involvement pre-dated their reception into care. It was apparent that young women who ran away from home or from care were particularly at risk of becoming involved in prostitution. Staff responses to their involvement varied enormously. The Departmental Management Team concluded that staff needed guidance and training on dealing with sexuality and sexual behaviour, including training to enable them to respond to the needs of young women. Managers were asked to ensure that young women in care had access to groups exclusively for them, where they could discuss issues of self-esteem as well as sexuality. The establishment of a number of girls-only children's homes (see chapter 7) provided a safe environment for some of this work.

Information for children and families services

Much of the work which BACC undertook in keeping people informed has already been mentioned, in the historical account of the Project in chapter 4. It included Newsletters, Findings Papers and Working Papers, other papers and reports, work on management information (the statistics prepared for managers), information packs for staff and leaflets for service users. All of it contributed to dealing with the problem of 'low cloud' – BACC's metaphor for poor communications in the Department, which was described in chapter 3. BACC's publications and reports are listed in Appendix 4.

Communicating with staff

Among the first actions taken by BACC staff was the distribution of newsletters: these were designed to reach as many staff working with children and families as possible, keeping them up to date with BACC's work as well as inviting them to contribute. Newsletters were complemented by other reports and papers. The series of Findings Papers provided information, summarising other publications or pulling together useful information, while the Working Papers presented some of the issues which BACC addressed. Other papers provided information on the Children Act and its implications. All these publications were distributed widely and introduced a new standard for communication in the Department. Work was also undertaken on basic information packs for child care staff, in a loose leaf format – completion of this project was held up while changes in the Department's management structure were incorporated, and the packs will be issued in 1993.

BACC produced numerous reports for both the Departmental Management Team and the Social Services Committee, and some of these were also widely distributed once they had been approved. These reports were instruments designed to promote changes in policy and practice, and are referred to throughout this book. Members of the BACC Team undertook extensive work to improve the usefulness and accuracy of management information in the Department. The importance of statistical data for managers in the Department was given added urgency by the need to tackle and monitor the problem of unallocated cases, which was described earlier in this chapter. The work undertaken by BACC on all aspects of management information for the children and families services was set out briefly in chapter 4.

Communicating with service users

Extensive work was undertaken by the BACC Team to produce a series of information leaflets for parents, children and other carers, setting out the Social Services Department's work. These were published early in 1993 and provided local information in an accessible form, supplementing booklets produced by the Department of Health on aspects of the Children Act 1989. A general leaflet entitled *Services for Children and Families* was translated into minority community languages, in both written and audio-taped versions. There were ten other leaflets, covering the following topics:

- Aftercare;
- Child protection;
- Children and young people with a disability or special health need;
- Children's homes;
- Day care for children under eight;
- Foster care;
- Juvenile justice;
- Social work services for deaf people and their families;
- Social work teams;
- Social work teams in hospitals.

The cost of translating, typesetting and printing all of these in minority languages was considerable, and initially audio-taped versions were produced and made available on loan from libraries, Neighbourhood Offices and social services offices.

Conclusion

This chapter brings together BACC's work under the general heading of services for children in need. It describes the beginning of a cultural change in social work in Birmingham. First, there is a growing emphasis on diversity – while all children have the same basic needs, the different ways in which these may be met, in accordance with families' ethnicity, religion, language and culture, are acknowledged and given priority. Second, there is a movement towards a service in which the rights of users are clearly spelt out and communicated, and where they have access to procedures for making representations and complaints. Third, there is a gradual shift away from a focus on child protection to providing support to children in need. Finally, there is an emphasis on communication – on providing information to managers, staff, service users, carers and the public. All these trends complement each other and reflect a common philosophy – one which values the individual and works in partnership.

All of these changes will take time to achieve. Ensuring that children and families receive a service appropriate to their culture, religious convictions and language will be a continuing commitment.

Development of good practice in this area is still evolving and will always need review and reconsideration as society itself changes. It is an area where anxieties and emotions run high. Working to develop and promote best practice, BACC recognised that there were no enduring 'right answers'. Whilst guidance could be provided, everyone must take responsibility for examining their own attitudes, policies and practices.

In Birmingham, provision for service users to make complaints was made ahead of the requirements of the Children Act 1989 and the NHS and Community Care Act 1990, and the Department had already moved on to develop a children's rights service and to set up a Young People's Forum. Dealing with complaints from children and parents in an open and impartial manner required a new approach from managers. Some of the difficulties encountered in making this change were described in this chapter.

Changing the focus of the Department from child protection to providing support for children in need was only beginning – there were real difficulties to overcome in the process of shifting emphasis away from crisis intervention to preventive work. This is not to imply that preventive work was not undertaken before 1989. It has always been the case that the majority of the children on the child protection register, including many children subject to care orders, live at home and are supported by social workers in the community. BACC's work was designed to enable children and parents to be given help and advice at an earlier stage, through development of services for children under eight, and of out-of-school care, and the imaginative use of family support budgets. In the process, the need for crisis intervention should be reduced. Without massive new resources, this change can only take place slowly.

These services also complement the work being done with children in care. Children can be returned home to live with their families at an earlier stage if there are facilities in the community to support families. The system of reviews will help to ensure that all options are considered.

Providing information and improving communications underpinned all BACC's work. The adage, 'knowledge is power', is as true in social work as elsewhere. Without knowledge, managers and staff are seriously hampered in their work. Without reliable and usable information, children, young people, parents and foster carers cannot work in partnership with the Department nor can they exercise their rights.

Nevertheless, the Department's major financial investment in children's services remains in its placements services – foster care and residential care. These services were given extensive consideration by BACC and are the topic of next chapter.

7. Looking after Birmingham's children

> When a court is considering whether or not to make one or more orders under this Act with respect to a child, it shall not make the order or any of the orders unless it considers that doing so would be better for the child than making no order at all.
> [Children Act 1989, Section 1 (5)]

The requirements of the Children Act are designed to ensure that local authority provision for children makes a positive contribution to their welfare. Thus, a court may only make an order committing a child to the care of the authority if it is clear that this will be better for the child than not making an order at all [Children Act 1989, Section 1 (5)]. This has two consequences for social services departments: before seeking an order, they should have exhausted voluntary approaches (such as agreements with parents) to safeguarding and promoting the child's welfare; and when an order is sought they must be able to show that the provision they are making for the child – such as accommodation in a children's home – is of positive benefit to the child. Accommodation provided by the local authority – in foster homes or residential care – can be part of a package of support to a family; it is not to be seen as a last resort when all other options have failed [Department of Health, 1989c].

Parents who seek this kind of help are not to be regarded as having failed their children. Parents continue to hold parental responsibility, and share it with the local authority even when a court order is made; their views, and those of the child concerned, must be taken into account. The implications are that both foster care and residential care must be of a high standard if they are to represent a positive choice. Placement of children must give 'due consideration' to the child's ethnic origins, religion, culture and language, and, wherever consistent with his or her welfare, the placement should be near to home and with brothers and sisters. Taken together, these principles represent a philosophical shift, away from viewing 'care' by the local authority as a last resort, towards a concept of the local authority sharing parenting with natural parents, as a good parent itself. Such a shift requires social services departments to reconsider their attitudes to children and families, as well as to review their procedures and provision for residential and foster care.

Improving the foster care service

Amongst the first Topic Groups established by BACC was the Fostering and Adoption Topic Group, which was set up in recognition of the pressures on the fostering service, and the consequent impact on children's homes. At its early meetings, this Group concluded that the task of reviewing both adoption and fostering simultaneously would be unmanageable, and decided to concentrate on foster care. Moreover, the Department of Health had announced its review of adoption law, with a first consultation paper published in September 1990 [Department of Health, 1990]. In these circumstances, a Departmental review of the adoption service might be premature. Nevertheless, adoption was not neglected by BACC, which organised consultation meetings in connection with the adoption law review and sent in submissions to the Department of Health.

The Foster Care Topic Group met regularly for eight months, and received reports from its four sub-groups, which considered information; recruitment of foster carers; retention of foster carers; and children needing foster care. Its membership included managers and other staff, from adoption and fostering teams, residential care, day care, children's teams, mental health teams, general services teams, administration, Payments Section, Information Systems Section, and the Panel of Guardians ad Litem and Reporting Officers. There was a representative of the Birmingham Foster Care Association on the Group and also an independent member of a Fostering and Adoption Panel. As with other Topic Groups, this wide membership helped to ensure that fostering was not considered in isolation from other aspects of services for children and families, and that there was potentially an extensive network of people able to comment and contribute to development of proposals.

The Group's remit was to review the service and make recommendations to meet the needs of Birmingham's children for the next five to ten years, taking into account the implications of the Children Act 1989, and specifically its requirements in relation to the:

cultural, racial, religious and linguistic needs of the children and young people, their families and the foster carers themselves. [Birmingham Action on Child Care, 1991d]

The Group began its work by analysing the current state of the fostering service. It noted that:

historically, Birmingham [Social Services Department] has not provided a fostering service which is part of an overall policy or plan for the care of children unable to live in their own homes. [Ibid.]

Statistics indicated that the Department had a lower proportion of children placed in foster care than many other social services departments. Policy decisions in 1980, which led to the closure of residential nurseries and a reduction in the number of residential homes, had not been accompanied by additional resources for the new adoption and fostering (Homefinding) teams. By 1990, the service was still unable to provide for all children under ten-years-old who needed placements, despite a policy decision taken in 1984, that children under ten should only be placed in residential homes in exceptional circumstances. The service for children aged over ten was minimal. Foster carers complained of lack of recognition, training and support, and of children remaining for too long in short-term placements without an allocated social worker; they stressed the increasing demands of the task.

This analysis of the problems and pressures facing the foster care service demonstrated the wisdom of not responding to the events of 1987-88 in residential care simply by establishing an enquiry into children's homes. Clearly, there were links between problems manifested so publicly in residential care and issues facing the foster care service. Without a foster care service able to meet the needs – at the least – of younger children, the residential care service could not concentrate on working with those children who could most benefit from what it had to offer. A fostering service under pressure was also one where problems were likely to arise. Indeed, a later report:

speculated that recent revelations about practice in residential care may well be matched by similar investigations into foster-care in the near future. [Birmingham Action on Child Care, 1992b].

The Foster Care Topic Group presented its report to the Departmental Management Team in November 1991 and to the Child Care Sub-Committee in December 1991. Proposals were made for the development and improvement of the service in the context of the outline plan for children's placements services – *Looking After Birmingham's Children* – which had been approved in September 1991 (this report was discussed in chapter 5) [Birmingham Social Services Department, 1991e]. Progress had already been made in setting up a fee-paid short-term fostering service on a pilot basis, and the Department's new management structure would:

ensure the development of a foster care strategy and the necessary management and professional leadership to work towards providing a quality foster care service. [Birmingham Social Services Department, 1991h]

The Topic Group made over fifty detailed recommendations which fell into three main areas – management issues; resourcing issues; and strategic issues [Birmingham Action on Child Care, 1991d]. Many recommendations on management issues – for example, in relation to effective procedures for prompt payment of foster carers – could be acted on immediately. Those with major resource implications or with strategic implications required a different response.

The Topic Group Report believed that unless the quality of support and recognition offered to existing foster carers were improved, there would be little point in using scarce resources to recruit new carers:

A future fostering service must reflect the intrinsic value of the foster carer as a major resource. [Ibid.]

Much of the Group's Report, therefore, concentrated on the support and training needs of foster carers. It emphasised the importance of:

- training and development programmes;
- support to individual foster carers from social workers;
- support to the Birmingham Foster Care Association;
- representation and complaints procedures;
- sound but sensitive procedures for investigating allegations of abuse against foster carers;

- legal support and advice for foster carers against whom allegations were made; and
- adequate financial recognition of the service.

Given proper training, support and recognition, the demands made on foster care by the Children Act could be met. The Report described the changing nature of the fostering task, with foster carers increasingly providing placements for older children, for children with a range of disabilities, and for children with severe behavioural problems often resulting from sexual abuse. Foster carers had a critical role to play in promoting partnership with natural parents, in facilitating contact between children and their families, and in ensuring a child's ethnic origins and linguistic, cultural and religious needs were respected. It stressed the importance of partnership between social workers and foster carers, with adequate information, regular reviews, and involvement of foster carers in case conferences and planning meetings. In developing the service to meet the requirements of the Children Act, it was necessary to balance the need to recognise, train and support foster carers as an essential Departmental resource against the need to monitor and review homes, and protect children in foster care from poor practice and abuse.

Whilst the Report provided a comprehensive set of practical recommendations for development of a quality foster care service, it lacked an explicit statement of the purpose of foster care. In concentrating on the needs of foster carers for training, support, recognition, and proper remuneration, it almost lost sight of the priority which must be given to children's needs. Given the absence of a policy which acknowledged foster carers as partners in the care of children, and which recognised them as a valuable resource, the focus by the Foster Care Topic Group on needs of foster carers and their support services as preconditions for a good quality fostering service was almost inevitable. In the process, however, some issues crucial to the care of children were almost overlooked, such as the importance of recruiting foster carers from Black and minority ethnic communities, from working class communities, and from all areas of the city. The recommendations made by the Topic Group undoubtedly contributed to achieving these ends, but these and other issues required specific consideration. The principles and practices which will lead to a satisfactory placement were not tackled, and will require further work.

Foster carers work in considerable isolation, and children in foster care have less access to knowledge of their rights, for example, to the Departmental complaints procedure, than their counterparts in residential care. There is also no system for independent inspection of foster homes, as there is for children's homes. Although the system of reviews does provide for regular monitoring, it does not include opportunities for children in foster care to raise concerns with someone able to act as an advocate on their behalf. The potential for abusive situations in fostering was acknowledged by BACC when it put forward a proposal for a study of allegations of abuse against foster carers. The need to investigate these thoroughly but sensitively, recognising the particular vulnerability of foster carers, was stressed. The importance of children in foster care having access to the Children's Rights Officer and the complaints procedure was recognised. In practice there were difficulties in providing this access universally, especially as many of the children were very young. The task of enabling foster children to seek help if they are abused, or to make complaints if they are simply unhappy, is left with their social workers, who inevitably have an investment in placements continuing without disruption.

> Both foster carers and foster children are vulnerable to allegations [of abuse] and several recent cases of actual abuse by foster carers have revealed the vulnerability of children in foster homes.
>
> [Nixon, 1991]

There has been increasing awareness and concern nationally about the incidence of allegations of abuse against foster carers. These clearly need to be taken as seriously as any other allegations of abuse. However, a small scale research project undertaken by Birmingham University [Nixon, 1991] revealed 'that the allegations and investigations were major life crises for foster carers', even if allegations were unsubstantiated. The loss of potential and existing foster carers as a result of insensitive handling of allegations was noted. There were also major concerns about the impact of allegations on foster carers and their own children; on foster children when abused or when their foster carer is under investigation; and on the staff required to deal with the resulting stress and undertake the investigation [Nixon, 1992]. In February 1992, the Departmental

Management Team agreed to a proposal from BACC to participate in a research, development and training project to develop a 'risk management strategy in foster care' [Nixon, 1991], which would help to safeguard the Department's growing investment in foster care. In the meantime, interim guidance on the handling of allegations of abuse made against foster carers was to be produced and issued to staff.

> Foster carers have been carrying a much greater burden of the impact of child abuse than has been realised until now. The survival of foster care as an option in child care may be at risk. Hence there is an urgent need to consider how the risks for all concerned in foster care might be more effectively managed.
>
> [Nixon, 1991]

The establishment of a fee-paid fostering service

Amongst the issues considered by the BACC Team were the difficulties being experienced within the whole placements system. There was evidence of shortages of places in both foster and children's homes, and of children inappropriately placed. Action to deal with these issues could not wait for the Foster Care and Residential Care Service Topic Groups to report, and a proposal was drawn up in 1990 for the establishment of a pilot fee-paid fostering service. By June 1990, it was evident that there were not enough places in short term foster homes or children's homes to ensure that the majority of children and young people entering care or needing to move within the system could be appropriately placed. The most obvious manifestation of this problem was the presence on 31 December 1989 of 82 children aged nine or under in residential units (out of a total of 476 children and young people), despite a policy which stated that these young children should be in foster care. Thus, one in six residents of children's homes were aged under 10, and their presence made it difficult for the homes to focus their work on the needs of teenagers. In a discussion paper presented to the Departmental Management Team, BACC predicted that this situation was likely to deteriorate if nothing was done, and added that the Children Act would require:

(a) more user choice
(b) placement near home and with siblings

(c) placement in a family of the same race etc
(d) adherence to a timetable and stated plans
(e) comprehensive assessments
(f) partnerships with parents which can deliver specific services, which will involve new commitment from foster carers.
[Birmingham Action on Child Care, 1990c]

These requirements could not be met by the existing overloaded service. A solution was the recruitment of additional short-term foster carers, but experience showed that recent campaigns had produced only a small net gain in numbers of placements. A fee paid scheme – which would pay foster carers a 'wage' in addition to the boarding out allowance (designed to meet the actual costs of caring for children) – was proposed. It was hoped that some people – mainly women, of course – would be attracted to fostering as an alternative to other paid employment. Given the characteristics of many children being placed, and the demands made of foster carers, the task could no longer be equated with parenting as it is usually understood. The Department could legitimately require foster carers to be more 'professional'. The advent of the Children Act would make this even more necessary. A pilot scheme was proposed, and approved by the Social Services Committee in October 1990 [Birmingham Social Services Department, 1990h].

Evaluation of the scheme in early 1992 showed that it had exceeded its target of securing 25-30 new placements. 38 places had already been approved and a further 20-30 were being assessed. More than two thirds of the approved places were in Black and minority ethnic households. The pilot project's success was startling. During 1991 three specially appointed social workers covering only a fifth of the city had found more than 60 new placements, compared with 54 placements secured by all the Department's Adoption and Fostering Teams during 1989/90. As a result, it was proposed to extend the scheme to cover the whole city and all new and existing short-term foster carers [Birmingham Social Services Department, 1992b]. Initially, it was hoped that resources would be found in 1992 to launch the scheme, but the problems described earlier (Chapter 5) in managing the 1992/93 budget delayed the start until April 1993 [Birmingham Social Services Department, 1993a].

Remand and teenage fostering scheme

A small Remand and Teenage Fostering Scheme was established in 1989 to serve parts of South Birmingham. The original brief for the scheme was that a single Senior Social Worker would recruit three or four carers to offer placements to young people remanded to local authority accommodation. Interest in the scheme and the number of carers considered suitable for teenage fostering, however, led to expansion to six carers, with short term placements available for other teenagers. Time limited, task specific placements – from one night to six months – were offered, and during its first two years 67 placements were made.

Availability of growth money for foster care in 1992/93 led to plans for the expansion of this scheme, with an Assistant Team Manager (appointed July 1992), two social workers, and administrative support. *Looking after Birmingham's Children* estimated that the Department would need about 100 foster carers able to offer approximately 136 placements to children and young people aged over 11, if a realistic choice of placement for this age group were to be available. Expansion of the teenage fostering scheme was a first step towards this target, and it was anticipated that eventually short-term, long-term and emergency foster homes would be provided. Fees and allowances would be similar to those paid by the fee paid fostering scheme. The need for good regular support from the Fostering Team, available through an on call system at all hours, was recognised.

Support to foster carers

The support needs of foster carers was one of the issues addressed by the Foster Care Topic Group. Action to provide better support to foster carers had, however, already begun. In 1989, a series of meetings with the Director herself was held to enable the foster carers to discuss their concerns. With encouragement from the Department, foster carers formed a Birmingham Foster Care Association, and from October 1989 a small grant was given to the Association to enable them to produce newsletters, and pay travelling and telephone expenses. Shortly afterwards, the Department made an office and telephone available to the Committee of the Association, and regular meetings were established between its officers, managers from the Department, and members of the BACC Team. During the Birmingham Child Care Conference a Mayoral Reception for foster carers was held at the International Convention Centre. Foster carers responded to this new level of support by contributing to the BACC topic groups as well as to the Advisory Group. In the new Departmental structure lead responsibility for foster care was assigned to one of the two Assistant Directors, Children and Families, and regular consultation meetings were established from April 1992.

Residential care: improving children's homes

The Residential Care Topic Group was set up in April 1990 and met 35 times before its Report was received by the Departmental Management Team in January 1992. Its 28 members included managers, staff, young people from residential care, a foster carer, a councillor, and members of the BACC Advisory Group. It was evenly balanced between women and men and between Black and White people. Members came from residential work, adoption and fostering, fieldwork, family support, child protection, administration, and the BACC Team.

In many ways this Group faced the most obvious but the most difficult of the tasks undertaken by the Topic Groups. The crisis in residential care was common knowledge; but the task of developing solutions without further loss of morale was formidable. The Group inevitably began by rehearsing the history of residential care nationally and in Birmingham, learning lessons which, with the benefit of hindsight, were plain to read. This history was recounted in chapter 2, and will not be repeated here. It formed the background for the Topic Group's work. Given this history, it would have been easy to deal in blame and recriminations, and to fuel cynicism which already existed about the reality of the Department's commitment to quality residential care. The Topic Group brought an early version of its Report to the Advisory Group in April 1991. At that meeting considerable effort was expended in ensuring that the Report did not avoid the real problems which had faced and still faced residential care, but that in doing so it gave positive messages for the future and did not undermine progress which had already been made.

The Group's final Report, while capable of standing alone, had also to be considered in the context of *Looking After Birmingham's Children*, which set the strategic framework for the future of residential care. There was also common ground with the Report of the Foster Care Topic Group. The Residential Care Topic Group emphasised that:

the service for children looked after in homes cannot improve without appropriate foster care resources for children whose need can be met within a family setting. [Birmingham Action on Child Care, 1992a]

This sense of the placements services as a system was important in avoiding some of the mistakes of the past. During the 1980s:

the rigour which was applied to the restructuring of the residential sector failed to find its counterpart in the fostering sector... The consequence has been that most children who enter care aged 12 (and even 10) or over have no placement option other than residential care. [Ibid.]

The Group's Report recognised that improvements were already underway in residential care, with, for example, introduction of a children's management structure, establishment of induction training for new residential workers, a handbook and complaints procedure for children in care, establishment of the Inspection Division, and plans for appointment of a Children's Rights Officer and independent reviewing officers. The service was not, however, fully prepared to meet the demands of the Children Act for choice of placement, partnership with parents, and development of a positive role, with clear aims and objectives for residential care.

Providing for children and young people was taking place in a context of limited resources, and the Group acknowledged the necessity of balancing needs of children and young people to live in a home which is comfortable, personal and not institutional, against the Department's need to keep costs to a minimum. The Group's Report made recommendations for appropriate sizes of children's homes, and the number of places which would be needed in the future. It considered the merits of providing specialised units and the advantages of generic units, and concluded that both would be required. It also emphasised improvements made already through dedicated management, which would be stronger in the new structure (see chapter 5). Once the strategy set out in *Looking After Birmingham's Children* was implemented, the Report stressed that homes should be able to care for the majority of children requiring residential care, without recourse to other placements for example in Community Homes with Education or therapeutic units. Children and young people in residential care would therefore be able to expect continuity of care.

Although the Report began with management issues, it based its subsequent recommendations on an analysis of the basic needs of children looked after by a local authority – food, education, play, love and security. The rights of children were also of critical importance, and not in conflict with the responsibility of adults to look after their welfare and set limits on their behaviour. The Report therefore endorsed the setting up of a Children's Rights Service and the importance of ensuring its independence.

Other detailed recommendations dealt with support and training for staff working with children who have been abused; the physical environment of homes; provision of food, and the creation of a homely, warm and welcoming environment; appropriate use of sanctions in homes; and education and health needs of children. It emphasised strongly the importance of staff ensuring that the specific needs of children from different ethnic groups, and with different linguistic, religious and cultural experiences, were taken into account.

Review of community homes with education

BACC undertook a review of the Department's two community homes with education, which resulted in distinct statements of purpose being established for each of them. The primary focus of one of the homes was to be work with children with behavioural and educational difficulties, whilst the other would mainly cater for the needs of older teenagers and young offenders. Work was underway to improve facilities in both homes, and in particular to create single bedrooms. Some bedsitter accommodation was to be set up where young people could learn to cater for themselves before leaving care. New management structures within each home were proposed which it was hoped would improve the quality of care given to the children and young people.

Training for residential workers

A high quality residential environment cannot be achieved without investment in staff. The Residential Care Topic Group examined the status, training and qualifications of residential care staff. Hitherto, the view had been 'the way to get on is to get out', with qualified staff leaving the service in order to gain advancement [Birmingham Action on Child Care, 1992a]. The Topic Group Report stressed the positive impact of the recently introduced induction training for new residential workers, and proposed a programme of in-service training which would develop core skills required by all residential child care workers. It also emphasised the potential of the National Vocational Qualification for providing competence based training and accreditation for residential staff.

Following the publication of the Utting Report in August 1991, the Department of Health announced that the Training Support

Programme (under which the Department of Health contributed 70 per cent of the cost of approved training programmes) would include a special initiative for providing qualifying training (the Diploma in Social Work) for managers of children's homes and their deputies. In October 1991, there were 42 Managers of children's homes in Birmingham, of whom only eight were qualified; six of their deputies (out of 44) and two other social work staff (out of 462) were also qualified. Although the Director welcomed the training initiative, she was concerned about the disruption which could be caused by the absence of too many managers undertaking training at any one time. She also estimated that the true cost of training one Manager was £50,000 spread over two years. In the event, the Department was granted three places on a special programme at Leicester Polytechnic. The grant from the Department of Health for 70 per cent of the cost amounted to £32,025, for the first year (seven months). After all the publicity given to the Initiative, the outcome seemed insignificant.

> Follow up interviews with some of those involved in the Induction Programme indicated that:
> - the induction process was very positive
> - that it has created expectations of training and development in those workers
> - if those expectations remain entirely unrealised then so too will the positive impact of the induction – in effect contributing to a more profound disillusionment.
>
> [Birmingham Action on Child Care, 1992a]

Since 1988, the Department's training policy had targeted workers in residential and day care services for qualifying training, with a requirement that trainees should return to those areas of work after qualifying. Given the salary and conditions of service differentials between residential and fieldwork, some workers were resentful about this requirement (although it should be noted that managers of residential homes were on similar or higher salaries than field social workers). This policy of targeting residential work was continued until 1991, when opportunities for returning trainees were broadened to include all parts of the children's services, a reflection of the level of vacancies in children's and general services teams at that time. The numbers of residential workers with a social work qualification nevertheless remained low.

Single sex children's homes

During 1991, a number of problems led the Department to establish single sex children's homes. Social workers were aware that some parents, especially Muslim parents, were opposed to teenage children being accommodated in mixed homes. Muslim families were especially concerned to protect their girls and young women from living alongside boys and young men. Some girls and young women who had suffered abuse, especially sexual abuse, also felt vulnerable in mixed homes, and it could be difficult for social workers to deal with issues of sexuality in mixed settings. In practice, some homes had traditionally only accommodated boys, but there had been no equivalent homes for girls. In September 1991, the Child Care Sub-Committee agreed to provision of single sex children's homes in each Division, for both girls and boys.

The education of children in residential and foster care

The majority of children accommodated by social services departments are of school age. Yet until recently, little concern has been expressed about their educational performance [Jackson, 1989]. Such evidence as is available shows that the educational performance of children in care is on average low and that, while some of their underachievement can be attributed to their experiences before coming into care, the care system does little to help them improve. Low expectations from foster carers and residential staff, changes of placement and school, an unstimulating environment and lack of help with school work, could compound the impact of earlier disruption. In the 1990s, an additional factor can be added to these – the increasing incidence of children and young people excluded from school.

From an early stage, BACC was concerned about issues of education. Local management of schools and grant maintained (opted out) status for some schools, together with a stronger emphasis on testing and examination results, placed additional difficulties in the way of educating children in residential and foster care. Some of these children and young people were not 'attractive' pupils for schools looking to maintain or improve their test and examination results. Similar difficulties in joining mainstream education could be faced by children with disabilities, special health needs, or emotional and behavioural problems.

BACC staff made contacts with colleagues in the Education Department and opened up a dialogue on these and other issues. One significant outcome was a joint seminar between the management teams of the two departments held in November 1991, following which a joint report was prepared [Birmingham Social Services Department, 1992e]. This set out the areas for joint working:

- standards of care and education within the residential facilities run by both departments;
- planning for children placed in out-of-city schools or other facilities, including dealing with inspection, complaints, and child protection issues;
- education of children looked after by the Authority, and children with emotional or behavioural difficulties; and
- requirements of the Children Act 1989 for joint working, information sharing, and registration and assessment of children with disabilities.

Agreements were reached on joint standards and inspections of the City's residential special schools, and the cooperation already established between the Social Services Department's Children's Rights Officer and the Education Rights Officer was noted. Further work on out-of-city placements was commissioned, to ensure an improved exchange of information and progress towards fewer children being placed outside the city.

A commitment was made to working together to improve the educational achievement of children with emotional and behavioural difficulties and children looked after by the local authority. In particular, the need to focus upon young people who had been out of school for protracted periods, including those permanently excluded from school, was recognised, and a joint working group was established. The responsibility of staff in both Departments for children and young people's educational achievements was acknowledged. The Social Services Department undertook to give higher priority to educational issues in its child care planning process, and to ensure that social workers gave adequate consideration to children's educational needs, as well as to their personal or interpersonal problems. Amongst the means to ensure that educational issues received attention was the Department's system of reviews (discussed in chapter 6) and participation in the Department of Health's outcomes study which is discussed below. Children's educational needs could not, however, be met by social workers alone, and dialogue with the Education Department continued in order to ensure a joint approach. A joint working group was also established to look at the assessment of children with disabilities.

Social Services Department managers were rightly concerned that changes in progress and proposed to the management of schools and the education service generally could leave some children at a disadvantage. In particular, there were growing concerns during 1992 about the number of children and young people excluded from school, either on suspension or permanently expelled, and the difficulties then experienced in providing them with an education. Children in children's homes seemed particularly likely to be affected. Work on these concerns was to continue after BACC ended in July 1992, and the issues were still unresolved early in 1993.

The health needs of children in care

The health of children in care – especially that of children in residential care – were addressed by a sub-group reporting to the Children Act Implementation Group. The sub-group identified two main areas of concern: the implications of the Children Act 1989 for the provision of services to children with disabilities; and medical examinations of children in care and their consequences. A paper setting out some of these implications of the Children Act was prepared. Subsequently, joint meetings with representatives of the four Birmingham Health Authorities were set up, and these meetings considered the implications for children's health of the changes underway in both health and social services. Work began on joint planning for children's health, with consideration being given to developing a joint Child Care Plan.

The revised system of reviews being introduced in the Department included detailed questions on the health of each child being reviewed. As this system gained momentum, it was anticipated that it would ensure that the health needs of children in both residential and foster care would receive higher priority than in the past. Improved forms for medical examinations were devised which would meet the needs of children and adolescents; specific questions were included which would, for example, draw attention to signs of substance abuse.

In Birmingham, services for children with disabilities were integrated with services for adults. This had the advantage of continuity for the individual child growing into adulthood, but risked the possibility of some of the needs of children as *children* rather than as people with disabilities being overlooked. Initial review of the services led to the conclusion that responsibility for them should be transferred to the new Children and Families Divisions, but that this transfer should not occur immediately. Time was required for work to ensure good coordination of services with other agencies, including the Education Department, as well as appropriate mechanisms for transferring cases from children's teams to adult services. The transfer was expected to take place in October 1993.

Assessing outcomes in child care: participation in a pilot study

In 1987 the Department of Health and Social Security suggested that a working party be set up to consider the question of outcomes in child care. The impetus for this study came partly from acknowledgment of the familiar dilemma between providing resources to support children in their own homes or providing substitute care. There was little research evidence to show whether – or if – substitute care was beneficial for children, nor to enable an evaluation of which forms of substitute care were most effective and for which children. A meeting of leading child care researchers at Dartington revealed that there were few measures of outcomes available, and that indeed there was no consensus on how outcomes could be defined or measured. A small working party, chaired by Professor Roy Parker of the University of Bristol and funded by the Department of Health and Social Security, was established to give the issues further consideration [Parker and others, 1991].

By early 1990, the Working Party had developed some schedules for measuring outcomes, and these were being piloted in a number of social services departments. The schedules were intended to produce valuable data for researchers and to have a direct influence on social work practice. BACC offered cooperation from Birmingham Social Services Department in trying out the schedules in some of its children's homes. Participation at this pilot stage was to prove mutually beneficial. Social workers valued the focus provided by the schedules but were also able to help improve their design. Their regular use was expected to:

improve social work practice both in raising consciousness about a number of issues that are crucial to a child's development and in encouraging communication between all the parties, including parents and children, who are responsible for outcome. [Ibid.]

Help for young people leaving care

In Birmingham, a service to prepare young people for leaving care and to support them after leaving already existed, in the form of leaving care grants, 'minimal care flats' within children's homes, an Independent Living Project, supported lodgings, an employment project, and preparation work routinely undertaken within children's homes and by social workers. There were also some joint arrangements with the Housing Department and the voluntary sector to provide accommodation for young people leaving care. These services and informal arrangements, however, required considerable further development and coordination, in order to provide a city-wide, comprehensive service.

BACC established a multidisciplinary, inter-agency working group in August 1989 to review current practice and procedures and to develop detailed recommendations for the future. Other work was also undertaken for the Corporate Children Act Steering Group. Two reports brought to the Departmental Management team in June 1991 set out the way forward. The Management Team agreed to use its 1992/93 growth budget to establish a city-wide, specialist after care service. This would provide financial support in the form of leaving care grants, clothing and travel allowances; would produce and regularly revise a *Leaving Care Guide* for young people; and would provide advice, information, and access to other forms of support. In addition, it confirmed agreement with the Housing Department on responsibility for the accommodation needs of young people leaving care. The Housing Department was also asked to undertake specific work on the housing needs of young women, young people with disabilities, and Black and minority ethnic young people.

By September 1992, the Leaving Care Guide, *Moving On, Moving In*, had been published, in an attractive loose leaf format and as a video. The Independent Living Project was developing a training programme for residential staff to enable them to prepare young people for leaving care, and consideration was also being given to training foster parents. Other departments were asked to ensure that their services met the needs of young people leaving care or who had left care, through access to advice services, leisure provision and adult education [Birmingham Social Services Department, 1992f].

Unfinished business

There were a number of areas of work which BACC did not have the time and resources to consider fully. Preliminary work was undertaken by BACC on reviewing the Department's services for children with disabilities, but this was to be completed during 1993, when the services would transfer from Community Care to Children and Families. Child protection services were being reviewed during the period, but BACC was not involved with this work. The post of Head of Child Protection Services was to be established in 1993/94. Juvenile justice was another area of the Department's work which was not examined by BACC, although after the end of the Project the Children and Families management team undertook work on the implementation of the Criminal Justice Act 1991.

Conclusion

Although the impetus for setting up BACC came from allegations of abuse in children's homes, the Project undertook a wide range of work, with residential child care comprising only a part of the whole. BACC was concerned to examine residential child care in its context – namely as part of the children's placements services which were themselves part of a wider range of services to children and families. Traditionally residential care had been an isolated service within the Department, but BACC's work showed that the problems manifested in residential care were symptomatic of problems throughout the system. Two major groups looked at foster care and residential care, and the BACC Team was also involved in a number of other pieces of work concerned to improve services for children and young people accommodated by the Social Services Department. Whilst the establishment of a complaints procedure, independent inspection, a Children's Rights Service and Young People's Forum (as described in chapter 6) were essential safeguards for children and young people, other action was required to enable the Social Services Department to meet the requirements – in the letter and the spirit – of the Children Act 1989. This chapter described some of the work initiated by BACC to achieve these ends.

8. Changing child care: the management of change

Assessing and evaluating the work of Birmingham Action on Child Care

Throughout this book it has been clear that Birmingham Action on Child Care undertook its work during a time of unprecedented change in both the personal social services and local government. During the four years since it was established, a fundamental revision of the law relating to children – the Children Act 1989 – has been debated in Parliament, become law, and been implemented. During the same period, local authorities' responsibilities for community care for adults have been increased and restructured; the future role and structure of local government has been under review; and the Community Charge has been introduced and then replaced by the Council Tax. By the end of the period, the role of local government as a provider of services was itself in question.

Between 1988 and 1992, a number of key reports on children's services were published, including several which focused on residential care. These included inquiries into events in Staffordshire, Leicestershire and Gwent, as well as the Wagner Review (1988), the Utting Report (1991), and the reports of the Howe and Warner Inquiries (both 1992). Events in children's homes provided the impetus for setting up BACC, although there were other concerns which also contributed to its establishment.

Birmingham Action on Child Care was first and foremost intended to be an action not a research project. However, BACC's holistic approach and its arms' length relationship to the Department permitted the development of intellectual exploration. The Project carried out its own small pieces of research, and drew on academic research. There was also a commitment from the beginning to recording BACC's methodology and work, so that they could be written up for future reference. This book is the outcome of that commitment.

BACC operated in the constantly changing environment of a social services department; its staff acknowledged that this environment would continue to change and develop after the project ended and that they themselves would need to adapt continuously. Much of the work it initiated was inevitably unfinished when the Project ended. Some later initiatives existed only on paper, and formed the agenda for the new Children and Families Management Team which was itself an outcome of BACC. Despite the changing environment and unpredicted demands faced by BACC, it nevertheless achieved the aims and objectives set out for it, both in broad terms and in detail, including the details of *how* the Team should work which were included in the Project *Outline*.

This chapter attempts first to consider whether Birmingham Action on Child Care carried out the intentions set out for it in the Project *Outline*. It goes on to describe the local and national impact and reputation of the Project. The key messages about the process of managing change in the public sector are set out. The Project's outcomes are summarised, and the relationship between the outcomes and the process is explored. Finally, the transferability of the BACC approach to management of change in other contexts is considered.

The Project's task: aims, objectives, and the *Outline*

The Social Services Committee decision to set up Birmingham Action on Child Care charged it with responsibility to undertake the following:

to establish new objectives, priorities and resources which will enable the Child Care Service to make a clear and positive response to future demands.
(a) to analyse the needs of children and families who require the assistance of the statutory child care service and to draw up general principles for the development of the services.
(b) to review and develop child care policies, strategies and resources in the light of the redefined needs and principles.
(c) to propose an overall implementation strategy with specific plans and a timetable of action to put into effect the changes required [Birmingham Social Services Department, 1988d].

Chapter 5 set out the broad strategy for service development which BACC produced, whilst chapters 6 and 7 described the implementation strategies, specific plans and timescales for making the changes proposed. General principles were drawn up for the future direction of the children and families services. These principles, the broad strategy and the detailed proposals were based on analyses of service users and needs produced by the four Topic Groups and other work carried out or supported by the BACC Team. The methodology set out in chapter 3 and the chronological account of BACC given in chapter 4 showed how the Team worked from an analysis of problems faced by the service and the needs of service users to produce detailed recommendations for change. In choosing to develop a specific philosophy and methodology, the Team also committed the Project to a wider brief – to change the culture of the organisation and to achieve practical results – to action. To some extent, the wider brief was foreshadowed in the Project *Outline*, a paper produced for the Departmental Management Team which set out in more detail how BACC would approach its work [Coffin, 1989].

New objectives, priorities and resources for the child care service: BACC's key achievements

A strategic framework and basic principles.
An outline strategy for the children's placements service.
The new management structure.
The growth in real terms of the Departmental budget for children and families.

The Project *Outline* (an extract is reprinted as Appendix 2) was specific about how the Project would operate and what it would do. As the *Outline* required, the Team and its associated staff worked 'within existing and projected financial constraints'. Despite the *Outline*'s prohibition on 'major reorganisation of the Department', however, BACC advised the Departmental Management Team that modifications to management structures were required to meet the needs of the service and the new legislation. In practice, the Children Act structured much of BACC's work. The *Outline* also charged the Project with basing its work firmly in the City Council's equal opportunities policy, and this was fundamental to BACC's way of working and development of policy and practice.

> **Implementing the Children Act 1989: four key methods**
> Children Act Implementation Group.
> Corporate Children Act Steering Group.
> Children Act Training Strategy.
> Children Act Development Group.

BACC did not work as closely with the voluntary sector as the *Outline* had suggested it should. The voluntary sector was fragmented and diverse, so that relationships with it were time-consuming and problematic. It was recognised, however, that work with both the voluntary and private sectors will become more urgent in the future. The processes developed by BACC for developing good practice and managing change could be applied to working with and coordinating the independent sector. BACC concentrated on services provided by Birmingham City Council as its first priority, and was able to improve relationships with and secure help from other city departments in implementing the Children Act. In particular, it was able to develop a corporate response to the Children Act, as well as to children's issues generally.

It involved staff extensively in its work, establishing consultative groups, involving staff from all levels in working groups, and providing information, progress reports, and training opportunities. The Team itself and its associated groups included both Black and White people, women and men, and staff from all the Department's children's services. In consequence, it 'establish[ed] the mutual trust and respect with those who [carried] out its recommendations' that was urged in the *Outline*. Others were also involved in the Project's work. The *Outline* had suggested foster carers, and children and young people who were looked after by the Department, and these too were included. There were many 'positive spin-offs from the Project' – training and development for staff, guidance on good practice, and better communications throughout the Department.

As the *Outline* anticipated, BACC's largest commitment was to improving services for children looked after by the Department, whether these were in children's homes or foster care. However, it also invested time in bringing forward proposals for day care and other support for children in need in the community. Less work was done for children with disabilities than wished, and the Department's services for them were not integrated with the rest of the children and families services.

The *Outline* envisaged BACC producing an Interim Report and a Final Report, but in practice the Project produced a number of Progress Reports during its lifetime and a series of reports in its last months. Common principles and a policy framework were set out in two Reports *Directions for Strategic Planning* [Birmingham Action on Child Care, 1991c] and *Ten Basic Policy Statements* [Birmingham Social Services Department, 1991d]. They set the direction for the Department's child care services for the next five years, providing detailed recommendations for change as well as a work programme for the new Children and Families Management Team. The new Departmental structure was the safeguard for ensuring that the Project's work continued after it came to an end.

Raising the profile of child care issues: the impact of BACC, locally and nationally

From soon after its establishment, BACC attracted national interest as predicted in the *Outline*. The Project raised the profile of child care issues within the Department as well as making a national reputation for itself.

An indication of BACC's impact on the Social Services Department was the increasing amount of time given to children's issues by the Departmental Management Team and the Social Services Committee during 1990 and 1991. As the chronological account of the Project in chapter 4 (and Appendix 1) shows, in 1990 and 1991, they considered a series of major reports setting out new directions for the children and families service. The Children Act would have required the Department to review its children and families service during 1990 and 1991, but the work undertaken went beyond the requirements of the Act.

The April 1992 structure for management of the Department reflected BACC's analysis of the problems of children and families services. By establishing a Children and Families Management Team to continue the work started by BACC, the Director ensured that the needs of the service would continue to have high visibility and receive high priority when the Project ended later in 1992.

Similarly, the impact of BACC on the Department's approach to children's issues was reflected in the growth of the children and families budget, which from 1990 grew faster than inflation. Indeed, in 1992/93, the Social Services Committee budget was increased at the expense of some other Committees, reflecting the corporate commitment to implementation of both the Children Act and the Community Care Act. This was one outcome of BACC's work with elected Members and Chief Officers, as well as with senior managers from a number of other departments, which secured understanding of and commitment to the Children Act. The new resources for children and families services were the result of clearly articulated and reasoned bids developed by BACC; and they were allocated within a strategic framework inspired by BACC.

Nationally, BACC began to make an impact early in its life, with the Project Team making connections with key people in policy and practice throughout England and Wales. The BACC Team was keen to learn from research and work being carried out by other social services departments and other agencies. It actively sought opportunities to discuss its work with practitioners, policy makers, and academics. The Advisory Group helped to spread knowledge of the Project and of how it intended to approach its brief. The Team made links within Europe which were to be of increasing importance to the City Council from 1992 onwards.

The existence of a specialist team which had an early grasp of the principles and details of the Children Act 1989, ensured that Birmingham Social Services Department, through BACC, was able to contribute extensively to consultations on the Regulations and Guidance issued under the Children Act. The Department sent in responses to 15 out of 24 consultation papers, a considerable achievement in itself. The Project Team also contributed to the interpretation of 'children in need' put forward by the national In Need Implementation Group [In Need Implementation Group, 1991]. It challenged the restrictive interpretations being developed by some social services departments, interpretations which would have undermined the Children Act as a force for change.

The Team arranged for Birmingham Social Services Department to join in the development of work being undertaken by Bristol University for the Department of Health on assessing outcomes in child care [Parker et al., 1991]. BACC's own publications were widely circulated within the Department, but were also requested by other local authorities, voluntary organisations, and individuals (BACC's publications are listed in Appendix 4). Members of the BACC Team gave presentations on the Children Act and other aspects of social services for children to many local and national organisations and agencies.

The Birmingham Child Care Conferences in October 1991 and 1992 brought together people with an interest in child care issues from many parts of the United Kingdom and Europe, including staff from throughout the Department. They contributed to the Department's national reputation for commitment to creating a quality child care service, a situation few could have anticipated in 1988. Both conferences addressed key themes in child care, encouraging participants to share their views on how to develop quality services for children and families, without avoiding the real difficulties which faced local authorities in the 1990s. The first conference focused on how different agencies and organisations concerned with children could work together, and the second added a European dimension to this concept. Both conferences set local authority personal social services for families within a wider societal context of responsibility for the welfare of children. They brought together participants from other local services, private enterprise, voluntary and community groups, and national governments, in recognition of the contribution that working together could make to children's well-being.

A corporate commitment to implementing the Children Act was nurtured by BACC, so that relevant City Council Committees adopted its interpretation of 'children in need', and began to develop their own strategic responses. Developing corporate ownership of the legislation was a slow process, since there were few recent precedents for inter-departmental cooperation on children's issues. BACC ensured that children's issues were discussed by City Council Chief Officers at their weekly meetings. The establishment of the City-Wide Child Care Strategy (discussed in chapter 5) on the initiative of senior politicians was one response to this vacuum. BACC helped to shape the strategy, which had effective outcomes in provision of day care to parents in work or undertaking training, including provision for city employees. The Corporate Children Act Implementation Group was a second initiative brought about by the work of BACC. Positive commitments were secured to joint work on housing needs of young people leaving care; to prevention of youth homelessness; to provision of information for children, parents and others; and to education of children in care. The size of this task was noted in chapter 5, including the Social Services Department's difficulty in ensuring that children's needs were specifically included in the successful City Challenge bid. Increasing problems likely to be encountered in educating children in care and children excluded from schools were noted in chapter 7. Nevertheless, foundations for future cooperation between the Social Services Department and a number of other departments were laid by BACC.

Key messages: BACC's approach to the management of change

Birmingham Action on Child Care set out to understand the 'child care system', to discover where it was not working, and to review components of the system in the context of the whole. With a thorough understanding of the system and its components, the Team believed services for children and families could be improved. With informed management, the workings of the system could be harnessed to contribute to the development of services. BACC set out to develop the means of planning effectively, and to propose action plans which would result in better services for children and families. The means employed to achieve change were important, the process being inseparable from the outcomes.

In Birmingham, change in the quality of services could not be achieved without change in the culture of the Department. Therefore, the BACC Team had to encourage participation at all levels and with other services; to be willing to listen to service users, staff and foster carers; and to be open to new ideas, complaints and criticism. Real cultural change is difficult to achieve: it is relatively easy to promote new symbols and slogans, but much more difficult to change the underlying ethos of an organisation. The BACC Team set out to model through its own way of working the kind of Department it hoped to see develop. Whether it was successful may not be apparent in the short term. This issue will be discussed again in looking at a potential model for management of change later in this chapter. The key components of the BACC approach and process are described next, before outcomes for services are reviewed.

The children and families service constituted a system whose components could not be studied in isolation; change in one element affected all the others to a greater or lesser extent.

BACC's review of the history of residential care showed how problems in different parts of the children and families services interrelated. Although BACC necessarily looked at different areas of work separately, it did so in the context of the whole system, and framed its strategic reports with an awareness of the dynamics of the system. The report *Looking after Birmingham's Children*, despite some criticisms of its treatment of the residential care sector, epitomises the BACC approach to dealing with recommendations in the context of the system.

Improvement and development of children and families services, both in order to avoid a repetition of past problems and to implement the Children Act, required change in the culture of the Department.

BACC's approach to the management of change stressed a number of elements:

- consultation with service users;
- involvement of staff, foster carers and service users in development and improvement of services;
- working across formal service divisions and hierarchies;
- collaboration with other agencies and interest groups;
- being prepared to listen to new ideas, criticisms and complaints;
- valuing people and the contributions they made; and
- modelling good practice in the way the Project approached its task.

The Topic Group process embodied these elements, and created a climate in which staff understood the issues, helped to develop the solutions, and were therefore prepared for change, and willing to contribute to its advancement. Other groups then used this approach, and the new structure for the Social Services Department was developed through a process of wide consultation which ensured that there was a broad commitment to its main components. This represented a change of culture from the approach taken when the Child Care Review Group began its work in 1979. It also contrasted strongly with the way in which reorganisation of the Department was managed in 1982.

Other aspects of BACC's approach included 'networking' with a range of individuals and organisations able to assist the Project; personal support and 'championship' by the Director of Social Services; and using its insider/outsider status to promote change.

The Project's unique position in the Department – outside the formal line management structure, but with a direct relationship to the Director herself, and with the support of an independent Advisory Group – was an important aspect of its working method. It enabled BACC to make contacts directly with people at all levels in the Department, and with a wide range of people and organisations – networks which provided support, information and the means of disseminating ideas. The Advisory Group was particularly crucial to the Project, not just for the contributions of its members to development of policy and practice, but for the support given to the Team throughout its existence. This support was especially invaluable in sustaining the Team during the middle phase of its life cycle, when persistence in completing its task was required. In addition, the Advisory Group gave BACC a degree of independence from the Department, so that it could confront existing practice and challenge outdated policies. The Director's personal interest in BACC complemented the role of the Advisory Group, ensuring its recommendations were given a place on the agenda, and acted upon.

The process and its outcomes

The true test of the process must be whether it resulted in improved services for children and their families. Whilst cause and effect are difficult to untangle, it is clear that during the life of BACC, significant developments took place in the Social Services Department's provision for children and families, and that BACC was involved with all these developments. They can be summarised as follows:

- a strategic framework for development of children and families services and implementation of the Children Act 1989;
- a process and training strategy for implementing the Children Act 1989;
- policies, guidelines, procedures and services which empowered and protected children and young people looked after by the Department;
- a range of services for children in need in the community;
- policies and practices which improved the care of children looked after by the Social Services Department; and
- provision of information for management, staff, service users and the public generally.

Before enumerating these achievements in more detail, it must be acknowledged that the Social Services Department would have had to change during 1990-92 in order to implement the Children Act 1989. The question therefore arises of whether the new developments and changes would have taken place regardless of the management process. Birmingham Action on Child Care might have been merely the instrument of changes which would have occurred whatever approach was taken to managing change. There are a number of indications that BACC's impact was much greater than this.

First, the scale of developments in Birmingham was unusual, and the Department was often in the forefront of developments in implementation of the Children Act. Members of the BACC Team and other staff participated in national developmental work on the Act, and were asked to address conferences and seminars. Policy and planning staff from other local authorities visited BACC to learn more about its work. The Department and the Project contributed to the consultations on the Children Bill and later on the Children Act Guidance and Regulations.

Given the position in 1988, which led to the establishment of BACC, such a range of developments would have required a stronger impetus than merely a requirement to implement the Children Act. Experience suggests that there would have been considerable resistance to the Act and that staff would have argued that its implementation was impossible without major additional resources. There had been considerable staff resistance to implementing the Boarding Out of Children (Foster Parent) Regulations 1988, which came into force on 1st June 1989. By contrast, staff throughout the Department were well-informed about the Children Act at the time it was implemented in October 1991, and appeared to welcome the opportunities which it presented.

Some situations in which progress on BACC's plans was slow or blocked were related to lack of resources. For example, problems in completing the final stages of the Children Act Training Strategy were due to staff shortages related to financial constraints. The difficulty Birmingham and other social services departments had in ensuring that managers of children's homes were professionally qualified was also partly a resource issue.

Some other delays or problems arose from the nature of the organisation. There were specific problems which sprang from the sheer size of the Department (which made communications difficult at times) or from the kinds of frustrations which can arise in any organisation, regardless of size. It was apparent that individuals, simply by not responding promptly to a request for information, action or decision, could hold up the implementation of a programme, even when it had the weight of the Social Services Committee and the Departmental Management Team behind it. This is not to accuse managers of failing to manage or individuals of obstructive behaviour. It was a result of the many competing demands on staff at all levels in the Department and throughout the local authority. The merit of BACC's approach to managing change was that, in involving staff in developing solutions to problems which they had themselves identified, it provided staff with incentives to give priority to the resulting programmes of action. When successful, this had the effect of multiplying the sources of pressure for change. Where Councillors, managers or other staff were not committed to implementation of a decision, or were not convinced of the necessity of change, or failed to give it priority in their own workloads, difficulties were encountered.

Delays and problems resulting from these factors included slow progress in developing the Children's Rights Service; slow progress on setting up a panel of independent visitors; difficulties in securing the accuracy of management information; and delay in developing a procedure for dealing with allegations of abuse against foster carers. At other times, delays and difficulties stemmed from lack of agreement on the best way forward. For example, delay in appointing a Children's Rights Officer and lack of a clear direction for the development of day care provision. Simply enumerating this list makes clear the competing demands on managers' time. Some slippage of programmes of change is inevitable when the scale of change is so great. The impact on some of the same managers and staff of the parallel changes in community care for adults must also be taken into account.

The process developed by BACC was also flawed in operation at times. The critique of *Looking after Birmingham's children* in chapter 5 suggested that it failed to follow through the Project's own systems analysis thoroughly. The length of time taken for the Residential Care and Foster Care Topic Groups to produce their reports stemmed partly from lack of experience in working with the topic group process. With hindsight, the Team felt that the agenda and programme for these two groups should have been more tightly coordinated.

This analysis suggests that some of these difficulties and delays arose *partly* from resource or staffing pressures, but that resources were not the primary or only cause of blockages to BACC's programme. Usually, implementation problems resulted from interruptions in, or failure of, the process. The problems have been highlighted to emphasise the importance of the process as an integral part of the outcome; in themselves, they were often only minor, surmountable impediments to change. When the process worked, as in the main it did, the scale of work undertaken and the number of initiatives set in train was impressive.

BACC's work led to observable changes in the culture of the Department as well as changes in the services provided. The Project's way of working was transferred to other change programmes – for example, in thinking about the new structure needed for the management of the Department. There are inherent problems in creating change within a large organisation with diverse functions. Together with the long lead in time needed for change in the public sector they make changing the culture of the organisation difficult. BACC helped to create the climate that made change possible, as well as influencing *how* it was done.

Outcomes for the children and families service
Empowering children and young people
Throughout its life, BACC was committed to empowering children and young people. The Team saw procedures which enabled children and young people to register their complaints and make

---

Protecting and empowering children and young people: BACC's key achievements

Appointment of a Children's Rights Officer.
Establishment of a Young People's Forum.
New format for planning for children, together with the development of a carefully monitored system of reviews.
Appointment of Independent Reviewing Officers and an Independent Reviews Monitoring Officer.
Contributions to:
  Revision of the Children's Complaints Procedure.
  Guidance on inspecting children's homes for the Inspection Division.
  Proposals for recruiting and supporting dependent Visitors for children in care.
  The Department of Health study of outcomes in child care

their voices heard as amongst the best means of preventing abuse within the child care services. The Project employed two young people who had formerly been in care, and undertook extensive work on children's complaints and rights procedures, on improving the process for reviewing children's cases, and on setting up means for consulting young people looked after by the Department.

Children in need

In thinking creatively about the potential for change encapsulated in the Children Act, the BACC Team recognised the scope for positive support for children and families in their communities. A key

---

Children in need: BACC's work

A broad interpretation of children in need adopted by the Social Services Committee and other relevant Committees of the City Council.
Addressing the needs of Black and minority ethnic children and families — work on *Issues of race, religion language and culture*; work on a glossary of social work terms; publication of a checklist for children's placements; Reports of all the Topic Groups.
Analysis of the use of day nurseries.
Consideration of the appropriate future role of day care provision.
Appointment of a Day Care Review Adviser to undertake the review of day care services required by the Children Act 1989.
Publication of standards for the registration and inspection of day care.
New management structure for services for children under eight.
Analysis of the problem of unallocated child care cases, with a range of solutions: for example —
   Casebusters' teams
   Recruitment and retention incentives
   Workload management
   Establishment of an access service
   Meetings for Team Managers
   Establishment of a Family Support Budget, with guidance on its spending.
   A service for sexually abused girls
Work on responding to juvenile prostitution

concept of the Children Act, 'children in need' was given a broad interpretation by Birmingham City Council as a result of BACC's work, laying the foundations for the development of a corporate commitment to supporting children in their own homes, by provision of a range of services. The philosophical shift entailed was demonstrated at the second Birmingham Child Care Conference, where the concept of a 'child-friendly city' received support. Initiatives undertaken or set in train by BACC included work on improving the appropriateness and accessibility of the Department's services to Black and minority ethnic children and their families. Considerable attention was given to day care provision for children under eight: with new provision for working parents, additional staff to undertake registration and inspection, and a new management structure. Initiatives were also developed to reduce the number of children on care orders who were without a social worker. Additional services were developed or planned for children and their families, through the establishment of a family support budget.

Children looked after by social services
Detailed work was undertaken to improve the provision for children looked after by the department – both in foster care and residential care. These included improvement of recruitment, training, payment, and support of foster carers. A fee-paid fostering project was established and exceeded its targets. It was able to recruit a significant number of Black and minority ethnic foster carers. Foster care was made available to older children by the Remand and Teenage Fostering Project, which was later expanded to cover the whole city. The Residential Care Topic Group made an in-depth study of the state of the Department's residential child care service, and provided detailed recommendations for its improvement. BACC also contributed to the first induction course for new residential workers, and work was started on developing specific roles for children's homes. In cooperation with other departments and voluntary organisations, BACC also helped to develop services for young people leaving care.

Information and communications
BACC was committed from the start to improving communications within the Department. This included publication and dissemination of its own newsletters, papers, and reports, as well as work on information and statistics for management, information leaflets for parents and children, and information packs for child care workers.

Provision for children looked after by the local authority: BACC's major contributions

Two major reports on foster care and residential care – with detailed recommendations.
Work on a procedure for dealing with allegations of abuse against foster carers.
Establishment of a fee-paid fostering scheme, and its expansion throughout the city.
Increased recruitment of Black and minority ethnic foster carers.
Expansion of the teenage fostering project.
Improved support to foster carers – facilities for the Birmingham Foster Care Association, membership of the National Foster Care Association for all foster carers, and insurance.
Regular consultation with the Birmingham Foster Care Association.
Contribution to an induction programme for residential social workers.
Continued targeting of qualification training on residential social workers.
Development of specific roles for children's homes, and single sex children's homes.
Liaison with the Education Department on education of children in care.
Contribution to Bristol University Outcomes Study, with positive benefits for participants.
Establishment of a leaving care service.
Joint work with the Housing Department on housing for young people leaving care.
Establishment of a project for prevention of youth homelessness.
Production of the leaving care guide 'Moving On, Moving In', as a video and book.

Information for child care

Improvement of quality and use of management information.
Numerous publications – newsletters, research guides, summaries of key publications and of the Children Act – see Appendix 4.
Preparation of information packs for child care workers.
Leaving care guide.
Leaflets for service users.

Management of change: a strategy for local government

The difficulties and contradictions faced by management in local government were summarised in chapter 2. There can be no simple solutions to managing change and improving services, when some changes are not welcomed, and services must be improved in spite of restrictions or reductions in revenue. In the 1990s, local authorities are required to compete with the private sector, to enable private and voluntary organisations to provide services, to contract for services rather than providing them directly, to ensure consumer choice and participation, and to give value for money. While many local authorities see these requirements as challenges and opportunities, they also undoubtedly represent a threat to established ways of doing things, to people's jobs, and to their sense of security. Some of them are mutually incompatible. Local government is likely to function in a climate of continuous change for some years. At the same time, the recession in 1992/93 has made the expansion or improvement of services through growth of income unlikely. These constraints apply to the whole of local government.

Nevertheless, the approach to managing change and improving services developed by BACC was successful within a context of only marginal growth in revenue. It ensured that many staff were well-informed about the real possibilities and boundaries within which they worked. They were involved in helping to identify the problems and solutions, within the constraints of central and local policy, resources, and staffing. Consequently, they were motivated to cooperate in improving and developing services, whilst retaining a sense of perspective and commitment to giving good service when the organisation was under pressure. They began to share a sense of the organisation as a whole, which enabled them to value their contribution, and to work with, rather than in competition with, colleagues from other parts of the Social Services Department and elsewhere.

A full overview and evaluation of literature on the management of change is beyond the scope of this book, but some observations can be made about the relationship of BACC's approach to creating change to two management texts which have been influential in local government [Peters and Austin, 1985; Kanter, 1990]. Peters and Austin emphasise the importance of 'management by wandering about' – of being a visible manager, who talks to customers, and is available to employees. They stress the need to pay attention to detail, whilst striving to achieve a vision. Their approach combines giving employees the training, skills and resources to achieve results, with a brutal intensity of pressure to perform. It stresses leadership from the top, and a single minded 'passion for excellence', as well as emphasising that everyone in the organisation has skills and knowledge of value [Peters and Austin, 1985]. Despite the emphasis on caring for employees, however, the cost of excellence is high for individuals:

We are frequently asked if it is possible to 'have it all' – a full and satisfying personal life and a full and satisfying, hard-working, professional one. Our answer is: No. The price of excellence is time, energy, attention and focus, at the very same time that energy, attention and focus could have gone toward enjoying your daughter's soccer game. [Peters and Austin, 1985]

The contradictions are summed up by Kanter [1990]:

- Think strategically and invest in the future – but keep the numbers up today.
- Be entrepreneurial and take risks – but don't cost the business anything by failing.
- Continue to do everything you're currently doing even better – and spend more time communicating with employees, serving on teams, and launching new projects.
- Know every detail of your business – but delegate more responsibility to others.
- Become passionately dedicated to 'visions' and fanatically committed to carrying them out – but be flexible, responsive, and able to change direction quickly.
- Speak up, be a leader, set the direction – but be participative, listen well, cooperate.
- Throw yourself wholeheartedly into the entrepreneurial game and the long hours it takes – and stay fit.
- Succeed, succeed, succeed – and raise terrific children. [Ibid.]

The kind of management that requires total dedication to the organisation, at the expense of family and community, is not feasible for local authorities attempting to promote equal opportunities in both employment and service delivery. Whilst leadership and vision are important, knowing what the customers want and seeing that they get it are essential. The real world of local government management also requires attention to local political realities, to local opinion, to the media, to central government, to other organisations, and to a multiplicity of service users, their families and carers. The BACC Team was highly visible, in touch with service users, foster carers, and staff at all levels. It was committed to high standards, and to modelling those standards in the way in which it worked itself. While leadership, together with a 'vision' for the Department's future, was seen as important, so was the contribution to be made by staff throughout the Department. Development of policy, principles and practice was a cooperative enterprise, involving large numbers of people.

Kanter argued that the contradictions of the pursuit of excellence can be minimised, and stressed the importance of cooperation, communication, and valuing everyone's contribution [Kanter, 1990]. The first major component of her management strategy consists of seeking:

that combination of businesses, array of internal services, and structures for organising them that promotes synergies – a whole that multiplies the value of the parts. [Ibid.]

She suggests that achieving this can enable a company to 'do more with less' – as local authorities are constantly exhorted to do – but only if the transition is well managed:

Among the by-products of significant restructuring are discontinuity, disorder, and distraction... The management challenge is to retain value and increase it by handling transitions so that they reinforce commitment and build the cooperation that brings synergies. [Ibid.]

She believes this can be achieved by minimising the losses people must face, providing them with positive visions of the future, and reducing the uncertainty of the present by active communication. Once the transition has been made, the emphasis continues to be on communications, on promoting cooperation between employees, and on leadership from the top combined with organisational structures which encourage teamwork and innovation.

Second, Kanter's strategy involves developing close working alliances with other organisations – pooling resources and linking systems to create a larger joint capacity, but without the risks entailed in a take-over bid. Partnerships and alliances allow participants to retain their individuality and flexibility, whilst enhancing their responsiveness. In a local authority context, this is the development of corporate working across departmental boundaries, of partnerships with the private sector, and of service level agreements with voluntary organisations, rather than the 'empire building' which has sometimes characterised large local authority departments.

Third, Kanter emphasises creating a climate of innovation, where new ideas can be exploited and developed, through the establishment of 'newstreams' – 'official channels to speed the flow of new ideas'. 'Newstreams' are risky and controversial; they use up emotional energy, generate new knowledge rapidly, require good communications to bring ideas together, and need teamwork and commitment to achieve results. Because they function differently from the rest of the organisation and require a degree of autonomy from it, they may generate suspicion amongst traditional managers.

Throughout, Kanter emphasises the importance of paying attention to the process of managing change; her strategies will not work if they are employed mindlessly or casually:

Instead of being able to do more with less, companies that do not move in more people-sensitive and less bureaucratic directions, more cooperative and less hierarchical directions, will find themselves doing less with more. [Kanter, 1990]

There are, of course, crucial differences between businesses and local government; these were identified in chapter 2, and can be summarised as follows:

- day-to-day control of the organisation by politicians, with their own value systems;
- the requirements and constraints of the legislative framework;
- the multiplicity of 'customers' and others to whom the organisation is accountable – the electorate, elected members, service users (themselves with competing interests), the general public, and central government; and
- operation in a 'market' governed by very different rules – in which, for example, excess demand cannot usually be controlled by price rationing or be met by providing more goods and services.

In addition, other organisations and agencies may lack incentives to work in partnership with the local authority – for example, the health service. Others – such as voluntary organisations and community groups – may be so dependent upon it financially that their individuality and flexibility are swamped. Partnerships may be difficult to develop between departments of the local authority.

These differences make the task of managing change and transitions more complex. Nevertheless, Kanter's strategy can be adapted for local government.

The principles behind the three components of Kanter's strategy were apparent in BACC's approach to promoting change in the service for children and families. The emphasis on understanding and using the system, rather than allowing changes in one section to create unintended consequences for other parts of the service, creates the synergy – the whole which is more than the sum of its parts – which Kanter discusses. BACC's approach to changing the culture of the department through involving staff, service users and foster carers in locating, developing and promoting good practice; and the way in which its topic group process was utilised for the management of the departmental restructuring, were departmental strategies for managing transitions. The constant flow of information in and out of the Project was crucial to this strategy. The ability to implement the Children Act was enhanced by corporate working with other departments and cooperation with voluntary organisations. BACC itself functioned as a 'newstream', bringing together a small, committed team, to work intensively for a defined period, to improve the service for children and families. The outcomes indicate that the method was effective.

None of BACC's strategies for managing change is specific to children's services or to the personal social services. They can be used by any public service organisation, in the voluntary or public sector, to help it to face the constant demand to 'do more with less', and to give value for money and to raise standards.

The future: the world of the Citizen's Charter

In the 1990s, public services are being set more and more measurable standards to achieve, through the development and monitoring of performance contracts, the Citizen's Charter and similar initiatives designed to improve services. The emphasis is on choice for service users and consumers, on consumer rights, and on listening to service users. These developments are essential for the increased accountability which they permit. They may, however, present future difficulties if they take no account of the views, skills and needs of staff at all levels in the organisation. Staff may become cynical if their views are ignored while service users are repeatedly consulted. Professionals in the public service may suffer from declining morale if the judgements of lay assessors and inspectors are frequently preferred to theirs.

Performance management is essentially a top-down process, which does not combine easily with a commitment to involving staff at all levels. Aims, objectives, goals, requirements and information are 'cascaded' downwards, and there is no inbuilt mechanism for information to flow upwards, other than in the form of performance indicators. It complements the Citizen's Charter in setting clear standards for staff to achieve, sometimes with penalties for failure. There are, however, real dangers for a system without 'feedback loops'. It was the lack of good feedback about the impact of policy and practice guidelines at the grassroots which contributed to the problems identified in the children and families services in Birmingham in 1987/88. Measurement of performance would not have identified these problems. Moreover, as the analysis of the effectiveness of the BACC process for managing change showed, staff at all levels can, deliberately or otherwise, thwart the achievement of imposed objectives. In an economic climate where workers fear redundancy, and the powers of the professions and the trade unions have been eroded, there is a real danger of workers in the public services feeling disempowered and disillusioned. In a situation of constant change, the management of transition is a daily task.

The approach taken by BACC to managing change is costly in staff time; but the alternatives may be more costly. They include increasing numbers of complaints, disciplinary actions and grievances; even the possibility of strikes. Performance management on its own cannot protect the organisation from poor practice, which may lead to referrals to the Ombudsman, legal action and the payment of compensation, as well as costly inquiries and investigations. High standards and good services depend on people, and on their morale and goodwill. Staff in local government need to be actively involved in the development of their own services if their morale is to be maintained. Without the commitment of staff, there will be conflict within the organisation and with others in its field. The reputation of local government itself will suffer, giving arguments to those who would wish to see its eventual replacement.

The lesson to be learned from the history of BACC (and of child care in Birmingham) is that change can yield positive results if it is actively managed taking into account the impact of change on the whole system, and valuing the needs and views of service users and their carers, as well as the contributions, views, and needs of staff at all levels.

References

BACC – see Birmingham Action on Child Care

Bebbington, A and Miles, J (1989) The background of children who enter local authority care, *The British Journal of Social Work*, 19, 5, October

Bernard, J (1990) *Innovation in a Local Authority Social Services Department: Content, Context and Process.* Unpublished MA Thesis, Polytechnic of East London

Berridge, D (1985) *Children's Homes.* Basil Blackwell

Birmingham Action on Child Care (1990a) *Working Paper No 1: method.* Birmingham Social Services Department

(1990b) *Working Paper No 2: A systems approach to child care planning.* Birmingham Social Services Department

(1990c) *Discussion Paper: proposal to unblock the Placements System.* Birmingham Social Services Department

(1990d) *A Report on Unallocated Child Care Cases, Report to Birmingham Social Services Departmental Management Team.* Birmingham Social Services Department

(1991a) *Review form for children looked after, with guidance notes.* Birmingham Social Services Department

(1991b) *Local authority support for children and families, Report to the Birmingham Social Services Departmental Management Team.* Birmingham Social Services Department

(1991c) *The Children Act 1989: Directions for Strategic Planning in Work with Children and Families, Report to Birmingham Social Services Departmental Management Team.* Birmingham Social Services Department

(1991d) *Report of the Foster Care Topic Group, Report to Birmingham Social Services Departmental Management Team.*

Birmingham Social Services Department
(1991e) *City-Wide Survey of Day Nursery Usage*. Birmingham Social Services Department
(1991f) *The use and availability of day nurseries provided by the Social Services Committee*. Birmingham Social Services Department
(1992a) *Report of the Residential Care Service Topic Group, Report to Birmingham Social Services Departmental Management Team*. Birmingham Social Services Department
(1992b) *Allegations of abuse in foster care, Report to Birmingham Social Services Departmental Management Team*. Birmingham Social Services Department
(1992c) *Quarterly Progress Report on Unallocated Child Care Cases, Report to the Birmingham Social Services Departmental Management Team* (February). Birmingham Social Services Department
(1992d) *Notes of the BACC Advisory Group meeting held on Thursday 30th April*. Birmingham Social Services Department
(1992e) *Report of the Day Nursery Survey Consultation Exercise*. Birmingham Social Services Department
(1992f) *The Children Act 1989: Issues of Race, Religion, Language and Culture*. Birmingham Social Services Department

Birmingham Action on Child Care/National Council for Voluntary Child Care Organisations (1991) *Partnership in prospect? report of a BACC/NCVCCO Seminar*. Birmingham Social Services Department

Birmingham City Council (1988) *Minutes of a meeting of the Social Services Committee held on 14th September*
(undated (1992)) *Poverty in Birmingham: City Council Strategy*. Directorate of Community Affairs & Policy Co-ordination, Birmingham

Corporate Child Care Steering Group (1991) *Report of the Corporate Child Care Steering Group to the Chief Executive: Options for Child Care Development during the 1990s*

Birmingham Social Services Department (1988a) *Report of the Director of Social Services to the Social Services Committee: Procedure for dealing with complaints*, January
(1988b) *Report of the Director of Social Services to the Social Services Committee: investigation into allegations of complaints concerning the care of children...*, September

(1988c) *Report of the Director of Social Services to the Social Services Committee: Complaints by, and on behalf of, children in care*, October
(1988d) *Report of the Director of Social Services to the Social Services Committee: policy and service review: services for children and families*, October
(1988e) *Report of the Director of Social Services to the Social Services Committee: Members' enquiries, complaints and rota visit reports*, December
(1989a) *Report of the Director of Social Services to the Social Services Committee: Review of complaints by and behalf of children in care: a children's rights service*, October
(1989b) *Report of the Director of Social Services to the Social Services Committee: Complaints' Procedures*, December
(1990a) *Facts and Figures 1990*
(1990b) *Policies for People*
(1990c) *Joint Report of Directors of Economic Development, Education and Social Services to the Social Services Committee: Child Care – A City-Wide Strategy*, February
(1990d) *Report to the Departmental Management Team: Child Care Strategy: follow up report*, May
(1990e) *Report to the Departmental Management Team: City Child Care Strategy: significance for SSD*, May
(1990f) *Report of the Director of Social Services to the Social Services (Child Care Sub-) Committee: A Children's Rights Service*, June
(1990g) *Report of the Director of Social Services to the Social Services Committee: Requirements of the Children Act 1989 and the NHS and Community Care Bill 1990: inspection and registration*, June
(1990h) *Report of the Director of Social Services to the Social Services Committee: Recruitment of short term foster carers – proposal for a pilot project in East Birmingham*, October
(1990i) *Report of the Director of Social Services to the Social Services Committee: The Shape of Things to Come: the organisation and structure of the Social Services Department*, December
(1991a) *Facts and Figures 1991*
(1991b) *Report of the Director of Social Services to the Social Services Committee: The Shape of Things to Come: a new framework for the Social Services Department*, July

(1991c) *Report of the Director of Birmingham Action on Child Care to the Social Services (Child Care Sub-) Committee: Children in need – the local interpretation and the corporate response*, September
(1991d) *Report of the Director of Birmingham Action on Child Care to the Social Services (Child Care Sub-) Committee: Children Act 1989: Ten Basic Policy Statements for Work with Children and Families*, September
(1991e) *Report of the Director of Social Services to the Social Services Committee: Looking after Birmingham's Children: a five year outline plan for change*, October
(1991f) *Report to the Departmental Management Team: Independent Visitors*, October
(1991g) *Report of the Director of Social Services to the Social Services Committee: The Shape of Things to Come: a new framework for the Social Services Department: progress report*, November
(1991h) *Report of the Director of Birmingham Action on Child Care to the Social Services (Child Care Sub-) Committee: A Quality Foster Care Service for the 1990s*, December
(1992a) *Joint Report of the Director of Social Services and City Treasurer: Revenue and Capital Budgets, Probable Outturn 1991/92 and Provisional Budget Allocations 1992/93*, February
(1992b) *Report of the Director of Social Services to the Social Services (Child Care Sub-) Committee: Evaluation of Pilot Project in East Birmingham to recruit short term foster carers for children under 12*, February
(1992c) *Procedures for Comments, Suggestions, Complaints about Services for Adults: Your Right to be Heard*, July
(1992d) *Procedures for Comments, Suggestions, Complaints about Services for Children and Young People: Your Right to be Heard: Children's Representation and Complaints Procedure*, July
(1992e) *Joint Report of the Director of Social Services and the Chief Education Officer to the Social Services (Child Care Sub-) Committee: Joint Action Plan between the Social Services Department and the Education Department*, September
(1992f) *Report of the Director of Social Services to the Social Services (Child Care Sub-) Committee: The Children Act 1989 – After Care – progress report*, September
(1992g) *Report of the Director of Social Services to the Social Services (Child Care Sub-) Committee: Use of Social Services Day*

Nurseries for Children of Working Parents, September
(1992h) *Report to the Departmental Management Team from the Independent Reviewing Officers and the Independent Reviews Monitoring Officer*, October
(1993a) *Joint Report of the Director of Social Services and the City Treasurer: Provisional Revenue and Capital Budget Allocations 1993/94*, February
(forthcoming – 1993b) *The Language of the Children Act in Translation*
Blom-Cooper, L (1987) *A Child in Mind: protection of children in a responsible society: the Report of the Commission of Inquiry into ... the Death of Kimberley Carlile*. London Borough of Greenwich
Brown, B (1989) Children: only a beginning, in Philpot, T (editor) *The residential opportunity? the Wagner Report and After*. Reed Business Publishing/Community Care
Bryson M and Roering, W D (1987) Applying Private-Sector Strategic Planning in the Public Sector, *APA Journal*, Winter
Butler-Sloss (1988) *Report of the Inquiry into Child Abuse in Cleveland 1987*; Cm 412. HMSO
Clarke, J and Langan, M (forthcoming) Restructuring Welfare: the British Welfare regime in the 1980s, in Cochrane, A and Clarke, J *Issues in Social Policy: the UK in International Context*. Sage
Clarke, J and Newman, J (1992) *Managing to survive: dilemmas of changing organisational forms in the public sector*, Paper presented to the Social Policy Association Conference, Nottingham, July
Cliffe, D with D Berridge (1992) *Closing Children's Homes: an end to residential child care?* National Children's Bureau
Cochrane, A and Clarke, J (forthcoming) *Issues in Social Policy: the UK in International Context*. Sage
Coffin, G (1989) *Birmingham Action on Child Care: An outline of a major project to review the services for children and families provided by Birmingham Social Services Department*. Birmingham Social Services Department, January
Community Care Special Action Project (n.d.) *Community Care: Building a Common Agenda*. Birmingham City Council
Cornish, D and Clarke, R (1976) *Residential Treatment and its Effect on Delinquency*, Home Office Research Study No 32. HMSO
Curtis, M (1946) *Report of the Care of Children (Curtis) Committee*, Cmd 6922. HMSO
Department of Health (1989a) *An Introduction to the Children Act 1989*. HMSO

(1989b) *Caring for People: Community Care in the Next Decade and Beyond*, Cm 849. HMSO
(1989c) *The Care of Children: Principles and Practice in Regulations and Guidance*. HMSO
(1990) *Inter-departmental Review of Adoption Law: Discussion Paper No 1: the nature and effect of adoption*, Department of Health
(1991a) *Child Abuse: A study of Inquiry Reports, 1980-1989*. HMSO
(1991b) *Patterns and Outcomes in Child Placement: messages from current research and their implications*. HMSO
(1991c) *The Children Act 1989: Guidance and Regulations: Volume 1: Court Orders*. HMSO
(1991d) *The Children Act 1989: Guidance and Regulations: Volume 2: Family Support, Day Care and Educational Provision for Young Children*. HMSO
(1991e) *The Children Act 1989: Guidance and Regulations: Volume 3: Family Placements*. HMSO
(1991f) *The Children Act 1989: Guidance and Regulations: Volume 4: Residential Care*. HMSO
(1991g) *The Children Act 1989: Guidance and Regulations: Volume 5: Independent Schools*. HMSO
(1991h) *The Children Act 1989: Guidance and Regulations: Volume 6: Children with Disabilities*. HMSO
(1991i) *The Children Act 1989: Guidance and Regulations: Volume 7: Guardians ad Litem and other Court Related Issues*. HMSO
(1991j) *The Children Act 1989: Guidance and Regulations: Volume 8: Private Fostering and Miscellaneous*. HMSO
(1991k) *The Children Act 1989: Guidance and Regulations: Volume 9: Adoption Issues*. HMSO
(1993) *The Children Act and Day Care for Young Children: Registration*, Local Authority Circular LAC(93)1, January
Department of Health and Social Security (1974) *Report of the Committee of Inquiry into the Care and Supervision provided in relation to Maria Colwell*. HMSO
(1985) *Social Work Decisions in Child Care: recent research findings and their implications*. HMSO
(1987) *The Law on Child Care and Family Services*, Cm62. HMSO

Department of Recreation and Community Services (1992) *Report of the Director of Recreation and Community Services to the Social Services (Child Care Sub-) Committee: Children Act 1989*, April

Eekelaar, J and Dingwall, R (1990) *The Reform of Child Care Law: a practical guide to the Children Act 1989.* Routledge

France, E (1990) *Inter-departmental Review of Adoption Law: Background paper No 1: International Perspectives.* Department of Health

Gardner, R (1991) A definition of need, *Community Care*, 30 May

Giller, H (1989) Young Offenders, in Kahan, B (editor) *Child Care Research, Policy and Practice.* Hodder and Stoughton

Handy, C B (1985) *Understanding Organizations.* Penguin (Third Edition)

Hennessy, E and others (1992) *Children and Day Care: lessons from research.* Paul Chapman Publishing

Home Office, Department of Health, Department of Education and Science, Welsh Office (1991) *Working Together Under the Children Act 1989: a guide to arrangements for inter-agency co-operation for the protection of children from abuse.* HMSO

House of Commons: Health Committee (1991) *Public Expenditure on Personal Social Services: Child Protection Services.* HMSO

House of Commons: Social Services Committee (1984) *Children in Care.* HMSO

Howe, Lady (1992) *The Quality of Care: Report of the Residential Staffs Inquiry chaired by Lady Howe.* Local Government Management Board

In Need Implementation Group, The (1991) *The Children Act 1989 and children in need: make it the answer not the problem.* c/o NCVCCO

Jackson, S (1989) Education of children in care, in Kahan, B (editor) *Child Care Research, Policy and Practice.* Hodder and Stoughton

Kahan, B (editor) (1989) *Child Care Research, Policy and Practice.* Hodder and Stoughton

Kanter, R Moss (1990) *When Giants Learn to Dance: Mastering the challenges of strategy, management and careers in the 1990s.* Unwin

Kelly, D (1989) Practice: the barriers and the principles, *in* Philpot, T (editor) *The residential opportunity? the Wagner Report and After.* Reed Business Publishing/Community Care

Levy, A and Kahan, B (1991) *The Pindown Experience and the Protection of Children: The Report of the Staffordshire Child Care Inquiry 1990.* Staffordshire County Council

Local Government Management Board (1991) *Survey of Social Services Employment, 1990.* Local Government Management Board

London Borough of Brent (1985) *A Child in Trust: The Report of the Panel of Inquiry into the Circumstances Surrounding the Death of Jasmine Beckford.* London Borough of Brent

London Borough of Greenwich (1987) *A Child in Mind: Protection of Children in a Responsible Society. Report of the Inquiry into the Circumstances Surrounding the Death of Kimberly Carlile.* London Borough of Greenwich

London Borough of Lambeth (1987) *Whose Child? The Report of the Panel Appointed to Inquire into the Death of Tyra Henry.* London Borough of Lambeth

Macdonald, S (1991) *All Equal Under the Act? – a practical guide to the Children Act 1989 for social workers.* Race Equality Unit, National Institute for Social Work

Marsh, P (1990) Changing practice in child care – the Children Act 1989, in *Adoption and Fostering,* 14, 4

Millham, S and others (1986) *Lost in Care: the Problems of Maintaining Links between Children in Care and their Families.* Gower

Monkton, Sir W (1945) *Report by Sir Walter Monkton on the circumstances which led to the boarding out of Dennis and Terence O'Neill,* Cmd 6636. HMSO

Morris, A and Giller, H (1987) *Understanding Juvenile Justice.* Croom Helm

Moss, M (1990) Introduction, in NAYPIC, *Abuse in the Care System.* NAYPIC (National Association of Young People in Care)

NACRO (National Association for the Care and Resettlement of Offenders) (1991) *Seizing the Initiative: NACRO's Final report on the DHSS Intermediate Treatment Initiative to Divert Juvenile Offenders from Care and Custody: 1983-1989.* NACRO

National Children's Home (1992) *The Report of the Committee of Enquiry into Children and Young People who sexually abuse other children.* National Children's Home

NAYPIC (National Association of Young People in Care) (1990) *Abuse in the Care System.* NAYPIC

Nixon, S (1991) *Unsubstantiated allegations of abuse against foster carers: a brief research report for Birmingham Social Services Department.* University of Birmingham, School of Continuing

Studies, June
(1992) *Outline proposals for a research, development and training project on abuse and allegations of abuse in foster care: developing a risk management strategy in foster care.* School of Continuing Studies, University of Birmingham, January

OPCS (Office of Population Censuses and Surveys) (1992) *1991 Census: County Monitor: West Midlands* (CEN 91 CM 43). OPCS (September)

Open University, The (1991) *The Children Act 1989: Putting it into Practice.* The Open University

Osborne, S P (1992) Lifting the siege? Organisational culture and social services departments, *Local Government Policy Making*, 18, 5, May

Parker, R and others (eds) (1991) *Assessing Outcomes in Child Care: The Report of an Independent Working Party established by the Department of Health.* HMSO

Parton, N (1989) Child Abuse, in Kahan, B (editor) *Child Care Research, Policy and Practice.* Hodder and Stoughton

Peters, T and Austin, N (1985) *A Passion for Excellence: the leadership difference.* Fontana/Collins

Phillipson, J (1989) Race and gender: a woman's chance to choose, in Philpot, T (editor) *The residential opportunity? the Wagner Report and After.* Reed Business Publishing/Community Care

Philp, A F (1963) *Family Failure: a study of 129 families with multiple problems.* Faber

Philpot, T (editor) (1989) *The residential opportunity? the Wagner Report and After.* Reed Business Publishing/Community Care

Poyser, A (1990) *From Dennis O'Neill to the Children Act 1989: presentation to the Advisory Group Conference 7 December 1989*, Birmingham Social Services Department

Pugh, D S (1978) Understanding and Managing Organisational Change, *London Business School Journal*, 3, 2

Renier, O (1990) Reflections on the Children Act 1948, unpublished paper, quoted Poyser, A *From Dennis O'Neill to the Children Act 1989: presentation to the Advisory Group Conference 7 December 1989*, Birmingham Social Services Department

Rowe, J and Lambert, L (1973) *Children Who Wait.* Association of British Adoption Agencies

Seebohm, Sir F (1968) *Report of the Committee on Local Authority and Allied Personal Social Services*, Cmnd 3703. HMSO

REFERENCES

Shorter Oxford English Dictionary, The (1973, revised 1984) Oxford University Press

Social Services Inspectorate (1989) *The Residential Care of Children: Birmingham Social Services Department: Report of inspection of nine children's homes*. Department of Health

(1990) *The Residential Care of Children: Birmingham Social Services Department: Report of follow up inspection of nine children's homes*. Department of Health

Thoburn, J (1990) *Inter-departmental Review of Adoption Law: Background Paper No 2: Review of Research relating to Adoption*. Department of Health

Utting, Sir W (1991) *Children in the Public Care: a review of residential child care*. HMSO

Wagner, G (1988) *Residential Care: A positive choice. Report of the Independent Review of Residential Care*. HMSO

Warner, N (1992) *Choosing with Care: The Report of the Committee of Inquiry into the selection, development and management of staff in children's homes*. HMSO

Wilson, E (1977) *Women and the Welfare State*. Tavistock

Appendix 1: Birmingham Action on Child Care: A Chronology

October 1988
The Social Services Committee agreed to establish a major review of services for children and families.
The Director of Social Services, Adrianne Jones, approached Barbara Kahan, Chair of the National Children's Bureau, and asked her to act as consultant to the new project and to chair its advisory group. Barbara Kahan agreed, and suggested that it would be important to record the work of the project once it was finished.

November 1988
Children Bill announced in the Queen's Speech.

December 1988
Children Bill published.

January 1989
The *Outline* for the project discussed by the Management Team, and the title Birmingham Action on Child Care agreed.

February 1989
The Project's Deputy Director Ben Brown appointed.
Ben spent his first three months visiting teams and establishments on behalf of BACC.

March 1989
Newsletter No 1 distributed; it focused on the terms of reference for the project, and the appointment of its staff, and included a request for comments and contributions.

April 1989

Newsletter No 2 distributed; it dealt with the appointment of the Project Director, reviewed the work undertaken by Ben Brown, explained how BACC would handle complaints, and again included an invitation to people to contribute.

June 1989

Project Director, Paul Sutton, took up his appointment.
Newsletter No 3 distributed, summarising the key messages in the Children Bill and looking at the implications for children with disabilities.

July 1989

Meetings held to decide on the membership and work of the Advisory Group.
Newsletter No 4 distributed, which brought readers up to date with BACC's progress – the appointment of Paul Sutton and other staff members, the move into the BACC offices, and the setting up of the Advisory group, and reviewed work underway.
The Departmental Management Team discussed:
- management information: children in care;
- managing a multi-racial workforce; and
- the Social Services Inspectorate's Report on Residential Care for Children in Birmingham; BACC was asked to prepare an action plan.

Community care proposals announced by the Government.

September 1989

BACC Planning Days held, to prepare the Project's programme of work; the Children Bill Seminar series was planned.
The Project Director went to London to work on the production of two key Department of Health Publications, *Principles and Practice* and *Patterns and Outcomes...* [see References].
The Director, Project Director and Barbara Kahan attended a conference, where BACC was presented and a number of useful contacts were made.
Plans for a children's rights officer announced.
A recruitment campaign for residential care workers for children's homes was run under the headline 'The toughest jobs in Brum'.
Children Bill 1988, Children Act 1989: a summary of its main provisions published by BACC and widely distributed.
The Birmingham Foster Care Association set up, with support from the Department.

October 1989

Children Bill Seminars run by BACC at the Department's Training Centre and attended by nearly 300 staff.
An Open Day held in the BACC Offices.

November 1989

First meeting with Rainer Foundation, to discuss work with sexually abused girls.
Newsletter No 5 distributed; it focused on news from the Project, the Children Act seminars, children's rights, and the Advisory Group.
Children Bill received the Royal assent and became the Children Act.
The White Paper on Community Care, *Caring for People*, published by the Department of Health.

December 1989

The BACC Advisory Group held its first meeting; members were briefed on child care history, terms of reference for BACC etc.
Second series of Children Act Seminars held at the Departmental Training Centre.
The Children Act 1989: a summary of its main provisions published and widely distributed within the Department by BACC.

January 1990

Findings paper no 1: Planning – summarised SSI Report, *A sense of direction: planning in social work with children – a review of SSI reports*, Department of Health 1989.
The Departmental Management Team discussed a first progress report from BACC and its Working Paper No. 1: Methodology.
The Social Services (Child Care Sub-) Committee received reports on:
- BACC: First Progress Report;
- The Children Act 1989;
- the Department's response to The residential care of children: SSI inspection of nine Birmingham children's homes.

February 1990

Planning for Children Topic Group held its first meeting.
Newsletter No 6 distributed; it covered the preparations being made for the implementation of the Children Act, including the establishment of Children Act Implementation Group.
Working Paper No 1: Project methodology published by BACC.
The first batch of newly-recruited residential social workers completed their induction training.

The Departmental Management Team discussed 'Major changes: community care and the Children Act'; Paul Sutton brought the Team up-to-date with BACC's work; the common issues in the Children Act and the NHS and Community Care Act as well as the tensions between the Acts were identified.

March 1990

BACC Advisory Group held its second meeting and discussed the BACC methodology papers, the proposal for a child care conference, and the brief for the three topic groups which were being set up.
First meeting of the Children Act Implementation Group.
Three seminars for middle managers on the Children Act run by BACC.
Newsletter No 7 distributed; it described the establishment of the Topic Groups, set out the 1991/92 budget growth, and included a number of small news items.
Findings paper No 2: Glossary, explaining jargon and abbreviations published by BACC.
Findings Paper No 3: SSI Report summarised the report of the SSI inspection of nine children's homes in Birmingham.

April 1990

Residential Care Topic Group held its first meeting.
City Wide Child Care Strategy Steering Group held its first meeting.
The Departmental Management Team discussed
- proposal for a Birmingham Annual Child Care Conference – agreed in principle;
- day nursery usage – small survey to be carried out to identify who the users of day nurseries are;
- divisional strategies for children's services – BACC offered assistance in producing these;
- management information: children in care.

May 1990

Adoption and Fostering Topic group held its first meeting.
Information packs on the Children Act 1989 and the NHS and Community Care Act 1990 prepared by BACC and staff from the Policy and Performance Review Division.
Working Paper No 2: A systems approach to child care planning: published by BACC.
Newsletter No 8 distributed by BACC; it again covered Children Act implementation and budget growth, as well as induction for residential workers, leaving care grants, and the outcome of a research study of Home on Trial.

The Departmental Management Team discussed
- the City-Wide Child Care Strategy (twice);
- management information: children;
- purchaser/provider split.

Children Act 1989: Consultation Paper No 1: Secure accommodation published and distributed by the Department of Health.

June 1990

The BACC Advisory Group looked at the conference proposal again, and discussed the progress of the residential topic group, implementation and training for the Children Act, attitudes, partnership and access to children in care (that is, contact).
BACC Project Director made a presentation to Chief Officers on the Children Act 1989.
The Services for Children Under Eight Topic Group started meeting.
Newsletter No 9 distributed; it brought readers up to date with the Children Act and gave the membership of the Children Act Implementation Group.
Findings Paper No 5: Principles and Practice, summarising *The Care of Children: Principles and Practice in Guidance and Regulations*, Department of Health, 1990. Published by BACC.
The Departmental Management Team discussed:
- child care issues generally;
- foster care – complaints procedure;
- implementation of the Boarding Out Regulations;
- insurance for foster carers;
- recruitment of foster carers – pilot fee paid project;
- the local authority as a good parent – participation in the Department of Health Outcomes Study;
- unallocated child care cases.

The Social Services (Child Care Sub-) Committee discussed:
- the local authority as a good parent – agreeing to participate in the Outcomes Study;
- a children's rights service;
- proposal for an annual Birmingham Child Care Conference.

Children Act 1989: Consultation Paper No 2: Policy and standards of day care and educational services published by the Department of Health.

July 1990

BACC Project Director gave a presentation to the Department of Recreation and Community Services Management Team on the Children Act.

Newsletter No 10 distributed; it dealt with the Department of Health Children Act consultation process, children's rights, the proposed child care conference, the topic groups, teenage fostering and the induction courses for residential workers.

The Departmental Management Team discussed the impact of social work language on Black and minority ethnic people – BACC offered assistance in dealing with language issues.

Children Act 1989: Consultation Paper No 3: LA provision of services for families with children in need
No 4: Aftercare
No 5: Co-ordination and duty to review day care services
No 6: Refuges for children at risk
published by the Department of Health.

Barbara Kahan began work in Staffordshire on the *Pindown Inquiry*.

August 1990

BACC carried out structured interviews with Team Managers about unallocated cases.

The Departmental Management Team discussed Inter country adoption, and established its policy.

The Social Services (Child Care Sub-) Committee discussed:
- allocation of child care cases;
- Children Act 1989: first progress report on implementation;
- implementation of the City-Wide Child Care Strategy;
- second progress report from BACC;
- SSI inspection of nine children's homes: second progress report.

Children Act 1989: Consultation Paper No 7: Criminal implications
No 8: Independent schools
No 9: Accommodation of children with parents etc.
No 10: Reviews of children's cases; arrangements for placement
No 11: Day care for children in need
No 12: Care and supervision orders
No 13: Emergency protection of children
No 14: Registration of day care facilities
No 17: Representations
No 18: Homes
published by the Department of Health.

September 1990

BACC produced a summary of *Consultation Paper 10: Reviews of children's cases*.

The Social Services (Child Care Sub-) Committee briefed on BACC and the Children Act 1989 by the Project Director.

BACC sent in responses to the Department of Health on *Children Act 1989:*
Consultation Paper 2: Policy and standards of day care and educational services
Paper 5: Co-ordination and the duty to review day care services.
Newsletter No 11 distributed; it set out the consultation timetable, and gave details of the child care conference, progress of the topic groups, and other news items.
The Departmental Management Team discussed:
• Children Act implementation;
• SSI Report on Birmingham's children's homes (timetable for the inspection).
Children Act 1989: Consultation Paper No 19: Independent visitors
No 20: Out of school provision
published by the Department of Health.
Review of Adoption Law issued by the Department of Health for consultation.

October 1990

The BACC Advisory Group met for fourth time and reviewed progress; the extension to the Project's life, to take account of the Children Act 1989 implementation date, was announced; the Group was briefed on the work of the Topic Groups, the Children Act Consultation Papers, and other work in progress. It spent time on specific questions of concern to the Project Team.
BACC sent in responses to the Department of Health on *Children Act 1989:*
Consultation Paper 17: Representations
Paper 18: Homes
Paper 4: Aftercare
Paper 8: Independent schools
The Departmental Management Team discussed:
• medical services for children in care;
• unallocated child care cases: analysis and proposals.
The Social Services Committee received a Report on the Recruitment of Short Term Foster Carers for Children under 12 (fee-paid fostering pilot project).
Children Act 1989: Consultation Paper No 21: Education Supervision Orders published by the Department of Health.

November 1990

International Children's Rights Day: BACC organised events in Birmingham.
BACC sent in responses to the Department of Health on *Children Act 1989:*
Consultation Paper 10: Reviews of children's cases – arrangements for placement of children
Paper 11: Day care for children in need

Paper 3: Local authority provision of services for families with children in need
Paper 7: Criminal implications
The Departmental Management Team considered:
- SSI Report: child protection services in Rochdale;
- unallocated child care cases (further discussion following from October report).

The Social Services (Child Care Sub-) Committee discussed:
- implementation of the Children Act 1989: interim initiatives and implications for Members;
- pilot subsidised childminders scheme (Joint report with Economic Development Department);
- recruitment of short term foster carers for children under 12: proposal for a pilot project in East Birmingham.

December 1990

The Departmental Management Team discussed:
- child abuse referrals;
- child protection – Review of child protection services set up;
- Children Act Training Plan.

Children Act 1989: Consultation Paper No 16: Foster placement published by the Department of Health.

January 1991

Corporate Children Act Steering Group set up and held its first meeting.
Work on after care, and on workload management began.
BACC held several meetings on the definition of 'children in need'.
Use of Language Working Group began meeting.
Children Act 1989 – further training planned.
BACC sent responses to the Department of Health on *Children Act 1989: Consultation Paper 16: Foster Placement*
Paper 19: Independent visitors.
BACC produced **Draft Review Format for children looked after, with guidance notes.**
Children Act 1989: a summary of the schedules within the Act published and distributed widely by BACC.
Newsletter No 12 distributed, bringing staff up to date with the Children Act and the Departmental training strategy.
The fee paid Fostering Project started recruitment of foster carers.
The first batch of childminders received their child care certificates after training.
The Departmental Management Team discussed:
- charge and Control Regulations – costs of implementation and incorporation into new Child Care Procedures Manual;

- meetings for Team Managers: BACC to hold regular meetings for all Team Managers working with children;
- personal information packs for child care workers.

The Social Services (Child Care Sub-) Committee received reports on:
- children's services information system;
- follow up inspection of nine children's homes.

Guidance on unaccompanied refugee and asylum seeking children issued by the Department of Health.

February 1991

Children Act training commenced with the series of five lectures aimed at wide staff audience.
BACC Project Director gave a presentation to the Education Department.
Findings Paper No 6: Guides to the Children Act listing and describing available guides to the Children Act 1989 published by BACC.
Working Paper No 3: Partnership with Parents published by BACC.
The Departmental Management Team discussed:
- Children Act developments: partnership with parents;
- children in need and other developments;
- city wide registration and training procedures for child minders;
- Revised Draft Statutory Review Form;
- unallocated child care cases: progress report.

First stage of the Outcomes study completed.
The Social Services (Child Care Sub-) Committee received reports on:
- allocation of child care cases: progress report;
- Children Act Training Plan;
- male prostitution;
- planning for the Birmingham Child Care Conference, 1991.

Guidance on adoption of Romanian children issued by the Department of Health.

March 1991

Service Level Agreement for a project for sexually abused girls and young women signed with the Rainer Foundation.
BACC Project Director gave a presentation to the Libraries Service on the Children Act 1989.
The Children Act 1989 and children's needs – make it the answer not the problem, NCVCCO, March 1991, published – with a contribution from BACC.
Work began on the new structure of the Department with the first meetings of 'The Shape of Things to Come' Working Group
Local SSI seminar on 'children in need'.
Guidance and Regulations, Vol 1: Court Orders published by the Department of Health.

April 1991

The BACC Advisory Group met; it reviewed progress and discussed the Residential Topic Group's draft report.
Last of the Children Act lecture series.
The Departmental Management Team spent two days discussing modifications to the Department's structure.
Guidance and Regulations, Vol 2: Family Support, Day Care and Educational Provision for Young Children
Vol 3: Family Placements
Vol 5: Independent Schools
published by the Department of Health.

May 1991

BACC Project Director gave evidence to the House of Commons Select Committee on the allocation of child care cases.
Children Act Training day for senior managers organised by BACC.
Partnership in Prospect? report of the BACC/NCVCCO Day Seminar, 23 May 1991, published.
The Departmental Management Team discussed a progress report on unallocated child care cases.
The Social Services (Child Care Sub-) Committee received reports on:
- Children Act 1989: reviews of children looked after by the Local Authority;
- review of child protection procedures in the Department.

'Pindown' Report published by Staffordshire County Council.
Virginia Bottomley at the Department of Health ordered the Utting Inquiry into children's homes.

June 1991

The BACC Advisory Group discussed the Fostering Topic Group report.
BACC produced an internal paper on Housing Support and Provision for Young People Leaving Care.
BACC started work on Adoption and Fostering Panels.
Newsletter No 13 distributed; it focused on Budget Growth, 1991/92 and the Department of Health Guidance and Regulations.
The Departmental Management Team discussed:
- after care for children looked after/leaving care;
- housing support and provision for young people leaving care (Joint report with the Housing Department);
- management information about children looked after by the Local Authority: new format agreed;
- personal information packs for child care workers.

The Social Services (Child Care Sub-) Committee received reports on:
- publication of Regulations and Guidance;
- the Department of Health draft guidance on child protection (*Working Together*).

Children Act 1989: Consultation Paper No 22: Working Together and *No 23: Children with disabilities* published by the Department of Health.
Circular from the Department of Health on lessons from the 'Pindown' report issued. All social services departments to make immediate checks on children's homes.

July 1991

BACC Project Director attended the Housing Department Management Team, and the Department of Recreation and Community Services Management Team.
BACC Project Director presented the Children Act at Chief Officers Group meeting.
House of Commons Select Committee reported as impressed by Birmingham initiatives to deal with unallocated cases.
BACC sent in a response to the Department of Health on *Consultation Paper 22: Working Together*.
Findings paper No 8: Review of residential child care services in Southwark, which reviewed the SSI Report with this title, published by BACC.
The Departmental Management Team discussed:
- allocation of the Family Support Budget – Formula and principles for allocation agreed;
- Children Act 1989: under eights issues;
- Children Act strategic direction and basic policy statements;
- Day care officers – funding for additional posts;
- Day care officers: roles and responsibilities;
- dogs in foster homes;
- fees and charges for services under the Children Act 1989 – new scales agreed;
- guidance for managers of residential and day care establishments;
- implementation of the Boarding Out Regulations;
- proposed research into implementation of the Children Act;
- support to children and families (Section 17).

Members of the Social Services Committee invited to attend the Birmingham Child Care Conference, 8-10 October 1991.
Children Act 1989. Consultation Paper No 24: GALRO Panel management and *No 15: Children fostered by private arrangements* published by the Department of Health.

The Local Government Management Board published results of a survey which showed vacancy rate in social work had risen.

August 1991

BACC sent in response to the Department of Health on *Consultation Paper 23: Children with disabilities*.
The Departmental Management Team discussed:
* the establishment of single sex children's homes;
* policy on charging for services for children and families;
* SSI follow up inspection of Children's Homes.

Report by Sir William Utting, *Children in the Public Care* published by the Department of Health.
Children Act 1989: Guidance and Regulations, Vol 4: Residential Care published by the Department of Health.

September 1991

BACC produced Equal opportunities checklist for children's placements.
Officer seconded to BACC to undertake work on after care.
BACC Project Director went to Lyon for a meeting of the Eurocities Network.
The Departmental Management Team discussed:
* implementation of the Boarding Out regulations;
* looking after Birmingham's children: a five year strategy for change.

The Social Services (Child Care Sub-) Committee received reports on:
* charges for services for children;
* Children Act 1989: 'Children in need': the local interpretation and corporate response;
* Children Act 1989: Consultation – the Black and Minority Ethnic Communities;
* Children Act 1989: ten basic policy statements on work with children and families;
* Children in the Public Care: a review of residential child care – Sir William Utting;
* Inspection of the Secure Unit;
* Looking after Birmingham's children – a five year outline plan for change to the system of children's placements;
* Pilot project to recruit fee-paid foster carers – proposed form of agreement;
* Research related to the implementation of the Children Act 1989;
* The establishment of single sex children's homes.

Children Act 1989: Guidance and Regulations, Vol 6: Children with Disabilities published by the Department of Health.

October 1991

CHILDREN ACT 1989 IMPLEMENTED

Birmingham Child Care Conference, 8-10 October 1991, at the International Convention Centre.
Children Act helpline run by BACC for two weeks.
BACC Project Director, Paul Sutton, appointed as General Manager/Children and Families.
The Departmental Management Team discussed:
- Children Act: independent visitors;
- The Birmingham Child Care Conference;
- unallocated child care cases.

The Social Services Committee received reports on:
- City-Wide Child Care Strategy: progress report – Joint report with Economic Development, Recreation and Community Services, Libraries, and Education;
- Children Act 1989: children in need...;
- Children Act 1989: position statement on implementation;
- filling staff vacancies in children's homes;
- information to support the implementation of the Children Act;
- Looking after Birmingham's children...;
- rota visits (members' visits).

Children Act 1989: Guidance and Regulations, Vol 7: Guardians ad Litem and other Court Related Issues
Vol 8: Private Fostering and Miscellaneous
Vol 9: Adoption Issues
published by the Department of Health.

November 1991

Newsletter No 14 distributed; it focused on Children Act issues – children in need, family support, aftercare, Section 27, liaison with health, Black and minority ethnic children, court timetable, day care; Children Act helpline; and the development of the aftercare service. It reported the publication of the Utting report, discussed Assessment, and gave news of the BACC conference.
Joint Departmental Management Team held with the Education Department.
The Departmental Management Team discussed:
- complaints procedure: children;
- Day Nursery Survey Report;
- The Foster Care Topic Group Final Report;
- The Birmingham Annual Child Care Conference, for 1992;
- workload management: progress report.

December 1991

BACC began work on the Criminal Justice Act.
The Social Services (Child Care Sub-) Committee received reports on:
- a quality foster care service for the 1990s;
- Children Act 1989: Aftercare: progress reports;
- Children Act 1989: the Library Services response;
- policy guidelines for the registration and inspection of daycare;
- proposal for the 1992 Birmingham Child Care Conference;
- SSI Follow-up inspection of nine children's homes.

January 1992

BACC Team met with several members of the Advisory Group for two days at Leamington to consider how to record the Project.
Findings from the Day Nursery Survey circulated to day nurseries.
The Departmental Management Team discussed:
- Birmingham Panel of Guardians ad Litem and Reporting Officers: spending of specific grant;
- Criminal Justice Act 1991;
- DipSW Priorities: the Team agreed that two thirds of secondments would be targeted at senior residential care staff in children's homes, and staff required to return to these posts;
- Residential Care Service Topic Group Report;
- review of the 'casebusters' initiative.

February 1992

BACC Team undertook work on City Challenge.
Project Director and the Director of Social Services undertook a major joint review of issues in children's homes.
SSI Day Conference: the Children Act 1989 – Three Months On: BACC Team made a substantial contribution as speakers.
The Departmental Management Team discussed
- allegations of abuse against foster carers;
- the development of Child Care Procedures;
- quality audit of fieldwork services;
- unallocated child care cases: progress report.

The Social Services (Child Care Sub-) Committee received reports on:
- a quality residential child care service for the 1990s;
- evaluation of the pilot fee-paid fostering project and its extension to other short-term foster carers;
- joint working between the Social Services Department and the Education Department: developing an action plan;
- proposal to send two representatives to 'The Child in the City' Sub-Commission of the Eurocities Network.

March 1992

BACC Project Director attended a Seminar of 'The Child in the City' Sub-Commission of the Eurocities Network in Lyon.
The Departmental Management Team discussed:
- Children Act: assessment issues;
- Day nurseries: income generation.

The Social Services Committee received a report on the Panel of Guardians ad Litem and Reporting Officers.

April 1992

Project Director, Paul Sutton, took up his appointment as General Manager, Children and Families.
BACC Advisory Group's last meeting held; it received presentations on the project's work since 1989.
The Departmental Management Team discussed the involvement of girls in care with prostitution.
The Social Services (Child Care Sub-) Committee received reports on:
- Children Act 1989: Representation and Complaints Procedure;
- the Birmingham Area Child Protection Committee;
- the Secure Unit.

May 1992

General Manager, Children and Families, to Lyon for Eurocities Network. Children and Families Unit established in the Policy and Performance Review Division.

June 1992

Planning for the Birmingham Child Care Conference continued.
The Social Services (Child Care Sub-) Committee discussed the management, registration and inspection of residential homes and independent boarding schools.

July 1992

The Social Services Committee received a report on the Children Act 1989: Representation and Complaints Procedure.
BACC officially ended and the BACC Team was disbanded.

October 1992

The second Birmingham Child Care Conference was held at the International Convention Centre.

Appendix 2: Extract from the BACC *Outline*

An Outline of a Major Project to Review the Services for Children and Families provided by Birmingham Social Services Department.

1. Context

1.1 The city

Birmingham is the second largest city in the United Kingdom, with a population of nearly a million. 7.5 per cent of the population is aged under five, and 20.8 per cent between 5 and 19 – over 280,000 children and young people in total. It is a multi-ethnic city – about one fifth of the total population are Black or minority ethnic people. In recent years, the city's industrial base has been severely affected by economic restructuring and recession. As a result, 21 per cent of the city's workforce is estimated to be unemployed, and, on one definition, half the population is said to live in or on the margins of poverty.

Major initiatives by Birmingham City Council to revitalise the economy, most notably through the Birmingham Heartlands project, but also through many smaller projects, have begun to make an impact. Nevertheless, the context in which work with children and families is carried out is often a bleak one.

1.2 The Social Services Department and its services for children and families:

Birmingham Social Services Department is the largest urban social services department in England and Wales, employing 8,600 people.

Budget: £21 million for work with children and families, 23 per cent of the total Social Services Department budget.*

Staff: 363 social workers employed in children's and/or general services teams, 44 in adoption and fostering teams, and 75 in three Juvenile Justice Teams.

Other resources: 217 temporary foster carers providing over 400 places for children; 562 beds in 34 children's homes/centres and two community

homes with education. 1,438 day nursery/centre places; one family support centre; one multi-disciplinary assessment and treatment centre; access to two NSPCC units.
Private and voluntary sector resources include 4,000 places with approved child minders; 750 places in private nurseries; and 6,500 sessional places for children in playgroups.
Unquantifiable resources: knowledge, experience, information, networks.

1.3 Demographic context

A number of demographic trends will have implications for the development of services for children and families:

There will be more under fives and therefore more demands for day care; but fewer teenagers and therefore less juvenile crime. A reduction in the number of young workers will mean women will be needed in the labour force, so there will be demands for both pre-school and out-of-school ('latchkey') care. A larger proportion of the Black and minority ethnic population will have been born in Great Britain; as a result, they will be more confident in making demands of social services.

1.4 Political context

Several recent child abuse enquiries, the formation of Childline, events in Cleveland, the Butler-Sloss report, and the publication of a new Children Bill in 1988 have drawn public attention to the front-line role of social workers in the protection of children from abuse and in providing support to families in need or at risk.

In Birmingham, disclosures of abuse at two children's homes helped to crystalise concern about the operation of the range of services for children and families. A full review, taking into account all aspects of provision, was overdue, and, accordingly, the Social Services Committee in October 1988 approved the establishment of a major project to review the child care service as a whole. A small project team will be recruited to spearhead the review, which is to take two years. Assisted by current departmental staff and supported by an independent advisory group, it will report directly to the Director of Social Services.

Clearly, the Project will be working in a highly sensitive area; child care workers have been under great pressure, from a mainly hostile press and public opinion. There is a danger of their closing ranks against outsiders or of their acting defensively rather than innovatively or imaginatively in their everyday practice.

Recently, Birmingham City Council's commitment to decentralising services to constituency based neighbourhood offices has led to the restructuring of the Department and relocation of staff. Staff now need a stable period in which to operate the new structures.

Initiatives now in progress, which the project will need to take account of in its work include the Social Services Inspectorate's study of children's homes, work on the expectations of managers being undertaken by the Senior Assistant Director, Bill Hendley, and the revision of the child care procedures manual.

1.5 Terms of reference

Aim: to establish new objectives, priorities and resources which will enable the Child Care Service to make a clear and positive response to future demands.

Objectives:
- To analyse the needs of children and families who require the assistance of the statutory child care services and to draw up general principles for the development of the services.
- To review and develop child care policies, practices and resources in the light of the re-defined needs and principles.
- To propose an overall implementation strategy with specific plans and a timetable for action to put into effect the changes required.

These objectives must be worked out within existing and projected financial constraints, with no necessity for major reorganisation of the Department, and with the likely impact of the Children Bill taken into account. All policy and practice must take full account of the City's equal opportunities policy. The contribution which may be made by the voluntary sector, including through self-help initiatives, will be considered.

1.6

The Project will begin work at a time when there is general acceptance of the crucial nature of services for children and families and a wish to develop high standards of practice. With the support of the Director and the Departmental Management Team, it will be able to draw on the knowledge and experience of Departmental staff as well as buying in expertise from outside. Many staff will welcome the opportunity to contribute to the review, but will also benefit from being involved, through the discussion and development of policy and practice.

While the Project will focus on Birmingham's services for children and families, both the methods to be employed and the outcome are expected to attract national interest.

2. The Project

2.1 Location in the department

The Project Director will report directly to the Director of Social Services and will be a member of the Departmental Management Team.

An advisory group, headed by Mrs Barbara Kahan will be established to provide support and expert advice to the Project Team; membership of the advisory group will be negotiated with the Project Director, and may change to meet the different needs of the Project during different phases.

The Project will work closely with existing staff, including the Children and Families Policy Group.

In addition, it is anticipated that the Project Team will wish to establish other consultative groups, bringing together (for example) residential staff or foster parents or children and young people in care.

2.2 The Project's subject-matter

The Project will review the whole range of services for children and families provided by the Social Services Department, although its primary focus will be on the needs of children in care or liable to come into care. Services for children with disabilities and/or special needs will be included, in line with the emphasis in the Children Bill on the duty of social services departments to this group. The department's relationships with the voluntary and private sector, with other City departments, and with other agencies, will be reviewed where appropriate. Although the Project is an internal Departmental project, it is anticipated that liaison with, and help from, other City departments will be necessary and available.

2.3 The Project's task

Services for children and families need to be reviewed and planned as a whole. In the past, services have been reviewed individually – for example, a recent review of homefinding services – but the emphasis for this major project will be on the whole range of services, and on the ways in which they relate to one another. Change in any one service has implications for all the others, and there will be a need to undertake thorough groundwork to establish a comprehensive picture of the services and their interrelationships before recommendations are made. (The Project Team will not, therefore, be expected to become involved in short-term pieces of work for the DMT or the Social Services Committee, unless the Project's Director agrees that these are useful and relevant for the Project's objectives.)

The Project will produce an interim report towards the end of its first year and a programme of phased implementation will begin immediately, with built-in evaluation and feedback. The final report will include a realistic plan, for the next five years, for the provision of services for children and families, with phased and evaluated implementation, clear agreed priorities, and criteria for monitoring practice.

Resources to implement the Project's proposals will be identified from within the Department's budget for children's services. There is a commitment to establishing systems to ensure that the Project's work continues beyond the end of its two years, with the implementation and continued monitoring of its proposals.

It is anticipated that there will be a number of positive spin-offs from the Project – for example, guidance on good practice, opportunities for staff training and development, and improved communications between policy-makers and practitioners. From the beginning the Project Team will need to establish mutual trust and respect with those who will carry out its recommendations.

2.4 The Project Team

Two new posts will be created, of Director and Deputy Director of the Project. These two officers will be supported by a team of staff seconded from within the Department for all or part of the Project's two years. In addition, other Departmental staff will undertake work for the Project as part of their normal duties. Administrative support will be provided.

The Team should include Black people and White people, men and women; and people with experience of residential work and/or day care as well as fieldwork with children. It will require access to Asian and Afro-Caribbean perspectives. A mix of skills and abilities will be needed in the team – for example, research literacy, the ability to present the Project and its work to committees, to staff and to seminars etc., and writing skills. Its members should include people with qualifications in social work, with access to local and national networks, with recent face-to-face experience of work with children and with management experience.

3. The Project's programme

The Project Team will be expected to develop its own programme in consultation with its advisory group. This will be presented to the Departmental Management Team early in the Project's life. The ideas that follow represent a basis only, but give some idea of the process and methods, and the size of the task.

Despite the emphasis on a thorough review of services before any proposals for change can be made, the Project will need to make an early impact on the Department, both because of its short timescale and because of the importance of gaining the cooperation of staff at all levels. Involvement of staff, foster parents and consumers, the dissemination of information, and the development and piloting of guidelines on practice should be attempted early. Good feedback to staff at all levels, through team meetings and seminars, and through a frequent, fairly simple, low-cost, widely distributed bulletin, would be a good investment. By the end of its first year, the Project needs to have completed most of its data collection and analysis and to be ready to make recommendations, some of which can then be implemented and evaluated during the second year.

There are a number of policy issues which can be identified now as central to the Project's work – the balance between preventive, remedial and crisis work with children and families, the provision of an ethnically sensitive child care service, and the balance between specialist child care services and a generic approach to social work.

Key practice issues which the Project Team will need to review include the Department's practice in dealing with child abuse including child sexual abuse, its provision of support to foster carers, the best use and management of residential and day care units, the processes of decision-making in respect of children coming into care, their placement and future needs, and the range and type of residential provision the Department should have.

The Project will need to undertake a review of staffing resources, in order to forecast future needs and produce a strategy for recruitment, training, redeployment and development. A similar exercise will be required in respect of other resources, such as under-fives and family centres, foster homes, residential resources, adoption services, intermediate treatment centres, specialist teams, and the provision made by the private and voluntary sectors, including ways of working with self-help initiatives.

Gill Coffin
24 January 1989

*These figures excluded expenditure on fieldwork, administration and training; when these are recharged to the appropriate client group budgets, the expenditure on children and families services amounted to £28 million, 32 per cent of the Department's budget.

Appendix 3: The interpretation of 'children in need'

The interpretation of 'Children in Need' should include the following elements [although] these categories are not exhaustive.

The city 'Strategic' interpretation

1. All children who are suffering from structural forms of deprivation (for example, those identified by the City Anti-Poverty Strategy), which the provision of services by the local authority might alleviate or whose welfare and upbringing by their families [the provision of services] might promote. Such children are most likely to be found in families:
   - eligible for or in receipt of free school meals;
   - eligible for or in receipt of family credit or income support;
   - eligible for or in receipt of community charge rebates;
   - from Black or minority ethnic communities;
   - where the child care responsibilities are carried out by a single parent;
   - who live in particular geographical communities;
   - who live in particular forms of housing tenure.

Such an interpretation is most likely to be of strategic value (for example, in carrying out the three yearly review of Day Care) in targeting resources towards those groups most likely to utilise them in pursuance of the aims of the Children Act.

The specific social services interpretation

2. Children who have suffered or who are likely to suffer significant harm – that is, children whose names appear on the Child Protection Register or where there appears to be a child protection concern.
3. Children who are eligible for inclusion on a register of children with disabilities (accepting that the precise definition [of disability] has yet to be arrived at).

4. All children currently receiving a broad 'preventive' service from the Social Services Department, including both statutory and 'voluntary' supervision.
5. All children who for whatever reason are denied equality of opportunity.
6. All children currently in care, on whatever grounds or otherwise enjoying accommodation (for example, respite care) or subject to any order under the public law aspects of the Children Act.
7. All children being worked with by voluntary or statutory services to prevent family breakdown.
8. All children with a statement of special educational needs under the Education Act 1981, or being worked with by the Education Social Work Service or excluded from mainstream provision, or in residential schooling, or in receipt of home teaching.
9. All children whose health is subject to specific forms of monitoring by the Health Authority through, for example Health Visitors, School Health Service and so on.
10. All children whose emotional development is the subject of specific work (for example, through the Child Advisory Social Work Service, Psychiatric Units, and so on).
11. All pregnant schoolgirls.
12. All children of homeless families.
13. All homeless children and young people.
14. All children for whom offending or its consequences are a significant feature of their lives.
15. All children in hospital, especially longer-stay or with conditions which disrupt life and education (for example, HIV/ AIDS), or sick children at home or children with long term illness of either parent.
16. All children who abuse drugs or other substances or whose parents are substance abusers (including alcohol).
17. Children of travelling families, to ensure access and entitlement to services.
18. All children whose 'home life' with their parents is threatened in any other way by their current circumstances.

The aggregation of the eighteen groups of children listed above will not, in all cases, lead to the identification of children in need by name. Rather it will identify those parts of the population of Birmingham whose children's health or development will be most likely to benefit from the provision of services by the local authority. However, a child who falls within one of these categories will not necessarily require services to meet his or her needs which may already be satisfied by others, for example parents. A number of caveats must be entered here.

First, the fact that a family might lie within one of the above definitions signifies that they are eligible for **consideration** for a service which the local authority has a duty to provide, not for the service itself. Guidance from the Department of Health notes that '**Local Authorities are not being asked to meet all and every need.**' Discretion and prioritisation will still be important judgements to be made.

Second, these services [set out in the Children Act] represent only some of those provided as a **duty**. The Local Authority has a wide range of **powers** to provide other services under the Act.

Third, the responsibility for providing services to children in need is a local authority duty, not purely a Social Services Department responsibility. The Act is quite specific about its intentions in this respect and this should properly lead to definitions of need which are less than pathological.

Fourth, even where the Social Services Department has accepted a responsibility to provide a service, there are different levels of provision, which might be listed as follows:

Indirect provision: for example, advice, counselling, practical assistance, peer and community support, referral on, networking, information.

Low level direct provision: for example, support groups, low-input services in terms of persons/hours/costs, small scale aids/adaptations, irregular consultation/contact.

High level direct provision: for example, intensive support to families, with a high input of persons/hours/costs, respite schemes, accommodation away from home, and so on.

Finally, whilst assessment is an important, indeed a vital, part of the process of service provision and meeting need, it must not become solely a process for deciding whether or not the potential service user falls within the 'in need' category.

September 1991

Appendix 4: BACC publications

Newsletters

1, March 1989: terms of reference for the project, appointment of staff, and request for comments and contributions.

2, April 1989: appointment of Project Director, work undertaken by Ben Brown, how BACC will handle complaints, and invitation to people to contribute.

3, June 1989: key messages in the Children Bill, implications for children with disabilities.

4, July 1989: BACC's progress – appointment of Paul Sutton and other staff members, move into the BACC offices, setting up of Advisory group, and work underway.

5, November 1989: news from the Project, Children Act seminars, children's rights, and the Advisory Group.

6, February 1990: preparations for implementing the Children Act, including establishment of Children Act Implementation Group.

7, March 1990: establishment of Topic Groups, 1991/92 budget growth, and small news items.

8, May 1990: Children Act implementation, budget growth, induction for residential workers, leaving care grants, and outcome of a research study of Home on Trial.

9, June 1990: Children Act news, and membership of the Children Act Implementation Group.

10, July 1990: Department of Health Children Act consultation process, children's rights, proposed child care conference, topic groups, teenage fostering and induction courses for residential workers.

11, September 1990: consultation timetable, details of child care conference, progress of topic groups, and other news items.

12, January 1991: Children Act news and Departmental training strategy.

13, June 1991: Budget Growth, 1991/92 and Department of Health Guidance and Regulations.

14, November 1991: Children Act issues – children in need, family support, aftercare, Section 27, liaison with health, Black and minority ethnic children, court timetable, day care; Children Act helpline; and development of the aftercare service; publication of the Utting report; Assessment; news of the BACC conference.

Working Papers

Working Paper No 1: Method (1990)
Working Paper No 2: A systems approach to child care planning (1990)
Working Paper No 3: Partnership with Parents (1991)

Findings Papers

Findings Paper No 1: Planning (1990)
Findings Paper No 2: Glossary (1990)
Findings Paper No 3: SSI Report: report of the inspection of nine children's homes in Birmingham (1990)
Findings Paper No 4: From Dennis O'Neill to the Children Act 1989: child care history 1945-1989 (1990) – by Arran Poyser
Findings Paper No 5: Principles and Practice (1990)
Findings Paper No 6: Guides to the Children Act (1991)
Findings Paper No 7: SSI Re-inspection (1991)
Findings Paper No 8: Review of residential child care services in Southwark (1991)

Other Major Papers

1989
Children Bill 1988, Children Act 1989 – a Summary of the Bill
The Children Act 1989: a summary of its main provisions
1990
Discussion Paper: proposal to unblock the Placements System
The Children Act 1989: implications for Black and minority ethnic children and families
1991
City-Wide Survey of Day Nursery Usage
Equal opportunities checklist for children's placements
Review form for children looked after, with guidance notes
The Children Act 1989: A summary of schedules within the Act
Ten Basic Policy Statements for Work with Children and Families
1992
Report of the Day Nursery Survey Consultation Exercise

APPENDIX 4 221

The Children Act 1989: Issues of Race, Religion, Language and Culture
1993
The language of the Children Act 1989 in translation (forthcoming)
Leaflets for service users
Information Pack for Social Workers

Reports

1990
A Children's Rights Service, Report of the Director of Social Services to the Social Services (Child Care Sub-) Committee
Birmingham Action on Child Care: progress report, Report to the Birmingham Social Services Departmental Management Team
Children Act Training Plan, Report to the Birmingham Social Services Departmental Management Team
Management Information – children in care, Report to the Birmingham Social Services Departmental Management Team
Proposal for a Birmingham Annual Child Care Conference, Report to the Birmingham Social Services Departmental Management Team
Recruitment of short term foster carers – proposal for a pilot project in East Birmingham, Report of the Director of Social Services to the Social Services Committee
Unallocated child care cases, Report to the Birmingham Social Services Departmental Management Team
1991
After care for children looked after, Report to the Birmingham Social Services Departmental Management Team
A Quality Foster Care Service for the 1990s, Report of the Director of Birmingham Action on Child Care to the Social Services (Child Care Sub-) Committee
Children in need – the local interpretation and the corporate response, Report of the Director of Birmingham Action on Child Care to the Social Services (Child Care Sub-) Committee
Co-ordination and the duty to review, Report to the Children Act Implementation Group
Day care services for school age children, Report to the Children Act Implementation Group
Housing support and provision for young people leaving care, Report to the Birmingham Social Services Departmental Management Team
Independent Visitors, Report to the Birmingham Social Services Departmental Management Team
Local authority support for children and families, Report to the Birmingham Social Services Departmental Management Team
Looking after Birmingham's Children: a five year outline plan for

APPENDIX 4

change, Report of the Director of Social Services to the Social Services Committee
Report of the Foster Care Topic Group, Report to the Birmingham Social Services Department Management Team
The Children Act 1989: Directions for Strategic Planning in Work with Children and Families, Report to the Birmingham Social Services Departmental Management Team
The Children Act 1989: Ten Basic Policy Statements for Work with Children and Families, Report of the Director of Birmingham Action on Child Care to the Social Services (Child Care Sub-) Committee
The Children Act 1989: Under Eights Issues, Report to the Birmingham Social Services Departmental Management Team
The establishment of single sex children's homes, Report to the Birmingham Social Services Departmental Management Team
Unallocated child care cases: progress reports, Reports to the Birmingham Social Services Departmental Management Team
1992
Allegations of abuse in foster care, Report to the Birmingham Social Services Department Management Team
Report of the Residential Care Service Topic Group, Report to the Birmingham Social Services Department Management Team
The Children Act 1989: assessment issues, Report to the Birmingham Social Services Department Management Team
Unallocated child care cases: progress reports, Reports to the Birmingham Social Services Department Management Team

Joint Publication

Birmingham Action on Child Care/National Council for Voluntary Child Care Organisations, **Partnership in prospect?** report of a BACC/NCVCCO Seminar (1991)

Appendix 5: Birmingham Action on Child Care Team

Paul Sutton	Project Director	June 1989 – July 1992
Jessica Anderson	Secretary	October 1989 – March 1992
Louise Bessant	Youth Project Worker	June 1991 – July 1992
Ben Brown	Deputy Project Director [Seconded to BACC from SSI, full-time]	February 1989 – June 1992
Graham Ballinger	Project Officer [Performance Review Adviser Seconded to BACC two days a week]	March 1989 – November 1989
Gill Coffin	Project Officer [Administrator, Guardians ad Litem Seconded to BACC two days a week]	February 1989 – October 1989
Billy Foreman	Project Officer [Social Worker Seconded to BACC initially half time, full time from January 1991]	February 1990 – July 1992
Delrose Gooden	Project Officer [Officer in Charge, Day Nursery Seconded to BACC two days a week]	January 1991 – July 1992
Claudia Gordon	Project Administrator	September 1989 – July 1992

APPENDIX 5

Neil Grant	Project Development Officer [Planning Officer, Children Seconded to BACC full time]	January 1990 – July 1992
Sandra Lawrence	Project Administrative Assistant	October 1989 – July 1992
Jane Middleton	Project Officer [Social worker Seconded to BACC Initially half time; 3 days per week from November 1990]	January 1990 – May 1992
Sylvia Miller	Youth Project Worker	December 1989 – June 1992
Dianne Parry	Clerk Typist	September 1990 – April 1992
Ruth Walsh	Project Officer [Co-ordinator, Children's Services seconded to BACC two days per week]	March 1989 – July 1992
Simon Westwood	Project Officer [Team Manager, Juvenile Justice Seconded to BACC full time for six months]	September 1991 – March 1992

Appendix 6: Membership of the Advisory Group for Birmingham Action on Child Care

Barbara Kahan, Chair

Sylvia Aston, Pauline Barr, John Beale, David Berridge, Dawn Cushnie, Audrey Douglas, Shane Ellis, Joseph Glenholmes, Delrose Gooden, Philip Green (observer), Barry Hindson, Adrianne Jones, Des Kelly, Ermyne Lee-Kin, Georgia Leon, Hilary Maslen, Steve McCabe, Sheila McGrath, Andy Merker, Nick Parker, Lea Pearson, Jane Prashar, David Priestnall, Rashpal Kaur Singh, Barbara Symons, Jane Tunstill.

Index

A

abuse of children in care 175
  children's homes 2, 8, 16, 21, 23, 24-7, 60, 117
  foster care 68, 69, 148-9, 173
  see also child protection; sexual abuse
action, BACC emphasis on vi, 53, 162, 164
Action on Child Care, Birmingham *see* BACC
adolescents
  in children's homes 21, 22-3, 102, 149
  remand and teenage fostering scheme 150-51
adoption
  increased use in 1980's 12-13
  not a focus for BACC 53, 144
  see also children in care
adoption law review 58, 69
Advisory Group *see* BACC, Advisory Group
advocacy *see* children's rights; Guardians ad Litem
assessment 76
Austin, N : *A Passion for Excellence...* 178-9

B

BACC
  Advisory Group
    initial meetings 62-3, 64
    later meetings 69, 78
    membership 51-2, 225

  network of contacts vi, 44, 167, 170-71
  anti-discriminatory work style 51, 165
  chronology 195-209, *see also* BACC, genesis; BACC, history
  Community Homes with Education review 69, 154
  day care work 76, **128-33**, 175
  departmental restructuring 52, 71-2, 77, 78, 80, **106-111**, 164
  emphasis on action vi, 53, 162, 164
  foster care initiatives 66-7, **144-52**, 173, 176-7, *see also* foster care
  future of achievements and initiatives 78-9, 110-11, 141, 166
  genesis vi, 2-3, **23-7**, 27-59, *see also* BACC, chronology; BACC, history
  history **56-79**, *see also* BACC chronology; BACC genesis
  implementation of Children Act 1989 **80-122**
  complaints, *see also* children's rights; complaints
  complaints and children's rights 117-22
  day care and out-of-school care 126-33
    see also day care
  departmental restructuring 71-2, 166-7
  family support guidelines 137
  monitoring 99, 100, 111, 124-5

INDEX

BACC implementation of Children Act 1989 *continued*
   see also monitoring and reviews
   response to consultation papers 66, 69, 70, 73, 167
   staff support 75-6
   strategic planning report 98-101
   training 69, 70-71, **96-8**
   see also Children Act 1989; Children Act Implementation Group
  improves staff retention and recruitment 79, 94, 135-6
  information about services 89-90, 98, 138-40, 160, 176-7
   see also BACC, publications; BACC, training
  interpretation of 'Children in need' 70, 82, **88-92**, 167, 216-17
  life-cycle *see* BACC, history
  management information work 66, 133, 173, 176-7
  method of working vi, 43-55, 164-6, 169-71, *see also* BACC, Topic groups
  national impact 75-6, 166-9, 172
  obstacles to achieving objectives 172-3
  personnel **223-4**
   later careers 77-8, 111
   recruitment 59-60, 61
  philosophy 3, 29, 34-44, 141, 168, 169-71
  priorities, selection of 49-50
  Project Deputy Director *see* Brown, Ben
  Project Director *see* Sutton, Paul
  publications **219-222**
   Directions for Strategic Planning... 98-101
   dissemination 49-50, 166-9
   final reports 77, 78
   information for staff and service users 138-40, 176-7
   Looking after Birmingham's Children... 74, **101-106**, 146, 151, 152-3
   Outline document 29, 163-6, extract 210-15
   see also BACC, Topic groups, reports
  relations with other Departments and agencies 73, 77, 91, 109
  care leavers 160
  Children Act implementation 45, 65, 71
  education 52, 156-8
  foster care 144-5
  in managing change 179-81
  out-of-school provision 132-3
  training 97
  Universities 65, 71, 97, 167
  voluntary sector 65, 165
  see also Children Act Corporate Steering Group; City-wide Child Care Strategy; interdepartmental liaison
  research 52, 162, 167, 178-82, *see also* BACC, publications; BACC, Topic Groups, reports
  seminars, *see also* BACC, training, 51, 61, 96, 157
  sexual abuse survivors' project 65, 137-8
   see also sexual abuse
  staff cynicism towards vi, 46, 51, 60, 96, 182-3
  staff involvement vii, 46-51, 60, 81-2, 165, 173, 178-82
  Topic Groups 47-50
   initial meetings 64, 144, 152
   later meetings 69, 128
   members 44, 50-51, 151, 159
   method of work 52-3, 173
   reports 70, 101, 128-9, 134, 146, 159
   see also BACC, publications; Children Act Implementation Group
  training 49-50
   on complaints procedure and reviews 121-2, 125
   foster carers 146-7, 149
   of other Authorities' trainers 97
   residential staff 20, 23, 51, 153, **154-5**, 176-7
   see also BACC, implementation of Children Act; BACC, seminars

INDEX

BACC training *continued*
  typical problems of limited-life projects 56-8, 163
  working method *see* BACC, method of work
  see also children in care; children in need, unallocated cases; children's homes; day care; foster care; Social Services Dept.; training
behavioural difficulties, education of children with 156-8
Bettridge, Frances 25
Birmingham 1-2, 113-14, *see also* Children Act Corporate Steering Group; City...; Social Services Dept.
Birmingham Action on Child Care *see* BACC
Birmingham Child Care Conferences 67, 168
  first 57-8, 72, 75-6, 151
  second 77, 79, 176
Birmingham Foster Care Association 151
Birmingham University 148-9
Black people *see* minority ethnic people
Boarding Out of Children (Foster Parent) Regulations 1988 66-7, 93, 172
Brown, Ben 59, 61, 116

C

Care of Children: Principles and Practice... 62
care leavers
  in BACC 51, 118, 175
  housing 71, 154
  increased budget 94-5
  planning for 99
care plans, *see also* permanency planning, 125, 134, 157, 174
case conferences, multidisciplinary, *see also* interdepartmental liaison, 11
challenge to care 24
championship of BACC by Director of Social Services 29, 44
change, slow pace of in child care 7-8, 169-70

change, management of *see* management of change
Charge and Control Regulations 93
child abuse 15, 175
  in children's homes 2, 8, 16, 21, 23, 24-7, 60, 117
  in foster care 68, 69, 148-9, 173
  see also child protection; sexual abuse
Child Care, Birmingham Action on *see* BACC
Child Care Act 1980 10
Child Care Review Group 24-5, 42-3
child care staff *see* social workers
child care in UK since 1945 8-16
  changing culture of 141, 144, 169-71, 174
Child in the City 77, 79, 87-8
child protection
  Children Act Corporate Steering Group 86
  Registers 11
  rejected as model by BACC 53, 99, 141
  in social services system 38-9
  unfinished work 161
  see also child abuse
child sexual abuse *see* sexual abuse of children
childminders 127, 132
  training project 85-6
children, services to *see* children in care; education
Children Act 1948 9-10
Children Act 1975 10, 11
Children Act 1989 3, 43, 58, 80-81
  BACC implementation of 5, **80-112**
  see also BACC, implementation of Children Act 1989
  budget implications 93-5
  child care orders 143-4
  Consultation Papers 65-6, 69, 70, 73, 176
  implementation as a whole 60
  inspection and registration 123-25
  interpretation of children in need 70, 82, **88-92**, 167, **216-7**
Children Act Corporate Steering Group 86-8, 95, 160, 168

INDEX

Children Act Corporate Steering Group *continued*
  see also BACC, implementation of Children Act 1989; BACC, relations with other Departments and agencies; City-Wide Child Care Strategy
Children Act Implementation Group 45, 50, 64, **81-4**, 168
  health issues 158-9
  membership 82-3
  replaced by Development Group 82
  report 73
  see also BACC, implementation of Children Act 1989; BACC, Topic Groups
children at risk see child protection; children in need
children in care
  abuse of see abuse of children in care
  budget increases 93-5
  complaints to BACC 61, 116, 148-9, 173, 174-5
  contact with family 14, 99, 144
  education 156-8
  health 158-9
  information for 139-40
  numbers 17, 93, 124-5
  outcomes 65, 159, 174
  services to, as system 37-43
  see also adoption; BACC; care leavers; children's homes; families; foster care; Social Services Dept.
Children in need
  BACC interpretation 17-6, 70, 82, **88-92**, 167, **216-17**
  services for 100, 113-142
  unallocated cases 66, 68, 69, 74, **133-6**, 175-6
  increased budget 93-5
  report 76
  see also social workers, shortages
children under five see early years
Children and Young Persons Act 1963 10
Children and Young Persons Act 1969 10, 12, 48
children's homes 17-18, 68, 74, **152-9**, 176-7

abuse in 2, 8, 23, 25-7, 60
  complaints ignored 117
  nationally 16, 70, 72, 76
  prevention 63
  BACC Topic Group 49-50, 70, 77
  report 101-6
  budget 93-5
  costs 22-3
  education of children 156-8
  emergency substitution for foster care 149-50
  inspection and registration 123-4
  management improvements 27
  national surveys of 13, 15, 70, 72
  reduction in use of 16-17, 93
  retention desirable 102-5
  review of management 24-7
  single-sex 156
  Social Services Inspectorate inspections 62, 70, 77
  in social services system 38-9, 161
  staff see social workers, residential
  stigmatisation 19-20
  visitors 117, 125-6, 173
  visits by Ben Brown 61, 116
  see also children in care
children's rights 100, **117-22**, 153-4, 173, 174-5
  budget for 94
  see also complaints
Citizen's Charter 182-3
City Anti-Poverty Strategy 92
City Anti-Poverty Unit 1-2, 113
City Challenge 77, 168
City-Wide Child Care Strategy 84-6, 100, 127, 128, 130-31, 168
  see also Children Act Corporate Steering Group
Cleveland Inquiry 14-15, see also sexual abuse of children
Colwell, Maria 2, 8, 11
Commission for Racial Equality 115
Community Care Special Action Project 28, 43-5
community care White Paper 1990, 60
  see also National Health Service and Community Care Act
Community Homes with Education 69, 153, 154

INDEX

complaints
  of children in care 61, 116, 148-9, 173, 174-5
  procedure 26, 27, 117-18, 120, 153
  budget 81, 94
  see also children's rights
consultation *see* complaints; participation
Corporate Children Act Steering group *see* Children Act Corporate Steering Group
Criminal Justice Act 1991 53, 58
cultural identity under Children Act 1989 53, 73, 144
cynicism of staff *see* BACC, staff cynicism

D

Dartington Social Research Unit 65
day care **126-33**
  after 1945 10
  BACC work on 76, 175
  budget 94-5
  in Children Act 1989 81
  City-wide Child Care Strategy 84-5
  inspection and registration 124
  in social services system 38-42
  training of workers 155
  in World War 2 9-10
  see also Social Services Dept.
decision making
  in child care 13-14
  in management of community care 43-4
  in management of social work 32, 42-3
Department of Health *see* Social Services Inspectorate
Department of Health & Social Security Development Group 48
  outcomes working party 159, 174
Directions for Strategic Planning... report 98-101
Director of Social Services *see* Jones, Adrianne
disabled children
  education 156
  management of services 158-9
  placements 104
  unfinished work 161, 165

disabled people
  in BACC 51
  demands on services 58
discrimination, racial 114-15, *see also* minority ethnic people
dissemination of research 49-50, 166-9
  see also Birmingham Child Care Conferences

E

early years
  budget 94-5
  priority work area for BACC 49-50, 175
  services for 126-33
  young children in children's homes 149
  see also day care
economic situation 1-2, *see also* financial issues
education 76
  of children in care 156-8
  community homes with 69, 153, 154
  legislation 58-9
  Supervision Orders 82, 86, 87
  see also training
emergency child protection 11, 12
emotional and behavioural difficulties, education of children with 156-8
empowerment *see* children's rights
Ethnic minority people *see* minority ethnic people
ethnicity *see* minority ethnic children
evaluation criteria 37
exclusion from school 156-8

F

families
  partnership with 143-4
  positive support for 49-50, 73, 99, 136-7, 175-6
  budget 94-5
  information 139-40
  services to, as system 37-43
  see also children in care; Social Services dept.

INDEX 231

family
  care of children within 10, 17, 81, 98-9, 136-7
  contact with children in care 14, 99, 144
Family Rights Group 13
feedback loops 37.183
financial issues 1-2, 30-31, 58, 93-5
  see also BACC, costs; poverty
foster care 24, **144-52**, 176-7
  abuse in 68, 69, 173
  BACC topic group 49-50, 70, 77, 101
  Boarding Out regulations 66-7
  education of children in 156-8
  expansion 18-19, 67, 93-5, 104-5, 150-51
  fee paid pilot project 67, 70, 77, 79, 105-6, 149-50
    costs 95
  independent visitors 125-6
  inspection and registration 124
  insufficient placements 2, 105-6
  minority ethnic children and carers 63, 115, 150
  priority work area for BACC 49-50, 74
  in social services system 38-9
  see also children in care; social workers

G

Guardians *ad litem* 31, 94, 124

H

Hartwell, Gemma 25
health of children in care 158-9
holiday care *see* day care
holistic approach *see* systems model
Home Office Development Group 48
House of Commons Health Committee 52, 75, 136

I

Independent Living Project 160
independent visitors 125-6, 173
information, provision of
  in managing change 181-2
  minority languages 53, 82, 115, 110
  to managers 66, 133, 173, 176-7

  to service users 89-90, 98, 138-40, 160, 176-7
  innovation, encouragement of 49-50
  inspection *see* monitoring; Social Services Inspectorate
  institutional care *see* children's homes
  interdepartmental liaison
    Children Act 1989 86-8, 98
    see also Children Act Corporate Steering Group
  children's rights 121
    see also children's rights
  day care 84-6, 128, 132
    see also City-Wide Child Care Strategy
  health care 158
  implementation of Children Act 1989 98
  management of change 180-81
    see also BACC, relations with other Departments and agencies
  intermediate treatment 12
    see also young offenders
  involvement in decision making *see* BACC, staff involvement; decision making

J

Jones, Adrianne v, 2-3, 25-7, 155
  championship of BACC 29, 44, 170
  departmental restructuring 109-11
  membership of BACC 61
Jowell, Tessa 43
juvenile delinquents *see* young offenders
juvenile justice, not a focus for BACC 53, 161

K

Kahan, Barbara v-vii, 48, 75
  Consultant to BACC 28, 34, 52
  establishment of BACC 59-61
  Pindown Inquiry 64
Kantner, R. Moss: *When giants learn to dance...* 179-82

L

languages, minority
  focus of planning under Children Act 1989 73, 99-100, 114-16, 144
  information in 53, 82, 115, 140
leaving care *see* care leavers
Leicester Polytechnic 155
library services for children and carers 95
Liddiard, Ronald 24
local government
  changing role of 58
  management in 30-31
Looking after Birmingham's Children ... Reports 74, **101-106**, 146, 151, 152-3

M

management
  of change 3, 23, 29-31, 106-111, **178-84**
  costs of varying approaches 54-5
  review of BACC's work **162-77**
    see also BACC
  staff issues 105, 179-84
  of children's homes 21, 24-7, 154-5
  of foster care 146-7
  information for 66, 133, 173, 176-7
  of public service vs. business 30-32, 181-2
  of resources 22
  of Social Services Dept. *see* Social Services Dept, management
  in social services system 38-9
manager contrasted with professional 30
minority ethnic children
  complaints of care experience 116
  disproportionate numbers in care 11, 115, 129-30
  focus of work for and post-BACC 53, 175-6
  foster care 63, 115, 150
  increased budget 93-5
  under Children Act 1989 49, 73, 98-100, 114-16, 144, 154
minority ethnic people 1, 82, 113-4
  in BACC 51
  services for 58, 114-16

social work staff 115-16, 129, 147, 150
minority languages *see* languages, minority
mixed economy of welfare 29-30, 58, 100, 178
  see also voluntary sector
monitoring and review of services 98-100, 111, **123-25**, 174-5
  children's homes 153
  day care 131-2
  focus on health 158
  foster care 148
  special schools 157
  unallocated cases 133-4, 175
multidisciplinary case conferences 11
  see also interdepartmental liaison
Muslim families 156
  see also religion

N

National Association of Young People in Care 13
National Health Service and Community Care Act 1990 1, 5, 58, 71
  implementation 82, 173
  inspection of homes 64, 119, 123
  management implications 108
  see also community care
networking 44, 167, 170-71, 180-82
newsletters 50, 60, 138-9, 176-7
nurseries *see* day care

O

O'Neill, Dennis 8, 9
Open University 64, 71, 97
out-of-school care *see* day care
outcomes
  of BACC's work 171-7
  in child care 65, 159, 174
Outline of a Major Project... 29, 163-6, extract 210-15

P

parents *see* families
Parker, Roy 159

INDEX

participation
 planning for 99-100
 Young People's Forum 122-3
 see also BACC, staff involvement
partnership
 focus of Children Act, 1989 98, 143-4
 in foster care 147
 in managing change 179-81
permanency planning 12, 104
 see also care plans
Peters, T. and Austin, N : *A Passion for Excellence*... 178-9
Pindown Inquiry 64, 70
placements sytem, restructuring 101-106
planning
 BACC Topic Group 49-50, 124-5
 see also care plans
playgroups 127-33
playschemes 132-3
positive support to families 49-50, 73, 99, 136-7, 175-6
 see also families
poverty 1-2, 113-4, 92, 21-2, see also financial issues
pre-school see early years
prevention of care 141
Price Waterhouse 24-5
prostitution
 BACC work on 138, 175-6
 review of response 76

R

Race Relations Act 1976 114
racism, see also minority ethnic people, 114-15
recession see financial issues
registration of service providers 123-4, 131-2, 175
 see also monitoring and review
religion
 focus of planning under Children Act 1989 99-100, 144
 focus of work post-BACC 53, 73
 Muslim families 156
remand and teenage fostering scheme 150-51, 176
 see also adolescents; foster care; young offenders

research
 BACC use of 52, 162, 167, 178-82
 dissemination of 49-50, 166-9
 see also BACC, publications
residential care see children's homes; social workers
respite care 104
reviews see care plans; monitoring and review
rights of children see children's rights
Rowe, Jane 62

S

schools see education
Seebohm Committee 11
seminars see BACC, seminars
sexual abuse of children
 budget for 94-5
 in care 68
 nationally 14-15, 21, 68, 70, 72, 76
 project for survivors 65, 137-8, 175-6
 single-sex children's homes 156
 see also child abuse; child protection; prostitution
Short Committee 21-2
Social Services Dept.
 budget 2, 93-5, 166-7
 changing culture of child care 141, 144, 169-71, 174
 competition with private sector see mixed economy of welfare'
 development 23-7
 increased concern with child care 166-7
 management
  reviews
  BACC involvement 52, 71-2, 77, **106-111**, 164, 166, 176
  day care 131
  foster care 151-2
  pre-1989 vi, 24-5, 106-7
  Team 53, 57, 65, 71, 109
  focused work 1991 74, 76
  see also BACC, reports
  see also management
 outcomes of BACC's work 171-77, see also BACC
 performance management 32-3, 183

INDEX

Social Services Dept. *continued*
  scope 2, 71
  as system 35-42, 130-31, 145-6, 152-3, 169-71
  see also BACC; Birmingham; Child Care Review group; children in care; children in need;; day care; social workers;
Social Services Inspectorate 26, 62, 70, 77
Social Work Decisions in Child Care 13-14
social workers
  DHSS criticism 13
  foster carers 144-52
  see also foster care
  increased recruitment and budget 94-5, 100, 135-6
  involvement in BACC's work *see* BACC, staff involvement
  media treatment 2, 8, 26, 58, 60, 63-4
  minority ethnic 115-16, 129, 150
  negative attitude to BACC vi, 46, 51, 60, 96, 182-3
  public criticism of levels of intervention 14-15
  reaction to organisational change 3, 25-7, 178-84
  residential
    low status and morale 19-21, 23, 28, 62, 155
    redeployment 105
    training 20, 23, 27, 51, 64, 73, 153, **154-5**
  shortages 66, 72, 74, 79, 129
  in social services system 38-9
  see also BACC; children in need, unallocated cases; children's homes; foster care; Social Services Dept.
staff
  cynicism towards BACC, vi, 46, 51, 60, 96, 182-3, *see also* BACC
  involvement in BACC's work vii, 46-51, 60, 81-2, 165, 173, 178-82, *see also* BACC
  issues
    complaints procedure 122
    in managing change 105, 179-84

staff, child care *see* social workers
Staffordshire children's homes, Pindown Inquiry 64, 70
standards of service 100
  see also monitoring and review; registration
Sutton, Paul vi, 58, 59-75
  appointed General Manager, Children and Families 76-7, 110
  Child in the City submission 77
  Directions for Strategic Planning... report 98-101
  In Need Implementation Group 90-91
  Social Services Inspectorate Advisory Group 62
  visits to social work teams etc. 61
systems model 4, 28, 34-42, 101-2, 169-71

T

teenagers *see* adolescents
Topic Groups *see* BACC, Topic Groups
training
  in social services system 38-9
  see also BACC, implementation of Children Act 1989; BACC, training
Training Enterprise Council 85
transracial adoption 60, 63
trouble-shooting 49-50

U

unallocated child care cases *see* children in need, unallocated cases
under fives *see* early years
underachievement, educational 156-8
unemployment 1-2, 113-4
Utting Report 70, 72, 154-5

V

visitors, independent *see* children's homes, visits; independent visitors
voluntary sector 65, 100-01, 137-8, 165, 168, 181
  see also mixed economy of welfare

W

Wagner Report 15, 123
Warwickshire, closure of children's homes 20, 68-9, 102-3, 106
Webb, Rita 75
women
  in BACC 51
  demands on services 58, 84
  see also families

Y

young offenders 11-12, 154
  Community Homes with Education 69, 154
  community-based provision 11-12
  intermediate treatment 12
  not a focus for BACC 53
  remand and teenage fostering scheme 150-51
Young People's Forum 120
younger children *see* early years